THE
ITALIAN
KID DID IT

THE
ITALIAN
KID DID IT

HOW I TURNED $3,000 INTO $30 BILLION

AND ACHIEVED THE AMERICAN DREAM

TOM GOLISANO

with Mike Wicks

HarperCollins
LEADERSHIP

An Imprint of HarperCollins

Published by HarperCollins Leadership, an imprint of HarperCollins Focus LLC.

Any internet addresses, phone numbers, or company or product information printed in this book are offered as a resource and are not intended in any way to be or to imply an endorsement by HarperCollins Leadership, nor does HarperCollins Leadership vouch for the existence, content, or services of these sites, phone numbers, companies, or products beyond the life of this book.

ISBN 978-1-4002-2999-4 (eBook)
ISBN 978-1-4002-2989-5 (HC)
ISBN 978-1-4041-1773-0 (custom)

Library of Congress Control Number: 2021949883

Printed in the United States of America
22 23 24 25 26   LSC   10 9 8 7 6 5 4 3 2 1

To my sister Marie—

you are my inspiration.

CONTENTS

Contents

INTRODUCTION

A close friend suggested I start the introduction to my autobiography with a short list of the highlights of my long and successful life. So here goes.

I founded a multibillion-dollar corporation. I owned a major sports franchise. I launched a political party. I ran for governor of New York State. I was invited to the White House to play golf with the President of the United States—he won. I was, at one point, asked to consider running for president—I didn't. Individually and through my family foundation I've given $300 million to good causes. What a life—and it isn't over yet!

For the past two years I've worked with a professional writer to help me pull the story of my life together. I suppose when you've been involved in so many things and affected so many lives across more than seven decades, colleagues, friends, and family expect you to pull it all together in a book, for posterity—whatever the heck that is. Also, after writing the bestselling book *Built Not Born*, which was published in February 2020, my literary agent said that people would want to know more about my life. Well, maybe—we'll see.

My ancestral roots lie in the sulfur mines of Sicily. My American roots lie in upstate New York. I grew up in Irondequoit, the son of an immigrant family. We weren't poor, but we struggled at times. My brother died a war hero in the Korean War when I was ten years old, which accounts for my poor opinion of politicians. I've been quoted as saying, "Every time a politician mentions war, they should be shot because politicians wage war, citizens don't wage war." My early life was eventful, and I was the sort of kid who learned lessons well—lessons that stood me in good stead for all that was to come in my adult life.

The Italian Kid Did It tells my personal story of course, but it's also a business story full of lessons and advice, I'll show you how I turned $3,000, a maxed-out credit card, and a business concept that no one thought would work, into a $30 billion company. I founded Paychex forty-nine years ago and am proud to say that I am still chairman of the board, even after taking the company public in 1983—a point in a corporation's life at which Wall Street often chooses to replace incumbent CEOs. Who would have thought an Italian kid from Irondequoit would have ended up building a business that today employs 15,500 people and services 670,000 customers?

If political intrigue is your thing, the story of how I started the Independence Party in New York State and the political shenanigans that followed are fascinating, and sometimes almost unbelievable. At times, it reads like an HBO television drama series (I'm open to offers, by the way). It follows my many attempts to bring a business perspective to politics and to make politicians more accountable—basically, to put people ahead of policy. Along the way, several major name politicians got in the way. Spoiler alert—they didn't fare well!

I give sports fans a behind-the-scenes look at my purchase and management of the Buffalo Sabres hockey franchise, and how I saved the team from having to move out of upstate New York. When I arrived, the franchise was bankrupt and toward the bottom of the league. Within a few years it was rated as the best-run sports franchise in professional sports by ESPN, ahead of 122 major professional sports teams in North America. At the same time, we managed to make hockey affordable for local fans. My secret? Unlike many owners, I ran it as a business, not a hobby.

I've been recognized for many things, but I'm most proud of being known as a philanthropist. Over the past twenty years I have donated more than $300 million to worthy causes personally and through the Golisano Foundation. People often ask me why I am such an active philanthropist. I suppose the simple answer is that you can't take it with you, or perhaps it's because I applied for immortality, but didn't get it. My family foundation focuses solely on helping people with developmental disabilities, including being the largest-ever individual donor to the Special Olympics. To date we have given the organization $37 million. Personally, I have had the pleasure of donating to hospitals, universities and colleges, and even a children's museum. I was asked by President Clinton if I would consider becoming a founding sponsor of the Clinton Global Initiative. I agreed and gave him $3 million to get the initiative off the ground. I continued as the major underwriter and sponsor for eight years, during which time the organization did some amazing good around the world.

Over the years, I've been intimately involved with about twenty-five companies as a result of entrepreneurs coming to me with intriguing business concepts. Although I'm now in my seventies, I am far from retired and continue to invest in new businesses that excite me. Like Paychex, the businesses that appeal to me are those that have recurring revenue.

Some people have called me a contrarian, and throughout this book you will see ample evidence to support that view. I do see things differently and my opinions are not always popular. Throughout *The Italian Kid Did It*, you will see me side with both Democrats and Republicans, which may lead you to question where I stand politically. Let me explain. I'm a fiscally conservative Republican, who is a middle-of-the-road moderate on social issues.

Want more? I give my honest opinion on some of the pressing issues of our time, including social welfare, education, congressional term limits, race relations, substance abuse, and gambling. I'm confident that my views will be a source of satisfaction to some and will madly infuriate others. And, you know what? That's good.

I hope you enjoy this book. If it makes you smile, laugh, shout, scream, cry, get angry, agree or disagree with me, have an *aha* moment, or make you feel anything in life is possible, then it was worth writing.

I DO THINGS FOR PEOPLE

Word on the street at one time was that I was in the mob. Maybe it was my name. Maybe it was my background, or the way I acted. Like most things said about me, it was completely false. It was said because people made assumptions. Wrong assumptions—about me, about what I was doing, and what I really did for people.

You see, a long time ago, when Paychex was in its tenth year and just beginning to thrive, I moved into a suburban house in Rochester, New York. It was well before the company would become one of the largest payroll processors in America, but the company and I were getting some media attention.

Shortly after my arrival in this suburban oasis, a rumor started to spread around the neighborhood. As virtually all rumors are, this one was spawned out of ignorance—largely because no one in the area knew what I did for a living.

One day I'm outside sweeping the driveway of my new home when the next-door neighbor woman comes dancing over and starts making small talk. I'm cordial but reserved. Finally, she gets to her true mission, asking bluntly, "What do you do for a living?"

I know where this is coming from, so I look at her with a serious expression, pause as if formulating a socially appropriate response, and then I deadpan, "I do things for people." She stared back at me blankly and speechless. As she walked away I kept sweeping my driveway, but now I had a big smile on my face.

A few months later, an article about Paychex appeared in the local newspaper accompanied by a photograph of me, featured prominently on the front page. It was only a few days later that the same neighbor woman came sauntering over to my property once again. At first she bore a stern expression, but as she approached, she started to smirk and it was apparent she was fighting back a grin. She laughed and said, "You son of a bitch!"

You might imagine I was initially offended by this woman's stereotypical assumption that, because I'm of Italian descent (even more incriminating, I have Sicilian roots), I must be a member of the Mafia. Though I can claim no links to the mob, I am fiercely proud of my Sicilian heritage. When I was growing up, I always thought we were just as normal as anyone else. Naturally, I often resented what people said, did, and appeared to think about us. But hell, all I knew was that we had the best food in the world! In some ways, I actually took an even greater sense of pride specifically *because* people criticized our heritage. To this day I've always felt that stereotypical assumptions about others, as well as resentments held toward those who do the assuming, are nothing but a colossal waste of time and energy.

I would, however, like to point out that there is a much broader and more meaningful aspect to "I do things for people," in that my entire career has been devoted to serving the needs of people and businesses. My early entrepreneurship activities, my business ventures, my runs for governor, my philanthropy, and even my time owning a professional sports team have all been focused, not quite on "doing" things for people, but more accurately on enabling people to do things for themselves and helping them reach their full potential. My basic philosophy is, if I can help them along the way, that's better for all concerned. So yes, I do things for people—it's what I do.

Though I was often ridiculed for it as a child, my Italian heritage is an important part of my story: from how my paternal grandmother and the Golisanos ended up escaping poverty in Sicily by emigrating to America and settling in Rochester, to my own upbringing as a Sicilian kid in a quintessentially American town. My personality and character along with my philosophies, especially as they relate to business, politics, and philanthropy, not to mention why people say I think differently compared to most other businesspeople, were forged during those formative years. I wouldn't be who I am today without them. And I don't think others can understand fully where I am coming from, until they hear the stories of my family and growing up as a "dago" in Rochester, New York.

TO AMERICA OR BUST— MY FAMILY'S BEGINNING IN SICILY

I was baptized Blase Golisano after my maternal grandfather—an Italian tradition that my unconventional father tried to avoid, before eventually bowing to my very conventional and traditional mother's wishes. She insisted on me being given an Italian family name.

My father, unhappy with the name Blase, suggested everyone call me Sonny. Like many immigrants of his day, my father was more interested in embracing the culture of his new country than he was in retaining the traditions of his old one, though he certainly would never forget, nor fail to revere, his Italian ancestral roots. Tom, the name I use today, was the name I chose at my Catholic confirmation when I was twelve. I chose it because my sister's husband Tom Graham was my sponsor. I also took his name as my middle name from that point forward. However, I never used it until I was in college and met Gloria, who became my first wife. I felt that Blase and Golisano was too much for people to handle, so, when I met Gloria I introduced myself as Tom, rather than Blase.

As I mentioned earlier, my father was Sicilian; his name was Salvatore and he was the final member of the Golisano family to escape the extreme poverty of Sicily at the beginning of the twentieth century. His father, Calogero, my grandfather, was a sulfur miner and for many years managed to survive the dozens of ways a miner can lose his life in one of the world's most horrendous occupations. Interestingly, the other name for sulfur is brimstone, from the Middle English for "burning stone," the substance that was thought to fuel the fires of hell.

Sulfur mining was work for the poorest of the poor in Sicily. It was terrifying and dangerous. My grandfather did not want any of his sons to have to endure life as a miner, so he came up with a plan to gradually send his five children to America. It was a simple plan, an unofficial version of what we today call chain-migration.

He labored six, sometimes seven days a week in the mine to save enough to provide passage for his eldest son to "escape" Sicily in the dark steerage hold of any ship voyaging to the United States. Once there, the eldest was instructed to find work and send money home to help save enough to send the next eldest son to join him, who in turn found work, and also sent money home. This continued until all four sons and daughter Carmela were safe in America. Calogero, Maria, and my father, the not-yet-born Salvatore, would follow last.

At forty years of age, Calogero was still remarkably healthy and Maria was pregnant with my father. Outwardly my grandfather showed no signs of silicosis (though chronic silicosis symptoms often do not manifest until years later), he had eluded cancer, and he didn't suffer from miner's disease (otherwise known as ancylostomiasis), or hookworm. He had survived years of inhaling hydrogen sulfide gas and endured heat so extreme many miners worked naked.

It's impossible to imagine working conditions like this. It's hard for me to imagine how anything good at all could have come out of those mines. In fact, my grandfather never did. Despite surviving most of the numerous perils that confront miners, my grandfather's fate was to die in a catastrophic cave-in along with thirty-eight of his fellow miners, just four months before the birth of my father. His body was never recovered.

In 1907, nine years after my grandfather's death, my grandmother had at last saved enough, with the help of her four sons and daughter overseas, to make the journey with my father to join them in America. My grandfather's plan had worked, just not quickly enough to save himself.

And so, my father and grandmother were reunited with the rest of the Golisano family in Rochester. Today, only 5 million Sicilians live in Sicily, compared to the 17 million presently living in the United States. Talk about a mass migration—it appears my family wasn't the only one who came to the United States for a better life.

It was not long before my father became Americanized enough to adopt the name Sam, despite living in the enclave of Rochester's Little Italy with his extended Sicilian family. Sam and Maria lived in an apartment behind a grocery store owned by his sister, my Aunt Carmela and her husband, my Uncle Peppinio. Living in Rochester, close to his four brothers and his sister, was good for my father. He went to school and learned to speak English, read, write, and do basic arithmetic.

My father worked in the small grocery store, sweeping floors, cleaning, stacking shelves, packaging fresh pasta, and learning to record purchases made on credit in the store's ledger. Like me, my father enjoyed arithmetic—he was always happy working with numbers—especially later in life when he would work out his potential winnings on the parlay bets that he placed on baseball games. The Golisanos were close and my father would see his siblings regularly; in true Italian tradition there was always a place for him at any of their dinner tables.

My father's schooling for all intents and purposes was finished by the time he was fourteen. By nineteen he had worked in the grocery store for ten years. His brothers were all much older: Tony and Charlie were laborers, Joseph was a baker, and Frank also worked at the grocery store.

It was Frank who came up with the idea of starting a wholesale grocery business, importing olive oil in bulk along with other products such as Italian-made macaroni by the barrel. The entrepreneurial gene is strong in the Golisano line. The five Golisano brothers went into business together; they had a truck, bought fresh produce from the wholesale markets to sell to their customers, and my father became the company's salesman.

My father met my mother Anna shortly after her parents opened a retail grocery store opposite Golisano Brothers Wholesale Grocers *Emporium*—a grand word for a storefront. Traditional Italian propriety was heavily involved, but her father liked my father and to cut a long story short, Anna and Sam courted and married in an appropriate amount of time and subsequently moved into a rented apartment in Little Italy.

It was 1925, and my mother continued to work at her parents' grocery store while my father sold imported Italian products along with local produce to retailers. Life was good: My father even had a car. But things began to change. Italians started leaving Little Italy and moving to non-Italian neighborhoods. Worse, they started eating more American food. It wasn't long before Golisano Brothers Wholesale Grocers could no longer financially support my father and his four brothers.

As a result, my father got a job selling life insurance for Prudential Insurance. Once again, he showed his ability to think differently. For example, the people of Little Italy had no money to buy "life" insurance. But my father knew Italians, especially his fellow Roman Catholics. They took their responsibility to bury their dead with honor and dignity seriously. It was their duty to hold a wake, a mass, have a decent casket, and an upright headstone, no matter the cost or the sacrifices that had to be made. So, my father took a different tack, he would ask prospects about their plans for when the inevitable happened to an elderly relative. How did they envision the funeral, how were they going to pay for it? And, then he sold them "burial" insurance. He may have been the first Golisano to identify an unmet need and find a way to fulfill it.

WORKING THE AMERICAN DREAM

My parents worked hard and in 1936 they bought their first home in West Irondequoit: a modest three-bedroom house with one bathroom and a two-car garage, a few blocks from the Genesee River. This was home for the first five years of my life.

At the time, my sister Marie was eight, my brother Charlie six, and things were going well. My mother was a seamstress and my father continued selling insurance. But Sam always had his eyes open for a business opportunity. In this case he recognized potential in the furnace in his own basement. He loved the fact it was fueled by oil, not coal, a refinement that the majority of homes did not enjoy in those days. He didn't have to constantly stoke it, and it burned much cleaner than coal. Converting a coal furnace to oil was expensive and beyond the means of most people, but he discovered a small company that had developed a conversion kit, basically an insert, that quickly and easily converted a coal furnace to oil. It was significantly less expensive than purchasing and installing a new furnace. More importantly, it was within the reach of many local homeowners. So, he started a furnace-conversion business and things went well as the business grew steadily.

Once again, it was an example of finding a solution to a need. He too could have easily said, if asked by a neighbor what he did for a living, "I do things for people"—from importing high-quality Italian olive oil, to selling burial insurance, to removing the hassle of hauling and shoveling coal in Little Italy. The Golisano family was doing well considering the United States was working its way through the Great Depression.

WAR CASTS ITS SHADOW

World War II broke out in Europe in 1939 and everything was about to change. For a while the war seemed a long way away, life went on much as it had before, and sales of the York Conversion Burner were on target. On November 14, 1941, another Sicilian-American Golisano was born: me.

Less than a month later, Japan bombed Pearl Harbor. War cast its shadow over the Golisano family for the first, but by no means for the last, time. This unpromising start to my life, however, was not the cause of my subsequent, often contrary, beliefs and theories on war and politicians. All that would come later.

War was not good for my father's furnace-conversion business, because it made consumers nervous about investing in their homes. Things got far worse when the government put a stop to the production of the kit he was selling, as part of the redirection of raw materials to the war effort. My father was forced to take a job as a timekeeper at the Sampson Naval Base and for a while I only saw him on weekends.

AN EARLY TRAGEDY

In 1943, the first of what were to be several tragedies occurred. Each would test our family's resilience in its own way. My then fifteen-year-old sister was working part-time at a supermarket and caught her hand in a meat-grinding machine in a horrific accident. Her right hand had to be amputated at the wrist. I was too young to grasp the full measure of the calamity, or to be affected by it at the time. But I grew up recognizing that she was an amazingly strong person who never once allowed her missing hand to become a disability, or to define her. I've always been very close to Marie; when she was courting her future husband Tom some years later, they would take me with them to the movies, to a restaurant, roller skating, or bowling. Over the years she has always been there for me and remains to this day one of my biggest supporters.

Later in life she would be instrumental in helping Paychex survive a financial crisis, but we'll come to the full Paychex story a little later.

SLOW TO TALK, BUT QUICK ON MY FEET
(SOME THINGS NEVER CHANGE)

I don't like small talk. Never have. I guess even when I was little, I wasn't a big fan of it. In fact, I never talked at all. By the age of four, my parents were getting concerned that I wasn't talking. I was taken to a doctor who assured them I would talk when I was ready. In this he was correct. Apparently, the formative moment came when the family drove past a closed hot-dog stand and I uttered the immortal words, "Hot dog sleep." It should be noted that not speaking didn't mean I wasn't thinking. I've always been someone who listens and watches. I also value speaking only when it counts, when you're making a point or have something meaningful to say. And, over the years, I've also learned how to leverage silence.

Though I was slow to talk, one thing that I did well was take risks. I wasn't afraid of much. My sister Marie loves to tell the story of the day I climbed into the family car at about the age of four, released the emergency brake, and took a seconds-long joyride the length of the driveway, in reverse, finally smashing into a neighbor's car. Apparently, I had the presence of mind to jump out, run into the house, and lock myself in the bathroom, presumably until I figured it would be safe to come out.

EARLY EDUCATION: IN SCHOOL AND AT HOME

I started school two months before my fifth birthday; in those days, you had to take an aptitude test if you were under five before being allowed to start school. They were different times: My mother took me to school for the first few days, but within a week I was walking to school on my own. I wasn't, however, allowed to take the family car.

I was good in math at school. But where I learned most of my skills was watching my mother and father—at work and at home. They were both entrepreneurs in their own right. It was about this time that oil prices started falling and the manufacturing of the coal-to-oil conversion kits my father specialized in recommenced. My father opened a storefront, advertised, and attracted new business. Sales were good and he soon had three employees, one of them my brother-in-law Tom. My mother, not to be outdone in entrepreneurial ventures, supplemented her day job as a seamstress in a clothing factory by making drapes in the evenings and on weekends. As this side business took off, she started her own small drapery enterprise in our basement. I grew up watching her sew drapes all day and all evening while my father was enthusiastically growing his business. Examples of a strong work ethic were not hard to find in my formative years.

My mother could save money, like every Italian mother. I remember, many years later after my father died, I visited her and sat in an armchair. My hands found their way between the cushion and the arm, where I found roll after roll of $100 bills stuffed into the depths of the chair. "Put them back, put them back," she yelled. Yes, she could certainly save, though clearly she did not grasp the nuances of sound financial investment. Although I've never stuffed my money down the back of chairs, I have been accused of being overly frugal.

I also learned from her mistakes. One day she announced she was going to buy a house in the city, which she then rented out. Her mistake was buying a house on the edge of a transitional neighborhood. The area around the house declined rapidly; collecting rents became a challenge. One day she decided to sell it and two characters gave her a minimum down payment; unfortunately, she never received another payment. When she visited the house a short time later with my father, she discovered it had been completely gutted. All the copper wiring, plumbing—everything that could be fenced or sold as scrap had been ripped out. She ended up just walking away from it and lost every penny she had invested.

Over the course of my business career, I have always carried out extensive research and gathered inside knowledge of the particular industry I am venturing into, whether that entailed launching a new business of my own or investing in an existing or startup business. Yet I, too, have made a mistake or two along the way, as we will also see.

LESSONS OVER PASTA

Dinners in Italian households are a big deal. We all sat down together, and we were all expected to be there—no excuses. My mother was an excellent cook and we ate traditional Italian food, made from recipes passed down from my grandmother: macaroni, pizza, fresh mozzarella, pasta, soup, and a medley of roasted vegetables. Good rustic food. Sundays were feast days and often we'd be joined by family. After dinner, the cards would come out and there would be poker at ten cents a hand, or sometimes gin rummy.

On weekdays, when I was in fourth and fifth grade, my mother would get out a deck of flash cards after dinner and rigorously test my math skills. She would show me a question and I had to work out the answer in my head. Math was my favorite subject, so I enjoyed this time with my mother. It certainly helped develop a level of mental acuity that has served me well throughout my careers in business and politics. She was a tough lady, but a great deal of what she taught me, either directly or by example, has played a part in my success.

Four years later I remember completing an algebra final exam before anyone else in class. My teacher suggested I recheck my answers. I told her I already had. I did miss one question, but my 98 percent score, achieved in record time, still amazed my teacher.

This is where my love of puzzle-solving may have originated. To this day, my grandchildren love to give me two three-digit numbers and challenge me to multiply them in my head. The ability to understand numbers and their meaning is a critical skill for any businessperson.

A SICILIAN MOTHER'S SHARP TONGUE

I am a pretty disciplined individual. Some might say I'm set in my ways. But I think having a disciplined approach to life is what got me to where I am today. Of course, it wasn't accidental; my mother was the disciplinarian in the house and used my father's shaving strap on Marie's and Charlie's backsides on occasion when they misbehaved. She was very Sicilian, in that she was adversarial with people—no demure pushover—and tough on me, too. She would confront me aggressively on anything I hadn't done that I should have, and I often ended up running up to my bedroom in tears. My father, however, would come and console me and bring me back downstairs.

My father never spanked me, but he did show me his belt on occasion—a warning I never ignored. He was a handsome, athletic, soft-spoken man. He was always friendly, and women were drawn to him—something that did not go unnoticed by my mother who was often jealous of the attention he received. I remember fondly the way he dressed. His everyday attire was a suit and tie, with a Windsor knot, and his shirt collars were always fastened. This must have rubbed off on me, because I dressed similarly every day I went to work at Paychex and expected all my employees to dress professionally as well. Paychex had an official dress code for the longest time, even when casual dress had become popular in many business offices.

Although my father was mild mannered to a fault, there was one occasion where he did stand up to my mother. On Saturday mornings, it was a tradition that he would go to the public market and bring back assorted Italian delicacies such as salami, ricotta cheese, mozzarella, black olives, and crusty Italian bread for lunch. My brother, sister, and I would wait in anticipation for him to return home with our Italian feast. My mother didn't feel the same. She would instead berate him; "Sam, can't you get something different? You get the same old stuff all the time." He suffered this tirade almost every week, though I'm not sure what he could have done much different. On one particular Saturday, he was laying the food out on the kitchen table and my mother started in on him again about buying the same old stuff every week. My father didn't respond but quietly picked up the ricotta cheese, which was in a small paper dish, and pushed it right into her face and mushed it in a little for good effect. Marie, Charlie, and I were laughing and crying at the same time because we didn't know what was going to happen next. My mother didn't say a word; she got up, wiped her face, and left the room. She never bothered him again after that day, at least not on that issue. And it taught me something else altogether: Sometimes the best way to deal with a complaint is not to say a damn thing. It's actions that count.

SOMEONE ELSE'S WAR TEARS OUR FAMILY APART

By the spring of 1950 you could say we were doing okay as a family. We had a lot of good times and my parents were managing financially, which is to say they were paying the bills. We weren't rich, but this Sicilian family had come a long way from the sulfur mines. My parents even gathered the resources to build their own house on Daley Boulevard, just three blocks north of where we were living. For a time, it seemed we had achieved my grandfather's dream for his family—I would go so far as to say, the American Dream. My parents had jobs, brought home steady money, and the family was growing and prospering. But all that was about to change dramatically.

On June 25, 1950, North Korean tanks crossed into South Korea; two days later President Truman ordered US forces to give the Korean government troops cover and support. The summer of 1950 saw 10 million young men register for the draft. My brother was one of them.

For Charlie, it was a case of either waiting to be drafted or enlisting and be able to choose which armed service he wished to serve in. Another advantage (if one may call it that) of volunteering was that his military service would be reduced by one year. My mother's brothers, Uncle Patrick (Patsy) and Uncle Anthony (Red) Liberti had both tried to persuade Charlie to choose to go into the navy. Anthony had served in the army in World War II driving an ambulance in the European theater: He spent the war at the front line retrieving wounded infantrymen and taking them to field hospitals. Patsy served during World War II as a ship's cook in the Navy. His ship was the USS *DuPage*, a *Bayfield*-class attack transport that carried infantrymen in the Western Pacific to various assaults throughout the region. The *DuPage* was hit by a Kamikaze aircraft in January 1945; he survived but 35 of his comrades were killed and 157 were injured. The aircraft left a 500-pound bomb lodged in the deck, which the brave seamen managed to dislodge and push into the ocean. According to the ship's official website, Uncle Patsy's ship received six Battle Stars, the most for its type of ship in the Pacific Fleet. Despite their harrowing experiences, the uncles felt Charlie would still be safer in the navy than the army during the Korean War.

Their sage advice, however, fell on deaf ears when an Army recruiter told Charlie that given his successful amateur baseball career, choosing the army might give him a chance to play baseball. The army had the best baseball teams; in fact, over a hundred Major League professionals were either drafted or enlisted during the war. The gentleman omitted the fact that in the army he also had a greater chance of seeing action—especially in the infantry, to which he was assigned.

By the end of the war, the infantry had suffered 70 percent of the casualties, while only accounting for 10 percent of army personnel. Friends and family did their best to convince Charlie to enlist in the Navy or Air Force. However, the appeal of swinging a bat and serving a one-year shorter stint was simply too great.

On January 2, 1951, my brother took his oath of enlistment and became a private in the US Army. His first posting was to Fort Dix in New Jersey for training. I went with my family and Charlie's sweetheart Donna to see him off at the railway station; Dad gave him his signet ring bearing the initials SG. It was an emotional scene: As we watched Charlie leave, we had no idea whether we would ever see him again. Charlie, looking distressed, turned back once more before boarding the train. Had this been a movie, that iconic moment would have dissolved in a prophetic fade to black.

He got to play baseball for the Fort Monmouth Signaleers and, for a while at least, it looked like he might spend the war playing the game he loved so much. In May, Donna and Charlie's engagement announcement appeared in the *Rochester Democrat and Chronicle.*

By July, it looked like the war might be coming to an end, but in August peace talks broke down. September and October saw a succession of battles, resulting in a staggering number of casualties. More soldiers were needed, and Charlie was reassigned to Korea.

On October 31, 1951, he arrived at a hilltop outpost overlooking the Samichon Valley and began learning about trench warfare and bunker life firsthand. He never got an opportunity to learn much, though. Just two days later he was killed in an attack on the station by a battalion of approximately a thousand Chinese soldiers. My brother died a hero; he remained on the front line to assist a comrade, Private E. Duncan, who had refused to fall back with the rest of their platoon. The two of them continued to inflict as many casualties on the attacking forces as possible with their machine gun, until Private Duncan was mortally wounded. My brother Charlie took his place and provided cover while his fellow infantrymen withdraw. Before he too could fall back, a stick grenade was lobbed into his foxhole and he succumbed to multiple shrapnel wounds.

It was from that remote hillside station overlooking the Samichon Valley that Charlie Golisano wrote his last letter home. It arrived more than a week after his death, but of course we had no knowledge of his passing. We continued to wait every day for another letter from him. At 9:00 p.m. on November 20, 1951, the doorbell rang. I was upstairs in my bedroom. I heard my father answer the door and a few seconds later my mother let out a howling shriek of despair. The news had arrived, coldly in my view, by telegram via Western Union. It took more than three months for my brother's remains to arrive home in a sealed casket.

During this terrible period the question of Marie's wedding to her fiancé, Tom Graham, hung in the air; it had been planned for the middle of February. My mother felt it should be postponed, but my father insisted it should take place as scheduled. By this time the invitations had been sent, the hall had been rented, Marie had purchased her wedding gown, and there was a sense of urgency as Tom, who was in the Army, was slotted to go to Camp Indian Town Gap in Pennsylvania.

The wedding went ahead as planned on the morning of Saturday, February 16, 1952. Family and friends attended, but there were few young people. My mother was dressed in black; she cried continuously. The reception after the wedding was a muted affair, as one would expect.

There was talk of there not being a honeymoon, but my father insisted, and the "happy" couple went to Niagara Falls. The honeymoon was cut short when a telegram arrived back in Irondequoit announcing that Charlie's remains were to arrive in a few days. By Wednesday, Marie and Tom were back home in time for Charlie's funerals (Catholic and military).

The effect on my family was catastrophic on multiple levels. My father had difficulty accepting that Charlie was dead. He held out hope that it wasn't Charlie inside that casket, that there was some colossal mistake. This was in spite of having had Charlie's personal belongings returned, including his dog tags and the signet ring my father had given him at the railway station the day he left. My father demanded the casket be unsealed, so he could be sure it was his son. He tried to convince the owner of the funeral home, who had known Charlie well, to unseal the casket. But he told my father he had no authority to do so and suggested he talk to our family doctor. He told my father that because Charlie had died three months prior, and had been killed by a grenade, he could not support my father's plea to view his son's body. He tried to explain to my father that it was for the best; that seeing Charlie's corpse now would likely haunt him for the rest of his days. Finally, my father acquiesced.

Charlie received both a solemn Roman Catholic mass and a military funeral with honors. At the cemetery, there were many fresh graves—it was an area reserved for soldiers. There was a bugler playing taps, a three-volley salute, and an honor guard. My father looked like a beaten man; I don't think I've ever seen a someone look so sad. My mother and sister wept. At ten years of age, I simply couldn't believe I wouldn't see my brother ever again.

For leadership and valor, Charlie was awarded the Bronze Star Medal with V device (denoting special acts of heroism in a combat zone). He also received the Purple Heart, the Combat Infantryman's Badge, the Korean Service Medal, the United Nations Service Medal, the National Defense Service Medal, and the Korean War Service Medal. The commendation cited Charlie for his heroism in action while determinedly and courageously defending the outpost and for his selfless devotion to duty. Later, my family was given Charlie's medals. They were meaningless to us.

I was just ten years old when my big brother died. To this day I still have the signet ring my father gave to Charlie.

It didn't help our family to consider that Charlie died a hero. In our opinion, he was a victim in what amounted to someone else's civil war. The US government sent increasing numbers of young Americans to the front, where they were slaughtered in an attempt to wear down the North Koreans and Chinese. It was as simple as that.

Why is all this important to my life story? Well first of all, I saw firsthand what my family went through. The effect it had on my parent's marriage. There was plenty of guilt and grief to be shared.

It also taught me that the difference between politicians and businesspeople is that you can have several companies in the same industry and all of them can be successful. But in politics there's only one winner. Because of this, politicians do bizarre things to get into office and to maintain their positions of power. It almost seems they lose their ability to have a conscience.

Winning becomes paramount because that is the only way they can maintain their jobs and their power over people. Nobody wants to be an electorally defeated president, senator, congressman. Ultimately, I have the highest regard for businesspeople and little to none for politicians. Yet it may have been these formative influences that drove me to consider, later in life, a political course myself. I thought I could do better.

Some forty years later, Marie and I were invited to a ceremony at White Haven Memorial Park, Rochester, to honor those who lost their lives in the Korean War. Several residents of South Korea spoke and reflected on how thankful they were that the United States had entered the war to protect them and save their democracy. It gave me a better understanding, and perspective, as to what we were doing in that war, and it made my sister Marie and I feel a little better about our family's ultimate sacrifice.

At the end of the Vietnam War there were a little over 2,000 soldiers missing in action (MIA), all of whom were eventually released or accounted for. What's interesting about the Korean War was that there were about 8,000 MIAs and we never heard from any of them again.

A FAMILY IN CRISIS

My father never recovered from Charlie's death. It not only devastated him psychologically, it also affected his business. Although Marie's husband Tom was working for him as an installer and the company seemed to be doing okay, the reality was far different. The business was just coasting without my father's full energy and attention that had been the company's driving force. It's often said of business that if you are not growing you are falling behind; there is no such thing as standing still. True to that adage, competitors entered the market as the business languished. The future of his company looked doubtful.

My mother's home-based drapery business, however, was doing well. During this period it was she who managed to catch up with missed mortgage payments and put food on the table. She was a very hard worker and a tough negotiator.

The next few years were rough for our family. With Charlie's death and Marie's marriage to Tom, the house was quieter, even somber, and my parents were not as content with each other. They had lots of friends, and family came by often for meals or to play poker, gin rummy, or pinochle. It was only when the house was full of people that my father seemed to come alive. Most of the time, he just seemed troubled and unfocused. Tom got a job with the Rochester Telephone Company as a mechanic maintaining the installer's fleet of Ford vehicles. He had run motor pools in the Army, and this was a great opportunity for him. My father wished him well, but it was the last straw for the company: Shortly after Tom left, he closed his shop. By that time business was very slow and the debt load had become unmanageable. He declared bankruptcy in the fall of 1954; in early 1955 he watched his vehicles and everything else vanish in a court-ordered sale. I watched it all, too. Though too young to understand what it meant or what actually led to his business's demise, I did take away something invaluable from this tragedy. I vowed it would never, ever happen to me. No one was going to break me. No one was ever going to take my cars or my money from me.

Eventually, with my mother's hard work, the family rallied. Somehow my father managed to get himself a new car not so long after filing for bankruptcy. And not just any old car: It was a brand-new, black-and-white Oldsmobile Super 88 hardtop. To this day I don't know how or where he got it from, but I suspect it was either charm or a bet that was responsible.

It reminds me of the time my friend Gary Muxworthy and I drove the Sea Breeze Expressway. His father had bought him the same model car but in maroon with a continental kit. I was in the death seat and he was lighting cherry bombs and throwing them out of the car. I remember telling him that I'd be more comfortable if he was actually driving on the road. But that was Gary, he loved having a good time.

By the time I was a freshman in high school, my parents bought a small ranch house on Long Acre Road, only about ten blocks from our old house. They had wanted to move for some time; there were just too many bad memories.

This was the house I most remember as my childhood home. It evokes memories of my high school years, of playing baseball and dating girls, and most importantly growing up with my two best friends, Gene Polisseni and Gary Muxworthy. We remained lifelong friends and many acquaintances referred to us as the three musketeers.

BASEBALL

I've always loved baseball; I started in Little League and made the high school varsity team as a sophomore. In Little League I was the first batter of the first game in the first year it was offered in the Rochester area. The damn pitcher hit me in the side of the head; luckily I was wearing a helmet.

Just like he had done with my brother, my father would take me outside and hit me ground balls and fly balls; he even put me through some batting practice. He came to every one of my games all the way through high school. One thing I remember was that he never yelled at a coach or criticized an umpire's decision. He just sat there and enjoyed the game. After the game we'd talk about the plays and such. He never put any pressure on me. He was a great parent and a wonderful baseball father. I remember he took me to three or four World Series, and we used to go and watch the Rochester Red Wings (a local minor league team) occasionally.

In high school, I played the outfield and was an above-average hitter. I got the winning hit for my team, the Irondequoit Indians, in the Monroe County championship, which made me a bit of a celebrity in high school. I credit baseball for building my self-confidence.

Our coach in those days made an impact on me. On the first day of practice he told us how to stand at the plate, how to swing at the ball, and then told us to run laps, after which we did infield practice. Some of the team disliked him for leaving us to find our own way, but his attitude was that we should go out and have fun. We ended up with a terrific team; in fact, five of the nine starters signed professional contracts.

One story from those days. We were playing East Rochester; I was about sixteen or seventeen, it was an away game, and I was in the outfield. One of the opposing team was on first base and somebody hit a ground ball to the shortstop. He flipped it to our second baseman and the runner came flying into second base with his spikes up, maliciously sliding into our guy. I saw it all. As luck would have it, two innings later I was on first base and someone hit a ground ball to the left side of the infield that was flipped over to the second baseman. It happened to be the kid that went in high. I didn't slide into base—I ran right through him. It started a fight, which was broken up quickly. The funny thing is, we became lifelong friends.

I had a strong arm and I was fast. I actually got invited to a Cleveland Indians tryout camp, but I couldn't hit with enough power. I was only 150 pounds in those days.

I continued to play semipro for many years and then went on to play fast pitch softball until I was fifty-three. I'm glad I never made it as a pro baseball player; it's a short career and I would not have appreciated the pay cut.

My brother Charlie was a far better baseball player. He could hit the long ball where I couldn't. At one point the scouts were chasing him, but in the end, no one ever signed him. He was an outfielder but at five-foot-seven, he was too short.

STEALING FROM THE CHURCH

In the summer of my senior year, a friend called and asked me what my plans were that evening. He suggested I join him at Christ the

King Church. They were having a fundraising festival and he had been assigned to work the hotdog stand. In a break between serving people, he showed me how he diverted some of the money he was taking into his own pocket. This bothered me but peer pressure won out and I found myself doing the same thing. It wasn't a lot of money, maybe $5 or $6, but it bothered me for many years. Some time ago, when I was in a better financial position, the guilt came flooding back. I finally got up the gumption to own up to my childhood thievery and sent a check for $1,000 to Christ the King Church. I thought nothing more of it until the priest at the church called me to find out why I'd sent him a check out of the blue. I confessed my adolescent transgression, and luckily, he saw the funny side of my story. I think he felt the guilt I had carried all those years was penance enough.

I remember the kid that led me astray. He was good-looking, tough, had a ducktail haircut, and looked like the Fonz from the sitcom *Happy Days*. I remember when we won the county baseball championship, me and three other team members held him down and cut off his hair. Kids can be cruel.

TOM GOLISANO—HOUSECLEANER

As I got older, I took over responsibility for cleaning the house; my mother's work consistently meant there were threads and lint everywhere and these would make their way into my bedroom, which annoyed me to distraction. No one asked me to do this—it just seemed a natural thing to do, since I hated living in a mess. As my mother and father were always working, I started taking it on myself to not only vacuum and mop floors, but to clean bathrooms and generally keep the place tidy. I started baking, mostly cookies and brownies, and all in all I became quite domesticated. Friends and colleagues know well that I've never seen a cookie I didn't like.

I was never obsessive about hygiene and neatness, but to this day I like both home and office to be clean and tidy. Even as CEO of Paychex, my desk was always clear to the polished surface—not a paper clip out of place—and if after hours I happened to see a messy desk anywhere in our offices, I would take everything and move it to a trash bin. To me, a cluttered desk is the sign of a cluttered mind. Okay; there may be some folks of my acquaintance who would tell you *I am* obsessive about neatness.

OF COURSE, THE ITALIAN KID DID IT

Being born and brought up in America didn't make me any less Italian, or more precisely Sicilian—a fact I was reminded of frequently growing up. During high school, in West Irondequoit, I was often called *greaseball, wop, dago,* or *guinea.* I remember one occasion in gym class, a kid a year older than me was harassing me relentlessly, throwing out insult after insult. So, one day I told him I'd had enough and that although he was probably going to beat the crap out of me I was going to hurt him, too. But when I finally said, "Let's take it outside," surprisingly he backed off. Later he saw me walking along the road and offered me a lift; we ended up becoming friends.

I learned early on I had to fight for respect—a revelation that gave me empathy for the underdog. This has become integral to everything I have done in my life, whether in business, politics, or with my philanthropic activities.

Racial profiling (as it has only lately come to be called) was not only prevalent at school, it affected my family life, too. During high school we lived in a WASPy middle-class neighborhood—and they weren't overly fond of Italians.

I remember we had a neighbor across the street who owned a Chevrolet dealership, and there were always a couple of brand-new shiny cars in his driveway. One Friday night I went over to a friend's house. The next morning, I went out someplace on my bike and when I got back, there was a police car in my driveway and my father said, "They want to talk to you." I was sixteen; they took me outside and told me that one of the neighbor's cars had been stolen and taken for a joyride the previous evening. The owner had told them he saw me getting into it. Fortunately, the mother of the friend I visited was at home and the police were able to verify my alibi: I was at her house at the time I was alleged to be stealing the car. At that time, it was not unusual for people to automatically think, "Of course the Italian kid did it. Who else?"

THE MACARONI TRUCK DRIVER

People often ask me about defining moments in my life, the moments that made me who I am today. Maybe, they are looking for secrets to success hidden among my Sicilian roots: an immigrant family upbringing haunted as it was by financial struggles and more than its fair share of tragedy.

Many successful people built their success on the foundation of inherited money, or an existing business. I had no such help. I built everything I have from the ground up through hard work and resourcefulness. Often simply because there was no other choice. I didn't do it completely alone though; early on in my life I came to recognize the inherent value of showing people respect and working closely with them.

In many ways we are the result of the things that happen to us and how we handle the situations that challenge us. More importantly, what did we learn? I remember one pivotal moment when I was sixteen. It was during the summer recess and my father, after he was forced to close his furnace-conversion business, had taken a job as a truck driver. He was delivering macaroni products for a local company and I accompanied him in his large panel truck to help carry boxes. I have clear memories of feeling sad that my sixty-year-old father had gone from running his own business to working for someone else. The company he worked for was owned by Italian immigrants from Sicily, like our family. This should have meant that there would be a sense of respect between the owners and my father, but sadly this was not the case.

I'm not sure what caused the confrontation but one of the owners began shouting at my father. I was stunned: He hollered at my father, told him he was incompetent, inefficient, useless, and worse. My father was obviously humiliated, especially as I was beside him. I didn't know what to do or say. I was extremely uncomfortable and shocked at the way he was being treated. My father didn't say a word to the man. He waited until the outburst was over and went to his truck and we drove off. We sat in silence keeping our thoughts private. It wasn't the only time he would be dressed down in this despicable fashion. Sitting in the cab of the truck I thought about what had happened. I saw things from my father's perspective: He had zero power in that situation—he badly needed the job—what could he have done?

I still remember the impact it made on me. I vowed that day that I would do everything I could to avoid ever having to work for someone else. I also made a resolution that if I ever had employees, I would never treat them so monstrously. Even at that young age I learned about the power one person can hold over another and realized that it came with a great deal of responsibility. I knew that if ever I held that power, I would use it with compassion and I'd always be fair and honest.

It doesn't matter what station in life people hold, everyone deserves respect. I have one caveat to this: I have no respect for drug dealers, murderers, rapists, pedophiles, and the like, but when it comes to an honest Joe or Jane doing the best job they can, they deserve and should receive respect and understanding.

Let me give you an example. Whenever someone met with me at my office and one of my staff brought them tea or coffee, I took note of whether they were polite enough to say thank you. If they didn't show common decency by acknowledging the server, I would immediately question whether I wanted to employ them or to do business with them. Furthermore, when they left, I saw it as a sign of disrespect if their cup was still on my desk and if their chair was not pushed back into place. This may seem a small thing, but by disregarding people who might not be in a position to help them, they demonstrate a degree of arrogance. In short, they have failed to earn my respect.

FROM PAPER ROUTE

TO BIDDERS GUIDE

Even before I witnessed my father's dressing down by his manager, I think I had a sense that I wanted to find my own way in the world and not end up working for other people. The idea of being independent, of having a few dollars in my pocket that I'd earned through my own endeavors, was deep-rooted.

Many years later someone asked me about the risks involved in starting a company, as opposed to the security of working for a large corporation or organization. I answered with a question: Do you honestly feel that putting your future in the hands of someone else is not without risk? Launching a business, of course, is not without risk, but that risk can be mitigated by good planning and calculated forethought.

FIGURING OUT WAYS TO MAKE A BUCK

Growing up in a household often plagued by financial difficulties gave me an appreciation of the importance of making one's own way in the world. I never got an allowance growing up and I didn't like the idea of not having money of my own. So, discovering ways to make a buck or two was important to me.

When I was about ten years old I went out with a friend and collected old newspapers from around the neighborhood, hauling them away in my small red wagon. My father would then take us to the dump where we'd earn a few pennies for our trouble.

I used the same wagon to deliver our local newspaper, the *Rochester Democrat and Chronicle*. I delivered to over fifty houses every day and more than a hundred on Sundays. I would also collect payments once a week and sometimes even received a hard-earned tip.

I saved the money from these enterprises and eventually amassed the grand sum of $600. I wasn't saving for anything in particular and I didn't spend much of it, I simply enjoyed being different, or just feeling independent maybe. When my father was going through bankruptcy, he came to me asking to borrow my nest egg. I had no qualms about giving it to him and never expected to be repaid. Which was just as well because I never saw that money again.

Back when I was fifteen, I had a friend, Dick Chesler. We used to hang out at the North Park Lanes bowling alley. Dick and I were always looking for ways to make some money and we noticed that once the place got busy, customers had to take a numbered ticket to wait for a free lane. We quickly saw this as an opportunity and started going down early and grabbing a few numbered tickets. Then when people came in later and realized there was a long wait for a lane, we'd offer to sell them a lower numbered ticket. This worked well until the manager cottoned on to what we were doing and threw us out.

We saw it as just providing a service to people and meeting a need at a reasonable price. Heck, sometimes we even just gave people a ticket—which sometimes resulted in a "tip" greater than what we would have sold the ticket for. The secret to the success of this ploy was astutely recognizing which patron might give a good tip and which would likely just take the ticket.

A year or so later, I got a job at Terrace Gardens Bowling Alley collecting sticky beer bottles and cleaning dirty, smelly ashtrays three to four nights a week. And of course, necking with the owner's daughter. An unusual but welcome bonus!

I remember one Christmas working briefly for the US Postal Service. It was my first eight-to-five government job—and also my last. Although I was told my delivery route would take eight hours to complete, on the first day I was back at the depot by midday. I was pleased with myself and expected compliments. I was wrong: My manager was not happy and insisted that I must have missed some houses. He ignored my assurances that I had been extremely diligent. In fact, he became quite threatening and made it abundantly clear I was not to return before five o'clock. I did as I was told, but I never forgot being paid full-time wages for working half-days. This may have been one of the experiences that led me to my long-held belief that government, at all levels, lacks the ability to manage anything cost-effectively and with any degree of efficiency.

I suppose, one way or another, I was always in the service industry. I've never been sure how much my childhood was responsible for the decisions I made in later life. I do know that I grew up surrounded by examples of people providing services to others in an honest, ethical, and fair manner.

My father was entrepreneurial, but I'm not convinced he was good at business. Starting and running his own company was something he felt he had to do to support his family. He had little education and he flew by the seat of his pants, rather than utilizing some sort of natural business acumen.

Some might say I'm smarter than my father was in terms of business. I'm not sure about that either, but I did inherit some of my mother's negotiating skills by osmosis, if not through direct teaching. In spite of my father's business failure, I knew early on that I wanted to be my own boss and to be in control of my own destiny.

Looking back on my childhood, I realize it helped form many of my opinions on business, philanthropy, war, government, and politicians—opinions that often run contrary to what most conservative businesspeople and especially politicians believe.

There were further lessons ahead that would ensure that no matter what, I would end up controlling my own destiny and bringing a large number of people along with me for a profitable ride.

Sandy Cissel was my high school sweetheart and my first serious romantic relationship. She was a year behind me, so graduated high school while I was working at the bank. We dated for two years and my parents liked her; she was a good student and went to Baldwin Wallace College near Cleveland, Ohio, and also studied at the Eastman School of Music.

Sandy's parents owned the Red and White grocery store, which was very successful. They lived in a far nicer house, in a better area of town than my parents. I got on well with her parents and was always welcome at their home. They even had a grand piano, which Sandy played. Having said that, I think her mother had some reservations that I wasn't good enough for her daughter. I sometimes wonder what she might have thought, just twenty or so years later, when Paychex went public.

Once we went off to college in different cities, 250 miles put a strain on our relationship. In the end, it was me who messed things up as we'll see later in this chapter.

GETTING SKUNKED

One thing I did learn during this period was to keep well clear of skunks. I was coming home from my friend's house and took a short-cut through the woods. It was about 10:00 p.m. and I was walking along this dirt path minding my own business when I heard a noise down at my feet. I looked down and there he was, Pepe LePew, looking right up at me. There was nothing I could do. I had to move, but the second I did Pepe sprayed me. I can still remember the smell: It was far stronger than the odor you get when you drive past a dead skunk on the highway. This was high-octane stuff. I vomited all the way home.

Walking through the woods that night wasn't my only mistake. My second was to walk into the house, which I realized a few seconds too late. I went back to the garage and took off my clothes, went back into the house and took a shower, and then a bath. The smell hung onto me for grim death. It had also now invaded the house. My mom threw a fit. When I woke up the next morning I went out and buried my clothes and went back inside to take another few showers.

Later at school I was standing by my locker and the girl who had the locker next to me walked up. I said, "Do you smell anything?" She wrinkled her nose and said, "It smells like skunk in here." I went to the nurse and she said, "You got a day off."

A year later I dug up the clothes and everything including my belt and shoes were still rank; perhaps they still are.

STARTING OUT IN THE BASEMENT— AND SEEING THE LIGHT

People often ask why I didn't go to college straight from high school. The truth is I didn't take my SATs because I never expected to go to college. We simply couldn't have afforded for me to attend college. Also, as a C+ student, getting accepted would have been a challenge. When I left school, I applied to several large local companies such as Eastman Kodak. They all turned me down. My father got me an interview at a local bank because he knew someone and called in a favor.

My first real job was counting money in the basement of the main branch of the Lincoln Rochester Trust Company. I was seventeen and spent day after day trapped in a dark, miserable, airless cellar in a mind-numbingly boring job. Cash would arrive by armored car from department stores—huge amounts of it. My job was to count the cash to ensure each wrapper contained fifty bills of the same denomination, and sort them so all the bills faced the same way while discarding damaged or worn-out notes. Hundreds of thousands of dollars a week would pass through my hands and none of it was mine. I suppose there could be some irony there, should you wish to look for it.

It was drudgery, lightened only by the company of my coworker, a very attractive young woman about a dozen years older than me named Ruth. She was high-spirited and a bit of a tease—I really liked her.

Our manager, Mert, was the head teller. He was a lifer and had found his own way to survive the vault of freshly counted money. He was cranky and cantankerous and whiled away his time between trips to the vault with tens of thousands of dollars by gambling and constantly checking the newspapers to see if he'd won. Perhaps there was a different sort of irony at play here—poor Mert, incessantly trying to win money while handling hundreds of thousands of dollars daily.

After about three months, I started to realize I might have to go back to school to escape a life of mindless tedium. A few of my friends had attended Alfred State College, which at the time didn't charge tuition, so the price was right. The downside was that I would have to pay for room and board in addition to buying textbooks. I checked out what they offered and got accepted to a two-year associate degree program in business management. Unfortunately, sessions for the course had already started for the year and in any case I didn't have the funds to start immediately. I resigned myself to going back to work, continue saving every cent I could, and enrolling the following September.

Back in the dungeon a few weeks later, it all got to be too much. I simply had had enough, so I walked upstairs and told my supervisor I couldn't do it anymore. He sent me home and said he'd call me in the morning. Perhaps he liked my gumption. I was never really sure but for some reason, he looked kindly on me and a few days later I received a promotion and became a bank teller.

Life as a teller was good. I got to meet people and the fact I was clean, well dressed, polite, and respectful did not go unnoticed. After a few months, one of the vice presidents asked me to make a presentation at a high school career day about working for a bank. It went well, and he told me he'd been very impressed by my performance. I'd enjoyed talking to the students and felt things were going well. I was living at home and saving just about every penny I earned to attend college, while relentlessly calculating how long it would be before I could begin the next chapter of my life. As is often the case when things are going well, I was about to experience a test of character.

When my paycheck arrived, there was a form detailing the company's affiliation with the United Way Community Chest. It was a donation form that gave the bank permission to deduct 50 cents from my weekly paycheck. At the time, I was saving every penny I had for my college fund so I threw the form in the trash. Besides, I'd never heard of the charitable organization.

A few days later my manager came to me asking for the form. I told him that I'd decided I couldn't afford the donation at this time, that I was saving to go to college. I thought this was reasonable, however, the bank did not. This was another occasion where I was put into a position where I was to learn a life lesson. I was called into the vice president of human resources's office and told that all employees were expected to contribute to the United Way. It became obvious to me that there was considerable PR value for the bank in having 100 percent compliance.

I once again gave my reasons for not donating and was told that my decision would mean a black mark on my employment record. Memories of my father being berated in the macaroni warehouse came flooding back. Another lesson learned and carried forward was that any company I owned would never make such demands on its employees.

I was glad at that time I wasn't relying on the bank for my future career. This negative experience was another nail in the coffin of long-term employment as a goal for me. I'd end up having a couple more jobs before finally striking out on my own, but my days as an employee were already numbered.

ALFRED BECKONS

Shortly before my nineteenth birthday I arrived at Alfred State Technical College. Unlike high school, this time I planned to take my education seriously. I'd saved enough money to allow me the luxury of not having to find part-time work. I was going to focus on business studies and learn things that would help me succeed in the real world.

The associate degree course I'd selected was in general business studies. As I wasn't interested in studying liberal arts, this suited me perfectly: My goal was to learn stuff that would make me money, not more cultured. That I could take care of later.

By working at the bank, I had managed to save enough for my first-year expenses and the occasional date—I was nineteen, so yes I was very interested in girls. My childhood sweetheart, Sandy Cissel, had also gone off to college in Berea, Ohio, over 200 miles away. I'd only been at Alfred a month when I called to break up with Sandy. It was a mistake, and a month later I tried awkwardly to get back with her. But by that time, she was dating a football player whom she later married. It wasn't the last time I saw her though; twenty or so years later we bumped into each other. She was divorced—we spent a very pleasant evening together.

I decided after much budget review that I could afford a car—a very inexpensive car. I found just the vehicle, abandoned on a vacant lot. It was a 1937 Nash, in rough shape, paint peeling, tires flat. It looked a little like something Al Capone might have driven. I got my brother-in-law Tom to take a look and he diagnosed that its condition was not terminal. It took me a while to locate the owner and a deal was struck. I paid $50, cash. I saw one for sale recently in about the same condition and it brought back fond memories—although the current price was over $9,000 "as is."

I thought a lot of my sister Marie's husband Tom, not least because he was so good to my parents. When my mother was making drapes, one of her responsibilities was to go to her customers' houses and hang them. They were heavy and she also had to install curtain rods, so my brother-in-law would go along and help her. He was thoughtful like that; he helped me with my cars, not just the Nash, and I'd hang out with him some evenings at the motor pool where he worked. I'd wash my car and do some maintenance. Marie and Tom were very happy and raised three fine kids. Tom died of a heart attack at forty years of age. He suffered a minor one and was in the hospital when he was hit by a second major one. Today the doctors would have probably been able to save him.

My original plan was to live on campus during the week and drive home on weekends. I now had the Nash and it was only a 160-mile round trip. I hadn't taken into consideration, however, that the journey would be undertaken in a twenty-three-year-old car that someone had previously abandoned. The drive to Alfred demonstrated that the Nash, now painted royal blue, was a fair-weather friend; it loved long, straight, level roads but balked at hills. On more than one occasion I thought I wouldn't make it to the top of the next rise. It occurred to me that this was one car Mr. Capone would not have wanted as a getaway vehicle.

On my next visit home, I said a fond farewell to the Nash and left it sitting in my parents' driveway. I soon learned that hitchhiking was a viable mode of transportation in those days, and never once had difficulty getting to and from college.

LIVING ON CAMPUS

My accommodation at Alfred was in a dorm, two students to a room. And there were rules. No alcohol, no girls, no parties, and no noise. None of that bothered me; I was there to work, learn, and study. Having spent a year after high school working, I was more mature than most of my fellow students. I had no interest in joining a fraternity nor spending my time partying. Girls, of course, were a different proposition. I always had time for that particular distraction.

It would have been helpful, though, if the list of rules had included one relating to hygiene. I soon discovered that my roommate was not too fond of water—in particular, such water as emanated from the shower. Three weeks later I could stand his stench no longer, it was him or me. In this case I did something for myself and managed to get him moved to another dorm, presumably to share a room with some-one possessing no sense of smell.

On my first day at Alfred, however, I was still full of anticipation. I remember being called to what I thought was an orientation—all the newbies were lined up in the dorm and we were addressed by the head of accounting. It was not the friendliest of welcomes; he was a miser-able person who rather gruffly stated that we should look to our left and our right and focus on three of our fellow students. "Only one of you," he said, "will graduate." I felt sorry for the three fellow students who caught my eye.

One of my first courses was basic accounting—a class I would take five mornings a week. My instructor was Professor Tom Dunn—he was a wonderful teacher. It was the first time I'd really studied balance sheets, profit and loss statements, and the like, but I felt at home with them—the world of accounting was incredibly appealing. I found every class absorbing, not just accounting but all the business courses. I found the world of business itself fascinating and I excelled in a way I had never done in high school. These top-ics made practical sense. There was a reason why one should learn them. They would be useful when I stepped out of academia and into the business world.

Professor Dunn was a real-world accountant. He had a commercial practice and would discuss actual client cases with us. He showed us where theory and practice sometimes went separate ways. I realized there were textbook or exam answers, and there were hard knuckle business-world answers.

I remember having to attend a compulsory lecture on the Cold War given by a Professor Woods. He went on at great length about how the United States was at risk, was in great and imminent danger, and that Communism had to be stamped out. To complete the course, we had to write a five-hundred-word essay on any topic relevant to the course. I chose to write about his lecture, putting forward a reasoned argument that it was complete propaganda. I got a D for the paper and a C for the course. This really ticked me off, as I had achieved As in all my other courses. I went to his office and asked why the low grade and he replied that I hadn't proven my point. I suggested it was difficult to prove a point in just five hundred words and that I thought the low grade had much more to do with me challenging his opinions. In the end, we begged to differ.

LIFE AS A BANK TELLER

Over the summer I went back to life as a bank teller, this time at Central Trust Company. I handled the job well and always balanced my books to the penny at the end of every day. However, my last few days working at the bank turned out to be a little fraught. During my final week, the branch manager called me into his office. He had three checks laid out on his desk. They were checks I had cleared. One was made out from a closed account, the second was a forgery, and the third had been returned due to insufficient funds—all in one week. He was not pleased and quite rightly asked me what the heck I was doing. In my defense, albeit a limited one, the checks had been deposited by regular customers and I knew each one of them. I was mortified: How could I have made three serious mistakes in one week when I'd had a perfect record up until that point? I told my manager I would fix it. I called each of the customers and urged them to come in and see me. By Friday at 4:00 p.m. I had collected all the money and balanced my ledgers to the last cent, before heading back to school. Making darn sure the numbers added up and everything was in order would be something I would continue doing for the rest of my life.

PROFESSOR DUNN, MENTOR AND FRIEND

I made the dean's list my freshman year and the following September moved into an apartment with four other guys, located above the Collegiate Diner in Alfred. I hated it, especially the immaturity of my roommates. I was determined to make the best of my time at college and come out with the knowledge I needed to become successful. At what I wasn't sure, but I knew my long-term future did not involve working for someone else. I was also a free, sometimes contrary thinker. I never simply accepted what people told me.

During my senior year Professor Dunn called me and I could immediately tell there was something wrong. He whispered, "I've got laryngitis. Could you teach my freshman accounting classes?" I asked him what kind of students they were and he said, "They're secretarial majors." And I said, "I'll do it!" So I taught accounting for a week or two and thoroughly enjoyed my time instructing a classroom full of women. My, but how things have changed!

Dunn also gave me part-time work at his accounting practice. This was an opportunity to put theory into practice. I performed bank reconciliations for him and started to learn hands-on the many financial issues and challenges small businesses faced. I really admired him and I'm friends with him to this day—as I write this it's only a month ago that my wife and I had lunch with him in Wellsville, New York, where he now lives.

Later in the year Professor Dunn, who was head of the accounting department, asked me, "Tom, what are you going to do after you leave Alfred?" I told him I'd probably get a job and he suggested I go to Albany State Teacher's College. "Get your bachelor's degree and I'll hire you as an accounting instructor," he offered. It sounded like a hell of a good idea and I was flattered, so I applied at Albany and was accepted. However, in April or May the college sent me the curriculum, which was mostly liberal arts courses. That was enough to make me run for the hills and I never looked back.

MEETING GLORIA, MY FIRST WIFE

It was around this time that I met Gloria. Alfred was a dry town, so students used to frequent a bar about ten miles down the road called the Beacon. It was a good place to meet Alfred University girls, even though traditionally the university girls didn't date the tech boys. On the flip side, the University boys loved to date the tech girls—life is rarely fair. I'd had my eye on one such young university lady, but she had so far rejected my advances. This made me even more determined to date one of these "out-of-bounds" girls.

Then one evening at the Beacon a few weeks later, a fight broke out and I happened to be standing close to another very attractive blonde who I knew frequented the Collegiate Diner. She was looking a little concerned about the fracas, which seemed to be getting worse. I told her I wasn't into fighting and asked if she would like to go outside. I discovered that her father was a dairy farmer and that she had once been voted the Steuben County Dairyland Sweetheart. I was impressed. Gloria was a math major, smart and beautiful. Three months later, I asked her to marry me. This may, to modern eyes, seem a little reckless but it was more the cultural norm in those days to get married younger.

Gloria's family and mine were polar opposites. Her family was rural—mine was urban to the core. My family was exuberant, fun-loving, and passionate about homemade Italian wine. Hers preferred soft drinks and was far more conservative. To accommodate these very different styles, we had two wedding receptions, one in West Irondequoit and one in Steuben County. One was a raucous, very Italian, affair; the other quieter and more reserved, but no less loving.

PROBLEMS WITH THE CATHOLIC CHURCH

The one thing that marred our wedding arose from how important it was to me to have my best friend Gene Polisseni serve as my best man. Unfortunately, the Roman Catholic Church had other plans. I was brought up Catholic and Gloria Protestant, so our wedding took place in a Protestant church. This posed a problem for Gene, who was a committed Catholic. The Church's ruling was that Gene could not stand up for me at a Protestant ceremony. He went to his priest and asked for advice, or perhaps permission to be there for his best friend on such an important day. The priest told him there was no way he was allowed to take part in the ceremony and that he could be excommunicated if he did indeed act in this capacity.

This type of insensitivity and overbearing power from any institution is abhorrent to me. It's something I have fought against all my life. Once again it makes me think of the manager screaming at my father. I have little respect for institutions that act in this imperious manner.

After the wedding, we moved to Wellsville, New York, where we lived in an apartment until I graduated. Another time when institutional rules ticked me off occurred over my last few weeks at Alfred. What happened lives with me to this day—a situation I regret not doing something about. I had a good friend named Ronnie, a business student from Rochester. He was handsome, athletic, charming—an all-round great guy. Three weeks before graduation he got caught with a coed while they were shacking up some place. They were thrown out of school and weren't allowed to graduate. I've always regretted I didn't make a fuss. I should have encouraged everyone I knew to skip graduation in protest. Sometimes it's the things we don't do in life that we regret the most. Failing to stand up to the system on that occasion, if only symbolically, remains one of my regrets.

After graduation, we moved to Rochester. Gloria had already dropped out of college by that time. I got a job at Monroe Savings Bank; my first post was a branch office in an Italian neighborhood. My name and the fact I could understand a little Italian apparently made me perfect for the position. There was a branch manager and five women tellers working there. I was the assistant branch manager, so theoretically the women reported to me. As a manager, I was awful; I thought I could talk to them like I talked to the guys and it just didn't work. They were all older than me and they chewed me up and spat me out—and rightly so. I learned some valuable lessons in that job about how not to treat people, particularly women. Many of my mistakes were due to youth and inexperience. For instance, I soon realized that any reprimand had to be carried out in private, not in the middle of the office, and that a calm voice was necessary to keep things professional and under control. The other lesson that has stayed with me throughout my career is to treat people equally and fairly.

BECOMING A LANDLORD

Soon after graduation, my father-in-law came to me with an offer to loan us the down payment on a house. He was the nicest person in the world. I said, "Myron, I don't know, let me think about it." I went back to him a week later and said I had an idea, "Rather than us buying a house, why don't I buy some multi-family dwellings? Would you loan me a down payment for that?"

To his credit, he wasn't thrown by his twenty-three-year-old son-in-law turning down the chance to buy his own home but wanting to invest in a business instead. He said sure, so I went out and bought a four-family property and a two-family property in downtown Rochester.

In spite of my mother's experience, I'd chosen a neighborhood with the worst of all tenants. I had to deal with people on social welfare, people who absconded in the middle of the night, and people who defaced and damaged my properties. I held onto the houses for about three years, then sold them and just about broke even. It was bad, but it was an education. The biggest thing I learned was to never tell tenants you are the owner. Tell them instead you're the manager. That way when you get the many "I want, I want" phone calls, you can tell them you will speak to the owner. Then you can go back and tell them the owner said no. However, I soon became an expert in all things electrical, plumbing, and painting; overall, my home-improvement skills improved greatly.

This foray into business, although not particularly successful, did nothing to dim my passion for owning my own business. All I had to do was remember how my father was treated in that macaroni warehouse.

EARLY MARRIED LIFE

My early married life was typical of that time, although Gloria became a bit of a feminist and that had a tendency to drive us apart. It seemed like she blamed me for anything negative that ever happened to a woman. We were married thirteen months before our daughter was born.

I remember the day Cynthia (Cindy) was born, I was in the hospital waiting room with another guy and we were talking and getting along fine. Then someone announced that a baby boy had arrived, and I immediately thought it was mine and rushed out to the hallway. As they wheeled mom by on a gurney, I leaned over, kissed her and said, "Nice going." Only to discover it wasn't Gloria. Thankfully the husband and real father was very understanding.

Two years later on September 30, 1965, Steven was born. It was wonderful to have both a son and a daughter. However, after a few months, we became concerned that he wasn't progressing as well as he should, or as Cindy had done. I'll tell the whole story of his developmental disability in chapter fifteen.

Cindy, on the other hand, was a very typical young girl. She did okay in school, was a cheerleader, and she played softball. But the most significant thing was that she really took care of her brother. She would babysit and play with him, nurture him, and do whatever she could to make him comfortable.

I was still young, and Steven made me realize I had an additional responsibility to my family, and specifically to his well-being. I recognized that as he grew older, he would need more care and the expenses would begin to rack up. He would need people to care for him, more than we could at least. I knew I would have to get myself into a financial position to care for him. The one thing we both knew was that we didn't want him to go into state care. There was a clear incentive for me to be successful in my career.

A FUTURE SERIAL KILLER ON MY COUCH

In the late sixties, when our children were young, Gloria and I used to go out on occasion and use a babysitter. One particular young girl was a high school senior. She was reliable and pleasant, and we never had any problems with her, until one night we returned to find her sitting on the couch with a young man. They weren't doing anything wrong and she introduced us to him. He was out of high school and working as a security guard. There was something I didn't like about him: Something didn't sit right with me about him. His name was Kenneth Bianchi.

When I took the young woman home, I told her that she should never invite a guest into our house when we were not there. She was fine with that, apologized, and all was forgotten. She eventually married a doctor and had children.

Between October 1977 and February 1978, Kenneth Bianchi and his cousin, Angelo Buono Jr., kidnapped, raped, tortured, and murdered ten women and girls between the ages of twelve and twenty-eight in the Los Angeles area. It turns out our babysitter had a lucky escape.

POP WARNER

During my late twenties and early thirties, I ran a Pop Warner junior football team for boys between ten and thirteen years. It taught me how to deal with parents even more than kids. I was president of the team, so parents were always coming up to me asking why their kid wasn't playing more.

We had some great players. There was one thirteen-year-old who was incredibly fast. On one occasion I raced him over a hundred yards, and he beat me. One year our team was undefeated and this kid led the league in scoring. But not all of our players played as well as he did, and his father came out of the stands and started talking to the coach, giving him advice. Coach Bob Bayer caught my eye and I knew he needed saving, so I went over to the father, put my arm around him, and whispered, "If you don't get out of here and get back in the stands, you and your kid are through with this team." That's what I did, very softly, not threatening, just a fact. He looked at me and he said, "Okay." We never had another problem with him. And then we went on to win the game.

It was Gene Polisseni who got me into managing the Pop Warner team; he was always doing community activities and he often tried to get me involved. He called one morning and said, "Tom, we got a game at one o'clock, and the freaking school district didn't cut the grass. Can you come over with your lawnmower?" Those are the kind of things we did back then.

We used the high school facilities to play our games. However, for the most part we weren't allowed to use their bathrooms, or the concession stand. The head of the football program at the high school was very much against Pop Warner. He didn't think it was a good idea for some inane reason. Of course, I constantly challenged him to allow us to use the facilities.

One day I had to go over to the school for some reason and there was a lacrosse game in progress. I'm watching the lacrosse game, and he comes up and stands next to me. We started talking and he says, "Now Golisano," talking down to me, "Now look at this program. This program is better than Pop Warner because this program is run by the state of New York." Without hesitation I replied, "Our Pop Warner program is run by something bigger than the state of New York." He says, "What?" looking confused. "The people of the state of New York." There was no answer.

I enjoyed my time as president of our football team and stayed on for ten years. Later, my nephew Chuck joined the team, which was another reason I stayed around for so long.

A NEW JOB

After my stint as assistant branch manager, I moved back to the main office of Monroe Savings. My desk was on what they called the platform, a raised dais on the retail floor. Customers would come up to me if they wanted to open an account, apply for a mortgage, buy savings bank life insurance—pretty much anything. I was making $110 a week and we had two children, so my primary focus became looking diligently for business opportunities where I could make more money.

At that time, Gloria's brother was attending Rochester Institute of Technology (RIT) in the engineering school. Nyhl was the complete opposite of Gloria. He was introverted rather than boisterous like his sister, but a heck of a nice guy. The program at RIT meant he did three months at school followed by three months of work experience. During one of his work experience stints, he got offered a job at Sybron, the dental company, and he asked me what I thought of the position and the compensation package, which was $120 a week. I was shocked, this kid was going to get paid more to do what was basically an internship than I was getting at the bank in spite of the high level of financial responsibility my job carried. Something was not right with this situation. I spent an entire weekend agonizingly thinking about nothing else, and on the following Monday I walked into the bank and handed in my resignation. The VP at the bank asked why I was quitting. I told him with all the responsibilities I had, I needed more money than they were willing to pay. Almost without thinking, he offered me a $20 weekly raise. In percentage terms that was quite good, but I'd made my mind up to leave and leave I did.

SELLING BUSINESS MACHINES

With two young children, I realized I need to be more in control of the amount of income I could earn. I thought a job in sales would pay more, especially if there was an incentive program or commission, so I interviewed at two companies, Rochester Telephone and Burroughs Corporation. They both offered me a job and I had to weigh the two offers. On the one hand, the telephone company paid better initially but Burroughs had a better incentive program. Even so, at first I was leaning toward the Rochester company, until Gloria intervened and persuaded me that working for a national corporation offered better long-term prospects. She was right. I soon became a sales rep with Burroughs, which many years later became Unisys.

It was a great experience because I dealt with small businesspeople. It gave me the opportunity to understand why certain companies were successful and others failed, how they operated and how they treated people. I entrenched myself in the world of business and loved every minute.

At Burroughs, I sold accounting machines; machines that carried out accounting applications; receivables, payables, payroll, general ledger, and the like. I was continuing to learn about the needs of small businesses and getting paid to boot—just what I needed at that time.

On one particular sales call I went to the village of Churchville, New York. The administration was interested in buying an accounting machine to do water billing. I made several presentations and followed all their processes. The town clerk liked the machine and seemed to like me. Things were looking good. Back at my branch I discussed the possible sale with my manager, and he asked me where they would be placing their bid advertisement. I wasn't sure what he meant but he gave me a lesson in how things worked when selling to school districts and municipalities. When they were planning to purchase something above a stipulated dollar amount, they had to advertise for bids. This was to ensure fairness and also to demonstrate that taxpayers' dollars were being spent prudently. He advised me to ask them to only advertise locally. That way our competitors were less likely to see the advertisement and therefore not bid. It occurred to me that perhaps our competitors were also using this subterfuge on us.

This interaction led to a legion of intriguing questions: What type of products are bid on? How many bid opportunities were posted every week or month? What was the total dollar amount? I did some good old-fashioned research at the local library and found out what it would cost to subscribe to every newspaper in upstate New York (there were 53 dailies and about 350 weeklies). It was a manageable cost. My thinking was that if I cut out all the bid advertisements and placed them in product order, with the product description, any specifications, and the bid opening date, into a master document and made copies, I could sell this as a subscription service to companies who would regularly bid on these opportunities, if only they knew they existed.

Back at Burroughs, the branch held a regular Friday night beer, ham sandwich, and poker night party. The salespeople would always talk boldly but unconvincingly about starting their own businesses— it was a perennial dream. I would listen to the chatter and add my two cents worth now and again. Then on one occasion, the branch manager walked in—he'd been eavesdropping—and he chided us, saying, "You guys are all the same. You talk about it but you never do it." On the Monday morning following the party I walked into his office with my resignation, and *Bidders Guide* was born. That was the day I became an entrepreneur.

THREE

HOME LIFE AND VITAL

INDUSTRY KNOWLEDGE

When I started *Bidders Guide*, Gloria and I were still living in the apartment in Rochester, the only difference being that we were owners of the three-family property rather than renters. I was running *Bidders Guide* out of the basement of the owner's unit.

We had a lot of fun during this period and I often used to hang out with my two best friends, Gary Muxworthy and Gene Polisseni; the three of us loved practical jokes. I remember lying on the couch one Saturday afternoon watching baseball when there was a knock on the door. I hauled myself up and opened the front door to find an orange crate on the front step. I opened it, only to find a viscous snapping turtle looking up at me courtesy of Gary.

On another occasion, I heard Gloria at the front door talking about a donation, so I went to see what was happening. There was a guy with long, stringy hair, grease marks on his face, wearing brass knuckles, motorcycle boots, and a leather vest with no shirt. To put this into perspective, this was during the rebellious and turbulent mid-1960s, so people were all a little on edge. He had handed Gloria a note asking for a donation; his disguise was so good it took us a minute or so to realize it was Gene. We laughed hysterically and then I asked him, "Let's do it to some of my other friends." I took him down the road and we repeated the trick with much hilarity. Then I turned the tables on him by sending him to a house where I didn't know the owners. As he was about to press the doorbell I could hold my laughter no longer and he realized he was being set up. That was probably a good thing as he could have been shot or ended up in jail.

It was during this time that things were getting tense in the neighborhoods around Rochester. There were several racially motivated incidents that led to a lot of property damage. Gary's father owned a hardware store and at one point in 1964 a major riot erupted that lasted for three harrowing days. At the height of the chaos, Gary, Gene, and I grabbed Gary's father's shotguns and camped out on the roof of the store overnight. I'm not sure what we would have done if the riots had spilled over to the area close to us and a crowd of protestors had decided to ransack the store, but thankfully that never occurred. It made for an interesting night, though.

One Saturday morning at home, we got a call from the water authority telling us the water would be shut off for forty-eight hours in thirty minutes. I called them back, only to realize that because it was the weekend, their switchboard was closed. I immediately told Gloria to fill the bathtub and I started to fill up any container I could find so that we'd have water during the shutoff. Sometime later Gene came over and couldn't contain his laughter when he saw all the containers filled with water. It was he of course who had called, disguising his voice—a talent he enjoyed, often to others' misfortune.

No matter how busy and dedicated I was to my business, I was always up for a good laugh.

BIDDERS GUIDE

For the next two years I made regular trips to the post office. I'd return to my basement office with large mailbags containing hundreds of daily and weekly newspapers. I'd sit there and clip the bid advertisements and separate them into product categories by putting them into envelopes. That was the extent of the filing system in those early days.

I had a mimeograph machine and an IBM Selectric typewriter. It would take me about an hour to work through the dailies and between two and three hours for the weeklies.

My business plan was simple. I'd worked out my overhead and figured how many subscriptions I needed to sell to break even. Anything over that target was what I earned to support my family.

I spent my days traveling around New York State selling subscriptions. I'd studied my target market and homed in on businesses that I felt were most likely to buy the service. These were mostly highway equipment and supply dealers, audiovisual equipment suppliers, school lab equipment manufacturers, food services equipment providers, and others who relied on institutional business for their sales.

My closing rate was about 50 percent and my subscription price was $95 for Western New York State, $95 for Eastern New York State, or $175 for both. My pitch was, "For $175 you get to know about every deal that's happening in the state—how can you go wrong with that?" I also told them it offered a good way to check that their salesforce was doing its job.

It was fun. I met a lot of interesting people and got to hone my sales skills, something that would become invaluable in the near future. I also learned something else that would open my eyes to the fact that business is not always fair and aboveboard. My sales visits often put me in contact with the people putting in bids, and it wasn't long before I realized the bidding system could be rigged. School districts pretty much followed the bidding process rules allowing fair competition in that they didn't take kickbacks, but the highway departments were often quite the opposite.

I once sold a subscription to a heavy equipment dealer who thought my guide was great. He said, "Now all I need to do is call up the highway supervisor and ask him, 'How much?'" He was that blatant about it—the supervisor making the purchasing decision could be bought. At that time, it was the norm in several product categories.

Another way I discovered the system could be rigged, was that bid information and criteria could be written in a certain way to ensure it was almost impossible for anyone but the pre-chosen supplier, who had greased the right palms with favors or cash, to win the bid.

I'd like to think *Bidders Guide* played a part in leveling the playing field at that time. For example, audiovisual equipment could not be sold in New York State without every audiovisual manufacturer or supplier at least knowing about it. Our guide created openness, although I am sure there was still some corruption for quite a while after *Bidders Guide* launched. It was, at the time, nevertheless a unique service. It helped prevent, or maybe simply deter, deals from being done under the table.

The challenge with *Bidders Guide* was that it wasn't generating sufficient revenue to meet the needs of my family. With a wife and two children, the youngest of whom was developmentally challenged, my income expectations from this venture were significantly higher. I knew I could grow the company, but I didn't believe it was worth the amount of time I would have had to put into doing so.

The idea of keeping it going and taking a second job was very appealing—I could more than double my income overnight. People have challenged me, stating, "Surely this was a step back. You were going from being your own boss to becoming an employee again." My answer: "Everything is temporary." And it was: A short-term setback can often open up tremendous opportunities.

BACK TO EMPLOYMENT, TEMPORARILY

With the realization that *Bidders Guide* wasn't going to meet my long-term financial goals, I went out and found another job as a salesman for Electronic Accounting Systems (EAS).

In 1970, EAS was a traditional service bureau handling routine payroll processing. It was also branching out into specialist accounting applications such as accounts receivable, accounts payable, general ledger, and inventory. That division required a significant amount of development time and mostly lost money. At the time, I thought it was a mistake and I'm sure it was a contributory factor in dragging down the company's overall growth rate. However, their payroll processing business was profitable.

The company was run by Ed Regan. The rest of the management team included Jim Doyle, John Woodward (of the Jell-O fortune), and Bill Selden, whose family founded the Selden Motor Vehicle Company, an early automobile manufacturer based in Rochester. Regardless of management pedigree, I came to think that the company felt a little too highly of itself. My opinion was to be proved correct on several occasions over the ensuing years.

My previous sales experience served me in good standing. I did well in sales and Ed Regan asked me whether I thought they should hire more salespeople. I replied that we needed at least another two salespeople on the road.

Sometimes I'd have to work late and when I got home, I had to read the papers, clip the bids, and prepare the *Bidders Guide*. I was working long hours, and on one particular evening, I had a longing for chocolate fudge. Gloria's stepmother made chocolate fudge that I truly loved, and we'd just returned from visiting her family. As I was getting my craving for a sugar fix, Gloria was heading to bed and I asked her, "How come you never make me fudge?" She replied, "You want me to make you fudge now?" I said, "Yeah, why not?" At first, she said no, she was going to bed, but then I heard dishes clanging upstairs. In a while, she came down with a Pyrex dish full of vanilla fudge which she presented to me with a flourish. I don't like vanilla fudge. My longing had been for chocolate fudge. So, I said, "What did you make that for? If it's not chocolate, I don't want it." Her face contorted in rage and she hurled the dish onto the concrete floor, where it smashed into a thousand pieces, globs of fudge flying everywhere. For a week or more, I was cleaning shards of glass and fudge out of my typewriter and mimeograph machine. I deserved it.

At that time, EAS and Automatic Data Processing (ADP) along with every other payroll processing company in the United States, only targeted companies with fifty or more employees. There was an industry-standard belief that outside payroll services were only viable for large companies. No one had ever thought to challenge that maxim.

In life, and especially in business, there are defining moments—moments in time when, should you take the wrong turn or miss a signpost, you will be in danger of either being destined to obscurity or serendipitously heading in the direction of great success. This was a time in my life when I was at that crossroads—of course, I didn't know it at the time.

THE PAYMASTER/PAYCHEX CONCEPT

One day I was driving along the street to my next sales call. I was idly looking at the names of businesses as I drove past, and it occurred to me that the vast majority of these companies almost certainly had fewer than fifty employees. Why wouldn't they need our services even more than the larger companies?

As with *Bidders Guide*, the library became my information source. I researched how many companies in the United States had fewer than a hundred employees and was surprised to discover the figure was 98 percent. Intrigued, I dug deeper into the statistics and was blown away to find 95 percent had fewer than fifty people working for them. That was a significant market being completely ignored by existing payroll processing companies, including EAS. I knew I'd recognized a massive opportunity and went directly to the EAS management team with a well-prepared business plan. I already knew a lot of reasons they wouldn't like the idea, the main one being that the small guys are not worth it because there's not enough profit in that market.

My business plan had three major components. First, we wouldn't get clients to fill out a confusing computerized input sheet, we'd get them to call in their payroll information by telephone. For fifteen employees, that would be a three-minute call. As a bonus, doing it that way would reduce costly errors. And there would be no need to have the information delivered, which saved time. Of course, this was long before email or even fax machines that would have made things a whole lot easier.

Second, the standard practice for payroll processors at that time was not to handle payroll tax returns. Payroll processors typically gave clients the information and helped facilitate the returns, but they didn't actually do the returns. This was a major hassle for employers—an employer with five employees in New York State would have a minimum of fifty-two payroll tax returns and payments they had to file every year.

The third element of my plan involved pricing. The minimum charge for payroll processing for any size company back in 1970 was $24 per pay period. There was no way a small business would pay that amount for a five- to ten-person payroll. I'd come up with a pricing plan that made sense; it worked for us and was affordable for the small business owner. Our minimum charge was $5 per pay period for the first five checks, then $1 per check after that.

My presentation over, I was hoping for a positive reaction. I'd discovered an incredible new market opportunity and presumed EAS would jump at an opportunity to explore it with me.

Unfortunately, their interest level was a lot less enthusiastic than I'd expected. They put forward several reasons why it wouldn't work, not the least being that certified public accountants wouldn't like it. I said, to the contrary, they will love it, because doing payroll tax returns was tedious work especially when they're on a manual system. And it wasn't very profitable. The EAS management team, however, was seriously short of imagination and gave an emphatic no to my business proposition.

I waited a couple of months, then, in early November, I went back into their offices and said, "You guys ought to rethink this. It's a massive market just waiting for us to service it." But they were adamant. Ed Regan stated flatly, "No, we still don't think we want to do it." I was dumfounded, but I wasn't going to be deterred. I had great faith in the concept.

I then took a different tack. I said, "I'd like to resign and start my own company. I'm going to call it Paymaster and we're going to specialize in payrolls under fifty employees. I'd like EAS to do the processing for me. Look at it this way, you can treat all my small companies like one big client of yours." I let that sink in, then with what I hoped would be the clincher I said, "I'll even rent space in your offices and reduce your overhead." This time they went for it—how could they refuse? They probably thought I was a fool, but that would soon change.

The deal I struck with them was that I would pay them a quarter a check. My revenue was approximately a dollar a check, which meant my cost of goods sold was about 25 percent. By these calculations I was virtually guaranteed to make a profit.

Four or five years later, we discovered there was another company out there called Paymaster. They had been in existence for over thirty years and even though they were not in the payroll processing business, we decided to change our name. I brought together some of my key players for a brainstorming session in which we came up with the name Paychex, a name we ended up liking a lot better.

When I started Paymaster, I sold *Bidders Guide* and with the proceeds I managed to pay off all my debts. I was left with the meager sum of $3,000. A couple of teachers, one of whom was already working for the publication part-time, purchased the publication. Forty-five years later two young men came up to me and told me they now owned *Bidders Guide*, which is still operating successfully and providing the same service as it did when I launched it all those years ago.

At that point, I was married with two kids and Gloria wasn't working—so what was I going to do with my tiny amount of investment capital? My first strategic move was to hire an employee, someone who had worked with me when I was at EAS. She liked the concept of Paymaster and was willing to take a chance on a startup with limited capital. All I needed was one employee. After all, I had no clients. I decided on a direct-mail campaign and sent out letters to as many local businesses as I could find. The hope was that we'd bring in enough customers to get the company off the ground.

Paymaster started as a sole proprietorship. It was just me, although I had asked Gene if he wanted to match my $3,000 investment and be my partner. He either couldn't come up with the money or didn't want to take the risk. A few years later, however, he did join Paychex.

My initial goal was to get three hundred clients. I had no idea how long this would take but I was hoping it wouldn't take too long given my "short" capitalization. In reality, it took me four years. Today Paychex sells over 2,000 clients every week. I've been asked many times how I came up with the figure of three hundred clients. In all honesty it was simply the number I had calculated I would need to give me enough money on which to survive.

Let me ask you a question (drumroll please). I expect the drumroll to be in the audiobook. If you sell payroll processing, which would you prefer to service, ten ten-person company payrolls or one hundred-person company payroll?

The short answer is, it's better to service ten ten-person company payrolls. And here's why. Let me explain some basic payroll processor pricing: The higher the number of units, or checks, the lower the revenue per check. The bottom line is I can do ten ten-person payrolls and earn two and a half times more revenue than that one hundred-person payroll. And believe me, the additional overhead is not proportional to the additional revenue. EAS never grasped this basic truth, even though I tried to convince them. I always felt this basic math offered insight into a huge potential market. And, I was correct.

Forty years on, Paychex's pre-tax profit is around 38 percent and ADP's is about 19 percent—the reason being, our revenue per check is so much higher. Let's explore this reasoning a little deeper. First, a hundred-person payroll company usually has someone on their staff to handle their payroll tax returns. Not to mention that bigger companies fight for better pricing and are generally more demanding. The other thing, believe it or not, is that it's less difficult to sell ten ten-person payrolls. The main reason for this is that your competition primarily focuses on the hundred-person payroll clients. The second reason is there are a greater number of smaller companies to target. Back in 1970, everyone was ignoring the companies with fewer than fifty employees. Today, due to the Paychex approach, more payroll processors are now targeting small business owners, so the competition is a bit stiffer.

The other major issue that EAS had with my plan lay in their unwavering belief in the myth that CPAs would fight against this intrusion into their business. In actuality, the reverse turned out to be true. We very quickly discovered the CPAs were terrific referral agents. As I had suspected, they hated doing payroll tax returns.

It's this counterintuitive approach that served me well over the years. In this case, don't always believe common business lore and especially the concept that it takes more work and is less profitable to cobble together a bunch of small customers than to land one large client. It's not always true—question it every time. Another consideration is that businesses that rely on one major client can't afford to lose that client, but a company with many small clients can manage a little attrition. Question everything.

In my case, I needed sixty clients to break even. I co-opted my nephews and nieces and they came in to help me. They sealed envelopes, licked postage stamps. They did whatever needed doing. We sent out the mailing in November 1970. The end result was that between the direct mail campaign and paying my only employee, I burned through my total investment within the first six weeks of operation.

FOUR

PAYCHEX, A ROCKY START

When people look at a successful company like Paychex, or the successful businessperson behind it, many are tempted to think a healthy measure of luck was involved, perhaps inherited money, or maybe an aggressive, step-on-people-and-claw-to-the-top-at-any-cost attitude. In my case none of this was true. The first few years of Paymaster (Paychex) were very tough.

I was hoping for sixty clients from the November mailing—I got six. Three thousand direct mail pieces and I all I got was a lousy 0.2 percent return on my investment. Right away, I knew I knew it wasn't going to be easy. It's often that way with entrepreneurs. I've often sat through presentations where a new business owner has a great idea and declares they can capture 10 percent of the market. It's never that simple. Never.

To help with the family finances Gloria took a job. She'd previously led an advocacy group for the developmentally disabled and was now working for a nonprofit with the same goals. This was an interest that grew from our experience with our son, Steven. That income helped a lot, but it still wasn't enough to cover the expenses of the business and take care of the needs of our family.

I managed to secure $10,000 through consumer loans to help us survive the next year or so. I couldn't access standard business loans as a startup, but fortunately I had friends at Central Trust Company. They had faith in the Paymaster concept and managed to arrange a loan for me through the Consumer Loan Department. I had to pay back $300 a month. They issued a payment book in which the installments were recorded. I still have it.

By the end of 1971 we had forty clients, still twenty clients short of breakeven. I was handling all sales myself and had worked out a strategy that was not only effective back then but is still used forty-seven years later by the Paychex sales team. It was simple: Whenever I got a new client, I would ask them for a contact name at their certified public accountant's office. I would then visit the CPA and let them know we had a common client. I'd make a presentation outlining the services we offered and why I could be of value to many of their clients. As I mentioned earlier, the EAS management team had been wrong in assuming CPAs would feel threatened, and they actually encouraged their clients to use our payroll and tax return services. My advice to entrepreneurs is always test assumptions.

Far from seeing Paymaster as competition, every new client led to several more clients as I continued to build solid relationships with CPAs across the region. Our client list grew from 120 in 1972 to around 250 a year later. We were becoming sustainable, payroll by payroll.

During this period, EAS were still handling our payroll processing and we were doing tax returns by hand. My first employee, Sharon Drogo, left the company after a year, so I hired a payroll specialist named Kathy Angelitis—one of the best hires of my entire career. Some forty-eight years later, I'm proud to say she still works for Paychex. Kathy probably knows more about payrolls than anyone else in the world.

Still, it was tough going; I remember one night in 1973, we decided to have a small dinner party at a restaurant for our half-dozen employees and I paid the bill with my American Express card, or so I intended. Instead, the manager came back to my table with my card and a pair of scissors—the charge had been declined. It wouldn't have been a problem were it not for the fact that it was my only credit card.

Fortunately, the restaurant was a client, so I asked, "Can you put my charges against your bill?" He smiled and said, "Sure, go ahead." The life of a startup is rarely dull. Times were so tight, Gary and Gene used to come by specifically to take me to lunch, or they'd invite me and Gloria and the kids over to their homes for dinner. I remember once Gary coming over to the house and mindlessly opening the fridge—it was completely empty. On another occasion Gary took us to the Oakhill Country Club for lunch and he told me he was there for me if ever I needed money. I never took him up on the offer, but I always felt more secure knowing it was there. It was four years before I got my first paycheck.

We survived that period and the company grew slowly but steadily. In 1974, things started to take a different direction. Until that point the company was myself and a few employees servicing the Rochester area. Then a pivotal moment occurred. Philip Wehrheim, who worked at EAS, came to me and said, "Tom, it looks like you're going to make it. How can I get involved?" He became a partner and opened an office covering Buffalo, Syracuse, and Albany. I had worked with Phil at Burroughs and later hired him to join the sales team at EAS, so I knew him well and trusted he would do a good job. Another colleague from Burroughs, Bob Beegen, joined at around the same time and opened an office in Detroit.

That same year, Iano Locurto became a partner. I had known Iano (short for Sebastiano) for a long time—we'd played baseball together. Gary had introduced us. He was the sort of guy who marched to the beat of his own drum. He was different, not to mention as hairy as a gorilla. Every winter he would head down to Florida and work as a doorman at the Boca Raton Hotel and Club. He said it was a great way to meet women and he thrived in warm weather. I liked Iano, but when he told me that he wanted to join Paychex as a partner in Los Angeles, I said I had to think about it. But in the end, I decided to give him a chance. My friends at the time joked, "Hey, even if he fails, it'll be a step up!" He ended up being just one of many colorful characters who at one time or another became part of the Paychex family.

My first franchisee came out of the blue. Chuck Wollmer, the operations manager for a client, came into my office one day to pick up the payroll for his company Bathtique, a chain of retail outlets selling bathroom fixtures and fittings. He told me how much he liked the payroll service we delivered and said he'd like to move to Miami, Florida, and start a Paychex operation there. I thought this was a wonderful idea and suggested we become partners. Chuck was blunt: He had no interest in being my partner, but instead wanted to open Paychex's first franchise. I hadn't thought of it before, but franchising seemed a viable option and I had someone else interested in going that route. As Paychex's first franchisee, we thought it important to create a legal agreement. We got together with a couple of lawyers to draft something up and it turned out to be a nightmare. The lawyers caused more difficulty than they were worth, so we ended up asking them to leave, and he and I worked out the details in about ten minutes. We then invited the lawyers back and handed them the draft agreement. My parting shot was, "Don't screw up the paperwork!" It wouldn't be the last time I threw lawyers out of my office.

At about the same time, I was talking to Bob Sebo, who some people later named the fourth musketeer, about a franchise in Cleveland. I had met Bob at Gary's ski store some years before and the four of us had started hanging out. Bob was a district manager for General Motors's Cadillac division. He worked out of a dealership a few steps away from my office, so he'd often drop in for coffee and a chat. He liked working for GM, but he was fascinated by the idea of recurring revenue (although he insisted on calling it residual income). He recognized the difference between selling someone a car and then having to wait several years before they *might* come back and purchase another, and the payroll business where you sold a customer once and they would very likely stick with you forever. He was right: Forty years on, Paychex still services some of Bob's original Cleveland clients. Now that's recurring revenue at work.

We were young back then, so when it came to him leaving a good job in the car business to join me at Paychex, Bob felt the need to run it past his parents. He asked me to help persuade them that this was a good career move for him. I was still virtually in startup mode at that time, so Bob's dad wasn't pleased with the news. I was at their house and he said, "Are you fricking nuts?" His dad was a short, feisty guy, and tough. He threatened to kick my ass, and at one point I thought he was going to do just that. In the end he calmed down and Bob joined Paychex. The funny thing was that his parents came to work with Paychex, too. His father delivered payrolls and his mom took computer classes and became a payroll specialist. Bob told me that some years later his father had apologized for almost talking him out of joining me in my new venture. Bob also confided that he himself had hoped to be what he called a "thousandaire." In the end he was able to add several zeros to that prediction.

Some of the antics we got up to during those early days are not for publication, but a memorable one was the time we stayed out until the early hours playing cards, euchre mostly, and drinking. Next day, Gene and I bumped into Bob's wife. She said, "You guys kept Bob out late last night." Gene and I without missing a beat said simultaneously, "We haven't seen Bob." It wasn't the first time we threw him under the bus—someone once placed a pair of lady's panties in his suitcase on his return trip from a business meeting.

These characters, and a lot more like them, are an integral part of the Paychex story and we'll hear more about their involvement later, but first I need to talk about how I ended up parting ways with EAS.

By the end of 1974 I had three partners and two franchisees, and the company was gaining traction; we had around three hundred clients. As partners and franchisees opened branches, I'd have them come to Rochester for several weeks of training. We'd also help them with their first year-end. Once they were back in their territories, they would start to bring in new clients. At that time, I owned all of the Rochester business and 50 percent of each of the partners' offices. The franchisees paid an initial fee and I then received a percentage of their revenues.

DIFFICULT CLIENTS

I remember during this period we were servicing a division of the Rochester Institute of Technology as a client. They had about sixty or seventy employees and it was run by a Middle Eastern guy whose accent was so strong he was difficult to understand. He would call in his payroll every other week and I had Kathy take it because she was the best. However, she would be on the phone with him for two hours because he was so disorganized. He would leave his office midcall to go get information. After about the third pay period, Kathy came to me and said, "Can you do something about this guy?" I said sure and called him up. I asked, "You know, your typical call-in is taking over two hours. It shouldn't take more than twenty minutes. We're eating up a lot of time here. Could you be a little bit more organized before you call?" He came back with, "You Italians are all alike. You think you run the world."

As you can imagine, this did not go down well with me. In fact, I was fuming so I called up the president of RIT and informed him we would no longer be doing this guy's payroll and explained why. Ten minutes later I got a phone call and the guy apologized. It was interesting that from that point forward he was always organized, and the calls took a more appropriate amount of time. The moral of the story is the customer is not always right and sometimes it's important to stick up for yourself and your staff—even to the point of having to cut a customer loose.

These small issues were annoying, but I had bigger things on my mind. I'd brought on board several partners and franchisees and began to think this might be a way to start a national organization. The average investment from each of the entities was between $30,000 and $40,000, and with each partner I had to come up with half that amount. Some of which I borrowed from the bank.

I went back to EAS again and said, "Guys, you've been doing my processing but you're running on these old Honeywell 200 computers, can I interest you in developing computer software based on the IBM System 3?" This was a small business computer, but it was expensive to rent at $4,800 a month. In those days, a low-end System 3 could hold a maximum of 10 MB of online storage. That's hard to imagine today when one can now purchase a laptop with 32 GB (32,000 MB) of storage for under $200. Even a midrange iPhone has 64,000 times more computing power than any of the computers we were using to process payrolls in the 1970s. I sometimes wonder what I could have achieved with that amount of computing power back then and at those prices. Today, of course, Paychex has state-of-the-art computer systems, and security has become a big issue. For instance, the company has forty full-time employees whose sole job is to try to hack into the Paychex computer network.

Back then, however, the EAS team thought I was crazy and questioned why I would even consider using such a machine. I explained that it was the most popular and commonly used computer among small businesses. Furthermore, we could go into any city in America and find a company using an IBM System 3 and rent time on it when it was not being used—usually during B and C shifts, which was an ideal time for us to run payrolls. I've always loved win-win situations, and this was one of mega proportions. The host company would make a little money and we had the use of as many computers as we needed across America, at a cost we could afford. True to form, EAS once again said they were not interested.

Finances were so tight though that at times I was unsure we would survive. I hit a particularly rough patch when we were developing the new software to run payrolls using these time-rented IBM System 3 computers. I was literally running out of money. I urgently needed an immediate influx of cash to help pay for the software development and to keep my accounts payable under control. I went to speak to my sister Marie, who without hesitation told me I could take what I needed from the insurance benefit she had received when her husband Tom passed away. Her generosity, and her belief in me, was even more inspiring when you consider she had three children to raise. I ended up borrowing $30,000 from her, which helped me survive those brutal touch-and-go startup days. I was eternally grateful for her support. As a result of her generosity Marie and her three children became significant shareholders in Paychex.

Before I tell you how I went from five partners and franchisees to sixteen, I need to share the story of the July Fourth weekend in 1975. It was the weekend when everything nearly came crashing down and I almost gave up.

THE JULY FOURTH PANIC

Prior to launching the new software program, which would allow branches to do their own payroll processing, we were still using EAS to process payrolls for ourselves and the five other branches, all from the Rochester office.

I'd hired a software engineer to work on developing new software that would computerize our payroll processing. This meant we'd no longer need EAS. The engineer assured me he'd have it ready in time for this vitally important weekend—a large number of our clients' employees were due to be paid before the holiday. But when the time came, the system wouldn't print the checks. One thing I learned the hard way was that computer programmers always underestimate the job and overestimate their ability to get it done. More to the point, they never get it done on time. The whole point of the new software and using downtime on other people's computers, of course, was that we'd be able to process them locally in each branch. But that would come later; at this point we were still processing all the payrolls in Rochester.

To give you some perspective of what this entailed, Cleveland franchisee Bob Sebo would prepare his payrolls and then drive to the airport to put them on American Airlines flight 73 that flew to Rochester at 7:00 p.m. every night. We would pick them up, keypunch them, and run the payrolls that night. At 7:00 the next morning the checks would be flown back to Cleveland where Bob would pick them up. He would then prepare them for mailing, go to the post office, and mail them out so they would arrive at his clients' offices the next day.

Eventually, as Bob's business grew, he ended up having to fly with his payrolls to Rochester. We'd process his payrolls at night, and he'd sleep on the couch. In the morning he'd edit his payrolls and fly back to Cleveland. Can you imagine doing that today?

In some ways, what we did was a lot of smoke and mirrors, as was the case when one of Bob's clients discovered that his payrolls were not being prepared in Cleveland. He went into Bob's office to collect them, but the plane was late and Bob had to confess that he didn't do the payrolls onsite. The client then asked, "So, what's behind that door then?" Bob replied, "The bathroom."

Back to my software issue. The holiday fell on a Friday, so everybody had to be paid by the preceding Thursday—no excuses. On Wednesday night, we still couldn't run the payrolls. This was an impending disaster. The one thing you can never do in payroll processing is fail to deliver employee checks to your clients on time. I thought to myself at the time, this is the definition of real pressure.

My second problem was that I had already notified EAS that we wouldn't be using them as our payroll processor from this point on, so there was an added degree of tension between us. Nobody could figure out what the issue was; I had four or five engineers from IBM plus our sales rep working on the problem, but still they couldn't print the checks.

So, hat in hand, I called up EAS and asked, "Guys, will you run our payrolls?" Surprisingly, they agreed to send a couple of people over to help out. Now, had they taken the time to ask me whether we were going to stay with them permanently, I couldn't in all honesty have said yes. But, they must have thought our grand plans to computerize had failed miserably and we'd be back with them long-term. So, they sent a few experts over to work with our people and we all worked through the night. We managed to finish the payroll processing by about 7:00 on Thursday morning. I then got all my friends and relatives and anybody else I could think of to deliver payrolls for us—it was far too late to mail them by that point. Jim Wayman even got a friend to deliver some of them by motorcycle. We were dealing with payrolls in Rochester, Buffalo, Syracuse, Albany, Detroit, Los Angeles, and Cleveland—and we were down to the wire.

YOU CAN'T QUIT NOW

That was a tough time, chaotic and worrying beyond belief. I didn't make it home for seven days and dropped around ten pounds in weight. I ended up going home in the early hours of Thursday. I looked a mess. I'd been sleeping on the floor of my office. I was toast—burnt toast. When I eventually arrived home, Gloria took one look and realized where my head was, and she said, "You can't quit—just keep putting one foot after another." I took her advice and we worked through it, a day at a time.

Two weeks later we received a letter from EAS saying they would no longer process our payrolls. By that time, we'd solved the problem with our computer software, so it was no big deal. However, the system was far from perfect—in fact, it was somewhat of a disaster. But somehow, we made it work well enough and didn't lose many clients in the process.

ORGANIC GROWTH

The media have given many accolades over the years to Paychex's high-level management, its training, its relationship with Wall Street, and my own entrepreneurial drive and acumen, but in the end it's about the quality of people who have worked at Paychex over the years. In this chapter I would like to talk about some of the characters who helped make Paychex the company it is today.

After things settled down, it became easier to go after more partners and franchisees. Many more would join Paychex between 1974 and 1977. How I grew Paychex with the help of this disparate group lies at the heart of Paychex's success and survivability. I'm sure if you look at other multibillion-dollar corporations, you will see them grow through the acquisition of known talent and by headhunting proven executives from the C-suites of other successful companies. As with most things in my life, I did it differently. I brought in close friends as franchisees and chose partners for their attitude and willingness to relocate to far-flung parts of the country. In all cases, I wanted people who could immediately bring in business and grow their territories.

GROWING PAYCHEX ONE PARTNER
AND FRANCHISE AT A TIME

There was one notable exception to my rule about only partnering with people I knew well. Jack Hartland worked for Pontiac, a division of General Motors, as a district manager, which was a pretty good position to hold in one of those companies. But he was not happy. His brother-in-law called me one day. Apparently, he lived in Rochester and knew of me. He told me that they had heard about people coming on board as partners and franchisees and wanted to meet me. It was flattering, but I said right away that I didn't know them and was only bringing on people I knew well. Jack's brother-in-law pushed, "Well, just meet with us." Not to be impolite, I agreed to a meeting at a restaurant where we had lunch and talked about Paychex. They asked me tons of questions, but I offered zero encouragement. Finally, I said, "Jack you seem enthusiastic about this, but I'm not going to go into partnership with you—I don't know you."

In an attempt to persuade me he showed me photographs of his family, his house, even his dog. I didn't want to be rude, but I told him that I wasn't interested in bringing on someone with whom I wasn't intimately connected.

About a month later he called my office. I'd forgotten all about him and barely remembered his name when my assistant tried to put him through. I picked up the phone and an upbeat Mr. Hartland, said, "Tom, I'm ready, I've sold my house. I want to move to Houston." I quickly learned that he had quit his job and was anticipating coming to Paychex. I remember thinking *what the heck?* I put him on hold while I thought about the strange situation I was in. Here was a guy who was incredibly keen to join my company and even move his whole family across the country for the opportunity. I took him off hold and said, "Be here for training starting in two weeks." He did all right—he was scared to death of computers, but he could sell.

It wasn't the last time Jack would surprise me. During a training stint in Rochester, he came into my office and told me that he had sold a fifty-person payroll. This was a great sale for him, and he was justifiably excited. He handed one of our employees, Judy Chapman, the personal payroll details on the way in, and shortly after he'd left my office she was at my door. "Tom, you're not going to believe this. This trucking company Jack just brought in—every mobster in the city is on the payroll!" I called him to let him know what he'd done and suggested this was one payroll that he might want to guarantee had no errors. As it happens, we kept that account for quite a long time.

EARLY PAYCHEX CHARACTERS—A ROGUES' GALLERY

I funded this growth, in part, through loans from Central Trust Bank. My bank officer was Tom Clark. Without his support, it would have been a tremendous struggle. He later became Paychex's chief financial officer.

I was incredibly fortunate to have been able to bring together the bunch of people I did, and for the most part we got on extremely well. As with any team, some people performed better than others, some parted ways soon after the company consolidated, and others spent their whole career at the company. I remained with the company the longest, which I think is the way it should be. I still own 10.5 percent of the company.

As some of these characters will make an appearance from time to time throughout my story, here's a quick who's who of the partners and franchise owners who ended up being part of Paychex when we consolidated into one company.

Jim Wayman became a partner in 1975. He lived in Rochester and moved to Boston to open up a Paychex office there. Much later, Jim and I became partners in another enterprise.

In 1975, Tom Tracey came to me asking for an opportunity to be part of Paychex. Formerly a salesman for EAS, he subsequently opened an office in Washington, DC. He had red hair and was a scratch golfer. I found it strange that he had taught basic accounting at the high school level because I was never sure he fully understood accounting principles. He was well known for two things: First, he made his Paychex office break even utilizing fewer resources and less money than any other office, and second, he encouraged the company to charge a delivery fee. A very profitable suggestion.

In the same year, Kevin Dugan and Tom Beaty joined Paychex as partners. Kevin came from EAS where he'd been in sales and opened offices covering the Philadelphia/Wilmington area. Tom's background was as an insurance salesman and he moved to Portland, Oregon. I used to say that if you cut off both his legs he'd still kick—all that man ever did was bitch.

In 1976, I brought on board Bill Hall as a partner. Bill was an elder statesman and opened a Paychex office in Phoenix, Arizona.

That same year saw a flurry of franchisees join Paychex. An old school friend, Ron Raab, not surprisingly known as Rabbit, opened an office in Denver. He went from being an electrical engineer at Kodak to Paychex franchisee. Ron Nowak opened a franchise operation in Atlanta in 1976. Ron was the IBM salesperson who sold us our first computer.

That same year, Gloria and I split up. I remember sitting down at the kitchen table and telling her how I felt. It was tough. We had two children, but I wanted it to be as painless as possible. I explained to her that I had no liquidity, all the money was in the business, so I wasn't sure how we would handle it financially. Then she surprised me and said, "I only want one thing from you." I said, "What's that?" And she replied, "I want the New York City franchise. You haven't sold it to anybody, why don't you let me have it? And, you finance it until I break even, and help me buy a house." In fact that was three things, but that's divorce for you.

I thought about it for a week and then we discussed it some more. She was determined: She wanted to be independent. It was very amicable. She went to Westfield, New Jersey, and bought a house. I gave her $10,000 more than we had agreed for the down payment and said, "Send me a check when you sell the house." Five years later I received a check in the mail for $10,000. What's more, she did an excellent job with the franchise and when we consolidated, she ended up with 5.5 percent of Paychex. Today, that stock would be worth over a billion dollars.

Some of my close friends thought I was too generous with her and not generous enough to them. All these years later, Gloria and I are still on pretty good terms.

Life in Rochester, at Paychex, went on much as before. My mind was focused on a consolidation strategy, and a new love interest in my life turned up unexpectedly. One day I was sitting in my office when Kathy Angelitis, my office manager, walked in and told me she had been interviewing payroll specialists and had decided to hire one of them. She asked whether I'd like to meet her. I shook my head and said it wasn't necessary. Kathy smiled and said, "I think you'll want to meet her." The new hire came in the next day and my life changed right at that moment. Her name was Diane; she was a beautiful young woman with two small children and she was going through a tough time after a failed marriage. I discovered she had to take two buses to get to the daycare center her four- and six-year-old boys attended and then walk a half mile to get to work.

I really respected her energy and drive in being able to balance work while looking after two young children. A few months after she joined the company, we managed to spend some time together and a relationship blossomed. We married four years later and had twelve happy years together.

A SOFTWARE THIEF

I remember one branch manager who decided to go out on his own. Nothing wrong with that except for the fact that he stole our software. This was many years ago when we were still renting computer time from companies. It all started when I got a call one day from a branch manager in Chicago who had just recently taken over the job. He said, "Tom, we've gotten some interesting feedback from some of our potential clients that software being utilized by another company looks exactly like ours."

We had invested significant sums of money into developing our proprietary software. It was used in Paychex branch offices across the country. The call bothered me so I went across to our computer department and asked them whether there was any way we could add something to our software that in certain circumstances would cause a mathematical error to appear in the payroll.

As the call had come from Chicago, and our branch manager there had recently resigned to set up business on his own, we suspected it might be him using our software to sell to payroll customers. In this way, he would not only be stealing our software but also our potential customers. However, we needed to be 100 percent certain. So, we set up a fictitious company that became a customer of his and then we waited.

Sure enough, when our fictitious company received its first payroll, there was the error; he was obviously using our software illegally. It was time to confront him, so I flew to Chicago. A couple of Paychex officers and lawyers and I planned to confront him at the offices where he was processing the counterfeit payrolls. Strangely enough, it turned out we were also using computer time at the same location. We hung around after we had finished our payroll processing, waited for our ex-employee to arrive, and caught him red-handed. Of course, he was shocked. As soon as he saw me, he knew he was in deep trouble. The fact I'd come all the way from Rochester to Chicago to deal with him spoke volumes. As I had lawyers with me, I presented a heck of a threatening presence. I said, "You got two choices. One, you can shut down and give us all your clients and we'll put them onto our processing system. Or two, I'm going to have you arrested for stealing Paychex software." It took him about ten seconds to make up his mind. By the following week, we had all of his clients. There weren't that many, maybe twenty or thirty, but if he'd kept growing, he could have become a significant problem. In business sometimes you have to go in hard and nip a problem in the bud.

Then, there's the story of Gene, my best friend.

GENE POLISSENI—MUSKETEER AND PAYCHEX FRANCHISEE

As I've already mentioned, Gene was one of my closest, lifelong friends—we met in eighth or ninth grade. He was an incorrigible practical joker, and you never knew when he was going to prank you. But he was always there for me through good times and bad. As I mentioned in chapter three, I offered him the chance to partner with me when I first started Paymaster. He was running a tire store in Rochester at the time, but he couldn't see the potential of the payroll processing concept. As the company expanded and the number of partners and franchises grew, there he was, my best friend, watching it all from the sidelines. I was running out of decent territories and partnership opportunities, so I attempted one last time to bring him on board.

I called and said that I wanted to come over to his house to formally present the opportunity to him and his wife, Wanda. I asked that their children be away from the house during the meeting, so we weren't disturbed. He agreed and I pulled together a professional presentation. Over a three-hour period, I took them through how the company operated, the financials, the product, and the sales process. In conclusion I said that I wanted them to move to Cincinnati, Ohio. I emphasized that it was the best market I had left and that the territory included Louisville and Dayton. I was serious. I knew they loved Rochester, that they were very active in several community initiatives, and that uprooting four kids was a lot to ask, but it was a great opportunity.

A few days later Gene called me and said they were willing to make the move. That was in 1977 and their first challenge was getting a mortgage. Gene came to me and explained that the lenders had said to him, as if in unison, "There's no way we're going to give someone starting a new business a mortgage." I told him not to worry, to just put me down on the application as his employer. I ended up doing this for six or seven of the guys back then.

Although he'd agreed and committed wholeheartedly to Paychex, he was nervous at the beginning. He ended up doing a great job. He had wonderful people skills and a sharp brain. As did Wanda. She ran the office and ensured the payrolls went out on time. She would later become one of Paychex's leading salespeople. After consolidation, they returned to Rochester and Gene became part of the senior management team, but that's a story for later. He died of prostate cancer in 2001, when he was only sixty-one. He spent his last nine months in the hospital. He is the reason I am an advocate for medical marijuana; the cancer itself isn't the only problem, it's the pain of depression that people have to deal with.

THE LATECOMERS

I was down to only a few available territories when Hank (Henry) Knapp joined the team as a partner. Hank is a good example of the diverse nature of the team I built. He had been teaching people with developmental disabilities. He'd wanted to be my partner for a long time, but I didn't think he had the right background and told him that if he wanted it that bad, he would have to come and see me every week for a year and remind me why I should give him the opportunity. He was determined. After several months of weekly visits, I gave him the chance to prove himself and he opened a Paychex office in New Orleans.

By the late seventies I was out of territories. However, there were two loyal employees I had made commitments to: Jerry Reynell, who was the Buffalo branch manager, and Tom Kubiak, one of our systems engineers. Both wanted to be part of the ownership group. I didn't have a territory to give either of them, but I gave them some equity and they later invested in Paychex. This, however, did not go down well with some of my other colleagues.

From 1975 to early 1979, we acted like a fraternity. We'd meet twice a year in some nice resort, and the guys would do what guys do when they're away from home. Some played golf, some partied, the single guys chased women, and maybe some of the not-so-single ones did the same. We had a lot of young guys and a few more mature souls. They were fun days. We were all growing our businesses—some, however, were more focused than others. I was running the Rochester office and managing the software for everyone. Partners and franchisees had to pay me two cents a check for the software, to cover my overhead.

Toward the end of 1978, I realized we were facing some issues, the biggest one being, how were we going to walk away from what we'd built? None of my partners could afford to buy me out, and I couldn't afford to buy them out—so I asked myself: *Where's the liquidity?*

The second issue was an imbalance when it came to how people were running their offices across the country. Some were great at sales; others weren't bringing in enough new business. Some were efficient at operations, and others were hopeless.

Concern number three was our inability as seventeen individual businesses to borrow sufficient money to fund growth. If we consolidated into one company, we'd have more credibility and consequently more borrowing power. So, Bob Beegen and I came up with the idea to merge all seventeen partners and franchisees into one company. And we came up with a five-year goal. The strategy was to focus on developing new cities and a national sales organization over the first three years of the plan, because the only people really doing the selling were the more entrepreneurial members of the group. After that, the following two years would focus on profitability. The great thing about Paychex was that once a territory was profitable, it was easy to expand to another city. Furthermore, it made sense that the new city would also be profitable. We knew we had a model that worked, we had plateaus to shoot for. It was very clearly defined.

The next agenda item was to pull the group together and see if they would support consolidation. In February 1979, we met at Nassau, in the Bahamas. It was a Thursday, I remember clearly, as we sat around and discussed the idea. I brought along my banking officer, Tom Clark. He and I had a great working relationship. He had also loaned some of the partners money to fund their operations, so I thought maybe he would be a good muscle guy to help me promote the idea.

I learned a very valuable lesson at this gathering. Have you ever heard the expression, "Never negotiate from an ultimatum"? It's usually good advice, but on this occasion, I rewrote the rule book as you will learn in the next chapter.

FIVE

CONSOLIDATION AND THE

TOUGHEST YEARS

NASSAU AND THE NO-NEGOTIATION CONSOLIDATION

The meeting in Nassau was challenging, to say the least. I had sixteen partners and franchisees and the mammoth task ahead of me was to ensure they all felt they were getting a fair deal when we consolidated into one company. My problem was how would I decide what percentage of the new consolidated company each person would receive?

Prior to the meeting, I sat down with Bob Beegen and Philip Wehrheim and we made a list of everyone's territories. Against each, we noted what they had accomplished to date and assessed their future potential. Based on this initial information, we noted what we felt each person should receive by way of shares compared to the others. This first step was crucial because it gave us a base from which to adjust for factors outside the primary formula.

My first decision was that negotiating individual deals wouldn't work, so we had to come up with a defensible way of giving each person a take-it-or-leave-it offer. Our approach was to look at the size of individual territories, the efficiency with which they were being managed, and their profitability. Our formula was highly complicated; if we changed one partner or franchisees' percentage of the new company, every other person's would change. And that would lead to chaos. I knew if we negotiated with one, we'd have to renegotiate with all—and that could not happen.

We brought all the partners and franchisees together in the hotel boardroom and I got straight to the point, "This is it; this is the deal—we're not changing it. If you don't want to join us that's okay, we'll protect your city and we won't go into your territory—no hard feelings."

I went to each person in turn and asked them whether they wanted in or out. Somewhat sneakily, I played my only trump card by starting with the two people I knew would say yes. Looking back, I'd bet half the guys, particularly the franchisees, didn't make up their minds until I called their name. By the time I finished, however, every single person had agreed to accept the package and join the new Paychex corporation.

Everyone got a good deal. How good? Today, the value of the shares received by the person who got the lowest number of shares at that meeting would be $200 million.

In July 1979, we all met again at Chicago O'Hare Airport for a mass signing to finalize consolidation. There were contracts and stock certificates to sign, and all the other legal paraphernalia involved in turning seventeen businesses into a single entity. The tables in the room were set up like some sort of signing factory—a conveyor belt of forms.

Shortly after we consolidated, Bob Sebo came up to me and said, "What in God's name did you just do, Tom? You created sixteen vice presidents. We need sixteen vice presidents like a freakin' hole in the head!" I told him not to worry, there was a method to the madness. He was right, though. That many VPs in a company with only about two hundred employees was pushing the envelope.

The next four years were my toughest period running Paychex. It was a time of tension and stress, not least because I now had these sixteen friends and colleagues—some of whom I called "nipple-suckers" because they required my constant attention. During one of our organizational meetings, for example, we spent almost an entire day negotiating whether employees or the company should pay for coffee. It was an incredibly heated discussion. I let them go at it, but Sebo shook his head and couldn't believe the amount of time I'd let it carry on. He still rags me about that meeting to this day. From my perspective, I saw that it was more about principle than it was about the cost of coffee. The new partners all wanted to voice their opinion.

I understood that the position my new partners found themselves in was a hit to their egos. One minute they were the presidents of their own companies, pillars of the community, business leaders attending Chamber of Commerce events, and the next they were a phalanx of vice presidents answering to me.

The adjustment was tougher on some than others, especially when I then changed the reporting structure. It became impractical for me to have sixteen field people reporting to me, plus the chief financial officer and the chief technology officer and other administrative staff. I decided to promote three of the sixteen regional managers (nay, vice presidents) to zone managers. If it had been hard for some of the guys to answer to me, they now had to report to someone who until recently had been their equal, and even more unnerving, a golf partner or close frat buddy. This caused a lot of contention because people had to answer to someone other than me. Some of them didn't like this, as they felt I was drifting away from them—or setting them adrift as the case may be. Now they had to go through a zone manager to reach me.

After consolidation, there remained some residual bad feelings and concerns. To alleviate this I was, in hindsight, overgenerous when it came to establishing salaries for the vice presidents. This, combined with the considerable amount of money we spent hiring more than fifty new salespeople to expand our sales force, quickly drove us into debt. Within a year the company owed a local bank $1 million. As a result, we all had to suspend our salaries for about six months. Fortunately, over the next year we worked through the situation, cleared the debt, and put the company back on sure footing. We had been too aggressive right out of the gate, and it taught me another valuable lesson.

If I had to do it all again, I'd probably try to manage with only half the number of partners and franchisees. Some of the guys I brought in were not of the highest caliber—good people in their own way, but I think the company was starting to outgrow them. I'll give you an example of what I mean by that. At one meeting, one of them inquired, "Tom, could we get something to commemorate this?" I asked him what type of thing he was thinking of, and he replied, "Well, like a founder's ring." I said to him, "Now wait a minute, I started this company in 1971, you joined the team in 1976 and you want a founder's ring?" That was the sort of immature and egocentric crap I was having to deal with back then. Another guy wanted to hang a complete set of all our portraits in the office, for heaven's sake! The one thing that meeting was useful for was helping me decide who was going to stay and who would be leaving. Over the years I've seen many reports in the media about people who supposedly "started" Paychex, but I was the only one who went four years without a paycheck and had to borrow money from family. And I was the one who came up with the original idea as well as the idea to consolidate into one company.

The problem was that these guys all thought they were high-performing entrepreneurs when in reality, only maybe half of them fell into that category. The rest simply didn't have the foresight to see the potential at the level the company was now performing. Now that they were vice presidents, many of them felt they could spend every other day on the golf course improving their handicap, and by doing so became a handicap to the company. One by one they left, or in some cases I helped them out the door. Some left to start other businesses and were moderately successful. However, if any of them had stuck it out and chosen to work hard at Paychex, they would have ended up considerably wealthier.

During this period, my father worked for the Rochester branch of Paychex delivering payrolls. He was extremely popular with clients, but he was getting on a bit—in his early eighties or thereabouts. One day we received a call from a client, a seniors nursing home, who needed something extra to do with their payroll. One of my staff asked whether Mr. Golisano, Sr. had arrived yet with the payroll and the client replied, after a long pause, "No he hasn't, do you want us to keep him?"

The worst thing I ever had to do in my life was to take away the keys to his car and tell him he could no longer deliver payrolls. He loved his job, that's for sure. I was never quite sure if he fully understood what we had accomplished with Paychex, but I'd like to think he had some idea and that it made up for me not becoming a professional baseball player.

THE NEW PLAN

Part of the original reason for consolidating the company was to develop an exit strategy, so as we came out the other side of the consolidation process we started to put in place accounting and business practices and protocols that would prepare us for going public, or perhaps selling the company.

As I said earlier, my broad plan was to facilitate three years of rapid growth followed by two years focusing on profitability. Memories of fun-filled, carefree, fraternity days were fading fast—things were getting serious and quicker than many of my friends were comfortable with. It certainly hit home harder with some than with others.

It was about this time that I thought my friend Gene would be more valuable back in Rochester in a corporate role—national sales manager, perhaps. I called him and told him how important he was to the company and how I felt we'd make a great team. I couldn't believe it when he hesitated; he said he needed time to think. I realized he was in a difficult situation, on the one side being loyal to a friend but also having to consider the happiness of his family. From my perspective, however, I was trying to offer him what I thought was a tremendous opportunity. It was frustrating, but I had to recognize that I had fought to get him to leave Rochester and take over the Cincinnati office, and now here I was fighting to get him to return.

I stewed a few days waiting for his answer, which, not forthcoming, got me even more riled up, so I called him back and left a message, "Gene, it's 1:30 p.m., if I you don't call me back to tell me you're coming to Rochester by 5:00 p.m. the offer expires." He called back before the deadline and said, "Okay, we'll come back to Rochester." Looking back, I regret talking to a friend like that, but I wanted him back in the main office—we had a company to grow.

Gene was a huge asset to Paychex. He was responsible for creating the sales organization and later formed the HR, training, and telemarketing departments. He was also responsible for starting our 401(k) services, which today are a major portion of Paychex's revenue.

I could see his office from mine. People would continually walk past my door to visit him. He was the company counselor: People warmed to him and he gave good advice. He'd listen. I didn't have the patience for that kind of stuff; I thought of Gene as the soul of the company.

When Gene and Wanda came back to Rochester, she worked out of the office for a while before asking to be given a chance in sales. She turned out to be a first-rate salesperson. In a matter of two to three years she was bringing in over four hundred clients a year. (The company average for sales staff at that time was only a hundred.) Gene and Wanda ended up with 3.5 percent of Paychex, so the move back to Rochester worked out well—it was certainly a good deal for them.

Once I overcame the difficulties involved in restructuring our operations, I set about initiating management reports. It was important that we had a way of gauging performance and results from branch to branch. Prior to consolidation, this information was not available to all concerned. Once stakeholders started receiving monthly reports for all branches, it was most enlightening.

For the most part if there was a debate on an issue and a decision had to be made about what direction we should go, I'd let the guys talk about it for a while. I wouldn't give them my opinion. At some point, I'd give them a small slip of paper on which they could place a non-binding vote for or against what was being proposed. A third party would read the result. That way I always got an idea of what the group really felt. It was very effective. Of course, Bob Sebo said to me one day, "Cut the crap, we know what you're going to do already." That made me smile—Bob knew me so well.

It was around this point I instituted a dress code, which was controversial even before many major, traditional companies started allowing more casual attire. I also brought in rules surrounding nepotism, and I stopped allowing spouses to attend sales conferences. Let me tell you my thinking on these topics and why they are so important for the effective running of any corporation, especially one that was about to go public.

Nepotism is easy to explain. If a supervisor is unhappy with an employee who is also a relative of a third employee, what can they do about it? They are immediately in a difficult, untenable situation. Now, you can't do much about coworkers dating; heck I was as guilty as the next person when it came to being attracted to female colleagues—and pursuing a few. The one thing we ensured though was that if a couple got married they could no longer report to the same vice president. Today, the rules are much more relaxed.

Dress code was a different matter, especially in the run-up to going public. We had analysts coming in and out all the time and we needed to present ourselves as a highly professional organization. I suppose it all started when I visited the San Francisco office. There was a young payroll specialist wearing an off-the-shoulder blouse, obviously not wearing a bra, and showing tattooed arms. It didn't exactly exude the professional image I wanted for Paychex (though it certainly exuded something else). So, I immediately initiated a dress code: no jeans, no sneakers—basically, professional office attire required.

One of my other, admittedly obsessive-compulsive penchants was for clean desks. I expected all desks to be free of clutter at five o'clock. Every six months or so, I would walk around a department at random and find a desk that was a mess. I'd then get that individual's wastebasket and sweep everything off their desk into it. Word soon got around that I was always watching. I know this makes me look and sound like a control freak. But it was important to me, and I think equally important to the brand of the company. I wanted us to look like order and precision were top of mind at all times.

For the longest time we operated a little like a private club rather than a business. As we grew, I realized that the corporate culture had to change. One example was our annual sales conference. We'd take our top salespeople to a hotel or resort somewhere like Hawaii, Arizona, Atlanta, or Disney World. But every year I'd get requests from people asking whether they could bring their significant other along. They would tell me that their spouse put up with their sixty-hour workweeks and supported them. I'd tell them that if we invited spouses it would double the cost; therefore, we'd have to invite fewer salespeople to keep to our budget. I also pointed out that it would cause issues where someone didn't have a spouse. Could they then bring a friend, mother, father?

The real issue was that the conference was about the sales team sharing ideas—however, the concept of it being work, albeit in a nice location, was lost on most of those attending. The thing is, one year we invited spouses and it had not turned out well. What happened was that some of the more ambitious spouses would approach their significant other's manager and demand they be promoted or be treated differently in some way. There was one other thing that turned me away from inviting spouse and that was the fact that most of our salespeople were in the midtwenties to midthirties and things could get a little wild at times. There were times when people got drunk and pestered their coworkers. And it wasn't only salespeople: We once had to fire a regional sales manager who pressured female employees. He was a nice guy when sober but didn't understand boundaries after a few drinks.

I believe that establishing a positive, distinct organizational culture is important when companies grow up. However, if overdone it can stifle creative thinking, encourage an overtly political atmosphere, and lead to backstabbing.

Once Paychex became a corporation, it started to get noticed. Two events stand out. I can't remember which came first because they occurred so close together.

The first was a call from our competitor ADP in 1981. They had done a good job of ignoring us up until that point, or at least pretending to. It was somewhat bizarre: They called me and offered $20 million to buy Paychex outright. Right over the phone, just like that, verbally. I was shocked. Given our bottom-line profits of around $1 million post-tax, this wasn't a bad deal. I said, "Okay, I'm willing to talk to you." Twenty times profit was worth a face-to-face meeting, that was for sure.

I went up to Roseland, New Jersey, and met with the guy who had called, Bill Neal. He was a good guy and we spent some time talking about Paychex. While we were discussing the potential merger, CEO Frank Lautenberg walked in. He would become a five-term senator for New Jersey. Personally, I thought he was arrogant. Anyway, he walked into the office and started talking to Bill while blatantly ignoring me. I was sitting right there, and he didn't even glance my way. I imagined he knew why I was there, but you would never have known it.

I thought to myself, *this is an interesting atmosphere*. It was then made clear that they would not be willing to pay the $20 million all at once; they wanted us to reach certain sales and profitability criteria over a three-year timeframe. The issue I had with this was that they would own the company from day one, which meant I had the responsibility to attain certain goals without the authority to make it happen the way

I wanted to make it happen. I considered this a bad deal, so my reply was, "That sounds like responsibility without authority," followed by, "No way. You either buy the company or don't buy the company."

They declined, which was fine by me, especially the way things panned out. Even then I think my instinct was that it would have been a mistake to sell at that time—that the company was worth more, maybe a lot more. I've learned over the years that it is important to follow one's instincts in business and, as I mentioned earlier, sometimes you have to ignore the conventional business wisdom.

The ADP offer reinvigorated everyone. Now we knew we were worth something—a lot of something—twenty million of something. It gave us all renewed confidence that we could make this work. The big boys were watching us, and they were getting nervous. They were right to be uneasy; we were rapidly becoming a force to be reckoned with and we were far ahead of the rest of the market.

The other event was the result of a discussion I had with Tom Clark, then my chief financial officer. We were talking strategy around going public. By this time, I was convinced this was the right course for Paychex to take. I asked him who he thought we should talk to about getting us in front of some investment bankers. He suggested we meet with some venture capital people he knew at the University of Rochester. He thought the best initial approach would be to have lunch with them and tell them our story, see what they thought. The lunch went well and we got the advice we were looking for. I think they suggested we use Hambrecht and Quist.

Before we left, the head of the university's venture capital department, Phil Horsley, asked, "Do you have any shareholders that would like to sell some stock?" I was thinking to myself; I know one: me. And, I knew some of the others would be interested in liquidating some shares. So, I asked him, "How much are you thinking of investing?" In my mind, I was thinking they might invest maybe $10,000 to $20,000; he floored me when he said they'd like to invest a million dollars. I told him that would get him 5 percent of Paychex.

When I got back to the office, I sent out a memo asking if anyone wanted to sell some stock. It took only a day to pull together a million dollars' worth of shares, and that's how the University of Rochester took a 5 percent stake in Paychex. A significant moment in the history of the company.

Six months later I got a call from Phil, "Tom, how are things going?" I said, "Pretty good." And he immediately asked, "Would you like to sell some more stock?" I said, "I'm not sure, let me ask around. How much are you looking to invest this time?" He said, "Well, another million dollars if that's okay?" I laughed and told him he wouldn't get as many shares, but we'd be kind to him and try to make it close. We all liked Phil, so after the second sale we put him on the Paychex board. He facilitated several very useful introductions, among them Grant Inman, a venture capitalist representing Hambrecht and Quist who also came in for a million dollars. We put Grant on the board, too. Phil and Grant recently retired after thirty-eight years of service on the Paychex board.

It's interesting to note that three months after we went public, the University of Rochester sold the 10 percent stake that they had purchased for $2 million for $7 million. They were, of course, pleased with the return. However, if they had kept their shares, today their stake would be worth approximately $3 billion. Talk about hindsight being 20/20!

By early 1983, after talking to investment bankers and other Wall Street pundits, we decided we should become a public company. The original partners had sold shares freely and we now had about a hundred shareholders. It seemed a good time to go public, so we chose Hambrecht and Quist and EF Hutton to be our underwriters.

Just before we went public I called up Ed Regan at EAS. I said, "Ed, Paychex is going public. I think we should sit down and talk because this could be really beneficial to you." He said okay and came over to the office. I told him what our plans were, who our underwriters were, and all that kind of thing, and then I said, "If you merge with us, you could get a degree of liquidity." At that time, taking his volume compared to our volume, he would have ended up with about 20 percent of the company. Unbelievably, he turned me down again. I discovered years later that he didn't even run my offer past his shareholders. The lesson here is that one should never underestimate any opportunity, nor dismiss it out of hand.

Taking a company public can be beneficial for many reasons, not least because it enables shareholders to buy and sell shares. Basically, it makes their asset liquid. It's all good in terms of marketing. If you're a public company your name is out there, and in the business of payroll processing it's important to have credibility.

The third reason is it makes recruitment of employees far easier. If you are a public company, people are far more likely to make a decision to come to work for you. You have a name. You are seen to have substance and permanence, as opposed, for example, to that of a privately owned company where anything can happen. They may also be able to benefit from stock options and have access to a 401(k) among other benefits.

While the years leading up to and including consolidation were stressful for me, I'm pretty sure that reading about them will be tougher for those who cashed out early. Nevertheless, I'm pleased to say there are a few shareholders from those days who are still enjoying their annual dividends.

If consolidation was stressful, going public brought great excitement, but it too wasn't without its fair share of traumas and challenges. Over the next few years I would learn a lot about Wall Street and how to run a publicly traded company.

GOING PUBLIC

My criteria for going public was based on the company reaching a $1 million post-tax bottom line. By mid-1983 Paychex had not only reached that milestone but had 25,000 clients and 500 employees. I felt at that point we were established enough and would generate sufficient interest and support for the company stock that I would be comfortable enough going public.

Once I'd made the decision, we had to plan how it would work in practice. I remember the day we had to decide on the share price, twelve years after I started the company, Friday August 26, 1983. The market was at the tail end of a bubble, and we were considering between $11 and $13 a share. That would give us a market cap of around $65 million. I remember explaining to a friend at the time that the market cap was calculated as the outstanding shares multiplied by the market price.

I was in Rochester with Bob Beegen, and our CFO and lawyer were in New York City. They were with some of our board members and we were all on a conference call with the investment banker, who told me the price should be $11. I had mixed feelings so I put the rest of the team on hold and muted the phone so I could speak to Bob. Although they could no longer hear me, I could still follow their conversation. Their feeling was that the act of going public was more significant than at what price the initial shares were set. I was sure the share value would rise, so I agreed that we went public at the suggested $11 per share. In the end the value rose steadily and we ended up raising close to $8 million, which we invested primarily in computer hardware.

BITTERSWEET DAY

The day we took Paychex public was both euphoric and devastating. The company went public at 9:30 a.m. and we should have been celebrating a major milestone for the company, the culmination of so much hard work.

Instead, we attended the funeral of my best friend Gene Polisseni's daughter Kimberly. Three days earlier she had been the passenger and victim of a DWI car crash. It was as senseless as it was tragic, and I quit drinking alcohol that day; to this day I think it serves no purpose. Gene quit, too.

As was the case with my brother Charlie, Gene and Wanda's daughter was so badly injured her parents were never able to say their last goodbyes at her closed casket funeral. For me, memories of Charlie's somber ceremony flooded back, along with lingering thoughts about how my mother and father must have felt that day.

GROWING PAINS

In 1983, we built a new corporate headquarters at 911 Panorama Trail South in Rochester, New York. It wouldn't be long before we needed to build an extension, such was the phenomenal growth of the company.

People often ask me if I've ever made any mistakes. A silly question really; of course, I have made a number of errors of judgment. A better question would be, "Are you willing to admit in public to any mistakes along the way?" To satisfy those curious minds, I will tell you about the time I upset Wall Street.

Within a couple months of going public I announced a new product. It was similar to what today's company Monster.com delivers, basically an employment agency. The problem was that back then we didn't have the internet, so we had to use a computer system and, to be brutally honest, it sucked. Wall Street was not happy with us. The feedback was swift and blunt—stick to what you know. After nine months, I shut it down and the investment community was relieved. Wall Street is far happier with predictability and consistency. They weren't the only ones.

Immediately after we became a public company, I started to review our entire operation and in particular its management structure. I felt it was my fiduciary duty to shareholders to ensure the company was running as efficiently and cost-effectively as possible.

After discussions with the management team, Gene came up with the concept of Paychex having two management organizations. The way we had been working up to that point was that salespeople reported to branch managers, whose job it was to ensure the delivery of services accurately and on time. While branch managers were usually good administrators who understood and interacted well with their operations staff, they worked less harmoniously with sales staff. Their focus was far more centered on the operations side of the business than on growing the business. The primary reason for this was that in many cases they simply didn't understand salespeople—they usually had very different personalities. Another reason for having two management organizations was the fact that our product was very well-defined. It wasn't something subject to specifications or which involved specialized pricing. Consequently, the salesperson could make the sale and the operations people could continue to service the client.

Gene's solution was to have both a branch operations manager and a branch sales manager, each looking after their own area of responsibility. I liked this idea with one caveat—it was important that the two managers have a high level of cooperation, communication, and mutual respect.

Introducing such a radical new management structure, I knew, would not be without its challenges. During consolidation, president-owners of companies became vice-president co-owners of a larger corporation. Later, some were promoted to senior positions leaving others to answer to people who were once their peers. Now, I was going to introduce further changes. My compulsory reorganization would further diminish the power of people who once owned the businesses they were now managing. They were of course still shareholders in Paychex, but on the ground in their branches their authority and power would be significantly diminished.

Which brings us to February 1984. I called a meeting of the partners at the Bahia Mar Hotel and Resort in Fort Lauderdale. On the first evening, we had a pleasant dinner. The next morning, I had to individually explain what would be happening in each territory. I had all nineteen managers gather on one side of the pool. I sat on the other side and called them over one at a time to outline the new structure and tell them about their new jobs. Some were happy with the new arrangement, others not so much. A few were so unsatisfied they left the company almost immediately after the reorganization. I've been asked whether lining everyone up at the same time was some sort of power move, and I can see why people might jump to that conclusion, but in reality it was about time management—I had a limited amount of time, there was nothing to discuss, and I did not want to get into nineteen long conversations.

Our new management structure was relatively simple. Zone managers would each be responsible for eight sales managers who were each responsible for eight salespeople. Once a region got to a size where it needed more salespeople, we hired a new sales manager. Once a zone had more than eight sales managers, a new zone was created along with a new zone manager. This system was very effective during a time of continued growth.

It was important for the new sales department to have sales quotas that were based in reality, based on past history. Justifying sales targets and making them reasonable was important because we didn't want salespeople coming back and complaining they were too high. We began the process by establishing what sales we expected for the entire company. Once we had that figure, we talked with zone managers and sales managers territory by territory to come up with figures that were both fair and attainable. By doing this we were assured of buy-in at ground level and reduced the potential for resentment between zones.

Regional targets were then broken down into weekly targets for each salesperson. Salespeople submitted a weekly report and back at the company headquarters, in those days at least, I would review them myself. I had a system: I expected each salesperson to make at least forty calls each week. I expected these to result in at least eight in-person presentations. From those eight, I expected to see no fewer than two new customers.

The important thing about this strategy was that I was able to compare salesperson to salesperson and zone to zone. As I said earlier, there's always a lot hidden in the numbers. Other managers and I could review the reports and the statistics and have a clear understanding of what was happening out in the field. More to the point, we could take action quickly if sales started slipping in any part of the country. Also, it didn't hurt that all parties were aware that we were collecting the data and that if we had to take action, we were doing so from a strong position.

The results of this restructuring were almost immediate: Sales productivity went through the roof. Revenues almost doubled during the three years after we went public.

While all this was going on at the grassroots sales level, I needed what I used to call a field general. Today, we might call the position vice president of operations. Choosing the right person for the right job was an important part of my role in the company at that pivotal moment, and I had lot of good people to choose from.

Bob Sebo, one of my zone managers, was efficient and had the personality and ability to run things with an iron fist. Sebo, therefore, became my field general. He kept all the bad stuff away from me as Paychex grew at an unprecedented rate. By bad stuff, I'm referring to gossip, internal politics—the sort of stuff that can bog you down when you're trying to manage and grow a company.

He'd go into the field and say, "This is what we're doing," and never try to blame it on headquarters, or on me personally. Even when I made decisions I knew he disagreed with, he still supported me and the direction I intended to go with Paychex.

Overlooking people for advancement, especially when they were former franchise owners, or my partners, was very tough—even more so because in one way or another they had all been my frat friends in the early days. By choosing Bob, I had to put a dent in the ambitions of another ex-partner, good friend, and stalwart supporter who subsequently sold his shares and moved on to another entrepreneurial venture. I had lunch with him a few years back: He regretted leaving Paychex and now considers it a mistake, a fact he tells me his wife never fails to remind him of every day.

During the 1980s, Paychex consistently experienced 20 percent annual growth and was often featured on best small companies and best employer lists in the likes of *Forbes* magazine. By 1986, we had fifty-eight offices in thirty-two states servicing 60,000 clients.

Much of our growth was organic, but we also made acquisitions. For example, in 1987 we acquired a company called Purchase Payroll, out of Minneapolis, which allowed us to immediately add nine hundred new clients to our books.

During this period the stock price, or market value of the company, did not change too much from the public offering date; it would fluctuate between $8 and $14 a share. I was in a different world now; no longer completely master of my own destiny. However, running a public company suited me, in part because it created an environment of discipline and structure. Institutional investors are mostly concerned about growth, but that growth has to have predictability; they don't like hills and valleys and they look for steady consistent growth. And that was where Paychex was fortunate. Our growth was always predictable. We knew that if we added a set number of salespeople every year and the sales team as a whole brought in the targeted number of new clients, given our retention rate, we were guaranteed consistent growth. Our formula for many years was to increase the size of our sales force by 5 to 7 percent, year over year.

During this period, I became well acquainted with a lot of people in the investment analytics community, some of whom became friends. It was a world I felt comfortable working in. I've known many CEOs who dislike that environment, mainly because analysts can be intrusive and pry into your business more than you might like. This is more prevalent when your business is unpredictable and I agree, in those circumstances they can make a CEO's life difficult. The bottom line is that analysts are far more likely to recommend you to their institutional shareholders when your profits are consistent and predictable. So, working with them is a vital part of a CEO's everyday business life. Both CFOs and CEOs need to feel comfortable interacting with financial institutions. Analysts have to trust you and your company or they may not play nice. The truth is, as far as the price of your stock is concerned, they can make or break you.

DIVERSIFICATION AND DIVERSIONS

Well-targeted product diversification also proved exceptionally beneficial to growth. Unlike the admittedly misguided—and ultimately doomed—employment agency idea, these were services aimed at providing more direct assistance to existing clients. In 1987, we expanded our core services by launching the new Benefit Services division, which tracked employee benefit plans for Paychex clients. This was followed a year later by the Personnel Services division, which provided clients with help in the development of employee handbooks to accord with federal and state employment laws and regulations.

Then in the late 1980s I got a call from First Data, which was owned by American Express; here was another suitor calling out of the blue. The voice on the other end said, "Tom, my name is Ric Duques, I'm a former senior officer at ADP. I'm now the CEO at First Data, I think we want to buy your company." I was always willing to talk, so we met on the front porch at my cottage on Canandaigua Lake. At that time, there weren't so many squawking and crapping geese around. (Geese became a major problem at my lake house some years later.)

We quickly reached a deal; it's amazing what you can achieve when there are no lawyers present. We shook hands and that was that. Some people have commented they were surprised that after spending all those years building the company, I'd be so quick to accept an offer. What they don't understand is that the CEO of a company has a responsibility to all shareholders. If someone comes along and offers a premium over the stock price, the CEO would be negligent in their duties not to consider it.

Duques assigned a ten-person team to visit Paychex and carry out due diligence, and they stayed in a local hotel for a week. It was quite the operation, file box after file box moved back and forth all week. The result was we got a clean bill of health. They loved the company and more importantly couldn't find one thing they were even a little concerned about. Ric said, "We've got a board meeting next week, we'll get back to you straight after that."

The following week he called and said, "Jim Robinson, the chairman of the board of American Express, shot down the deal." My inelegant reply was, "You bastards, you didn't clear it through him before you visited me?" I was thinking, first, they cut up my card in a restaurant now they do this to me? What's with these guys?

Once again, however, this turned out to be a fortuitous turn of events. In the grand scheme of things we all ended up making a lot more money by not selling. By way of an epilogue, I played golf with

Jim Robinson six or seven years later and he said it was the biggest mistake he ever made. I replied, "Thanks a lot, I sincerely mean that—thank you."

Around this time, ADP was our biggest competitor selling head-to-head in our market—in fact, they were selling to smaller companies at the same time we were beginning to move in on companies with larger payrolls. They had also just come out with a product that made payroll tax payments and filed payroll tax returns to the client's government jurisdictions.

My frontline salespeople were putting a lot of pressure on me to start a tax payment service to compete on equal terms with ADP. I wasn't sure at first but in the end, they convinced me, and it was the best move we ever made. I called Diane Rambo, our astutely competent branch manager in Chicago, and said, "Diane, I want you to move to Rochester and start a TaxPay department. You'll have no software to work with. You'll have to do it all manually initially. When can you be here?" Surprisingly she didn't hesitate, answering, "I'll be there next week." She did a wonderful job and ran it for fifteen years.

How TaxPay worked, was that when we processed the client's payroll we calculated the amount of payroll taxes owed to the federal, state, and maybe local taxing jurisdictions. Upon the due dates we took the funds out of our fiduciary account and made the payments on behalf of the client to those governments. At the end of the quarter and at the end of the year, we also filed the required payroll tax returns on behalf of the client electronically. The great advantage of this was that we had investment income based on the float.

However, the most exciting thing was it only required minimal additional work, yet increased revenues by about 30 to 45 percent for each client. Within a couple of years, around 50 percent of Paychex clients were using the service, and the sales team started to sell it as an integral part of our service, rather than as an add-on. Sometimes, it's highly valuable to take note of what your competition is doing well and copy them.

BREAKING GROUND ON THE NEW TRAINING CENTER

A mere six years after going public we had already outgrown the new offices we had built in 1983. We'd reached $101 million and had demonstrated 20 to 25 percent growth for each of the previous nine years. By the end of 1989, we'd have over 100,000 clients.

We needed more space to house our growing number of employees, not to mention the thousands of staff from branch offices who visited to undertake training. Rather than look for new premises, however, we decided to build a 107,000 square-foot addition, effectively tripling the size of our headquarters.

A major part of our success lay in our ability to bring on board new clients faster than our competitors. Excellent training was of paramount importance to us.

Paychex consistently differentiated itself from its competition—it was in some ways what I was known for—and I was about to demonstrate that again with our new training center. I met with our architect one day to go over the plans for the expansion of our offices and he said, "Tom, I have an idea—what do you think of this?" I was always interested in thinking outside the box so encouraged him to tell me what he had in mind. "Let's put your training department in the lobby, so that as soon as people arrive they are in the middle of the training department." Now, no one had ever done this before. Training departments were often offsite or stuck away in a basement. I loved the idea of visitors being able to witness the level of training we carried out on a daily basis. We literally brought in thousands of people a year from our branches to teach them about our products and services, and anything that would help make them more successful would be a plus. Without doubt, showcasing our training department right out front would give sales trainees a profound impression of the importance we placed on their performance and contribution to the company.

I've always believed in the importance of top-class training for staff. I also feel strongly that trainees should be treated well and with respect. When I was in my early twenties, I was flown to Detroit for five weeks of sales training. This was when I was working for Burroughs. The accommodation was not in a hotel, it was in a converted YMCA. My room was an eight-foot square and the bathroom was way down the hall. And it wasn't downtown—the area was a little frightening. By this time, I realized why they wouldn't let us drive; I am sure most of my fellow trainees would have turned tail and headed home. A loud bell rang at 6:30 every morning and an hour later a school bus would arrive; it felt like we were being shepherded to prison. The bus had no air conditioning even though it was midsummer.

The training center was in an old factory and was at least in better condition than our accommodations. We ate all meals at the factory and were then herded back to the Y—and this went on for five weeks. It felt like we were being punished rather than motivated.

Three weeks in I went back to Rochester for the weekend and got my car. Breaking the rules made me somewhat of a hero with the other trainees, especially because we could now at least explore the city a little.

Once again, difficult circumstances brought me a lesson. I knew that once I had my own sales team, training would be handled very differently. As a result of my experience, Paychex staff are always put up in decent hotels, provided good food, and treated with respect at all times. My own terrible training experience meant that once the new offices opened and I walked past the training department, I would always make eye contact and wave at everyone in class. During the day as I met them in corridors or the dining room, I would talk to them and build a connection. I wanted them to know that they were important to the company and that we truly valued them. I never lost sight of the fact that they were our frontline troops; it was they who would be building the business client by client.

I knew when they went back to their branches across America, they would talk about their training at our corporate offices, and I wanted them to realize that they were an integral part of a far bigger enterprise and be proud of that fact.

Wall Street loved our idea of putting training front and center of our corporate headquarters, and as I've said, if you can keep those guys happy, you are ahead of the game. Fast-forward to today, and over a million hours of employee training occur at Paychex with almost a third of those hours being instructor-led.

The new training center was at the heart of a lot of, shall we say, entertainment. Maybe because I am so approachable, both management and trainees liked to prank me on occasion. Of course, it wasn't always one way.

SEVEN

TRAINING, PRANKS, ACQUISITIONS, AND STOCK SPLITS

Formal training had been integral to the growth of Paychex since I founded the company. In 1991, we took that commitment to a new level by opening an impressive new state-of-the-art training facility, with eleven full-time instructors, front and center in Paychex's headquarters.

Our ongoing financial commitment to training was significant. Taking into consideration travel, accommodation, salary, and the cost of training itself, we were investing around $18,000 per new recruit. And, that was without the lost opportunity cost of not having their territory covered while they were receiving their training. This investment paid off. The majority of graduates reached 75 percent of their quota within their first quarter. This formal training meant new sales reps were up and running 35 percent faster than previously and consistently produced higher sales revenues. This focus on training, along with the discipline it taught our new recruits, gave us an advantage over our competition. It also impressed both existing clients and prospective customers, as well as those folks on Wall Street.

I was always a stickler for keeping the training rooms clean and tidy and insisted people dress professionally. I wouldn't stand for new recruits turning up for training in jeans and T-shirts, for instance. Business attire was always insisted upon. Whenever I talked to new recruits, I emphasized the importance of treating people, especially clients and clients' employees, with respect. I taught them to take their cup back to the break room or kitchen after meeting with prospects or clients, thanking someone when they brought them a coffee, and replacing their chair after leaving a meeting room table— small things that would distinguish them over our competition's salespeople. Basic manners maybe, but often sorely lacking in the business world.

During one particular graduation-day lunch, I was outlining the company's five-year plan. These lunches were formal affairs; people were expected to wear business attire. Although celebratory, they were serious—sometimes certificates were awarded.

I was several minutes into my presentation when someone started vacuuming at the back of the room. I was stunned and shouted to the cleaner that she couldn't be doing that now and couldn't she see I was in the middle of delivering a speech? She looked confused, came up to me at the front of the room and tried to hand me what looked like a work order. I barely looked at it and told her to leave; I was not pleased. Of course, the trainees in the room thought this was hilarious. After I quietened them down I got back to discussing the business plan. A short time later, there she was again; this time outside washing the glass walls surrounding the training room. By now I was furious. I went outside and brusquely shooed her away. As I turned to go back into the room my eye caught the entire HR department laughing from the dining room. Too late, I realized that the whole thing had been an elaborate prank. I'd been had, and good!

I wasn't always on the receiving end; I was known for being unpredictable and could come up with a good prank. I remember going into work one day and noticing that a group of management trainees looked particularly bored. A few evenings later I bumped into a group of these middle managers hanging out at a local bar. They were from out of town and I enjoyed spending some time with them.

One of the managers, a guy named Chris, impressed me so I pulled him aside and asked him if he'd like to help me play a prank.

As I've said, we used to have graduation-day lunches for our trainees and if I was available, I would speak at the event. The training instructors and the department head were always a little uneasy about what I might say as I often went off script. On this occasion, I kept to the standard line and didn't say anything contentious or provocative. I noticed they smiled and relaxed. I always allowed questions from the trainees on these occasions, and that was when the fun began.

Chris, who I was not supposed to know, of course, stood up and said he was disappointed with how our software handled local income taxes. I replied that I knew it wasn't up to par, but that the IT department was aware of the issues. As I looked around the room for another question, Chris jumped up again and told me quite aggressively that he wasn't happy with my answer. One of the instructors by this time had made his way to Chris and was standing next to him trying to calm him down. Or possibly warning him that he was on very dangerous ground.

For my part, I said angrily that we were working on the issue as fast as we could. At last, other people managed to ask some questions before Chris once again stood up and said loudly that he thought my answer was BS. I glanced over at my head of department; she had a horrified look on her face. The room was silent, and I let the silence last for a few long seconds before telling Chris that if he didn't like it, he could leave and not come back. He stormed out and my head of training's jaw dropped; Chris was one of her best graduates. You could have heard a pin drop in the cafeteria, until Chris marched back in with a broad grin and everyone started laughing and clapping like crazy.

I didn't only play tricks on our trainees; my partners were also fair game. My friend Gene used to drive a bright-red Mercedes SL sports car all winter long in Rochester, New York. One day when I drove into work, I saw a large crane that was starting construction on the addition of our new headquarters. A short time later, I asked the contractor to build a platform big enough to hold a car. We then sent Gene out to lunch for a business meeting and got his spare set of keys from his wife. On his return there was his car swinging from a crane five stories above the ground. Unfortunately, the wind had come up quite strongly and I was beginning to worry that this might become an extremely costly prank. Gene on the other hand was unperturbed and just said, "Boy, I wish I'd thought of that."

Occasionally, I'd drop into a sales conference to see what was going on and ensure the material and information we were delivering was up to standards. On one occasion, based on Gene's recommendation, we brought in an outside consultant to make a presentation, so I was particularly interested to hear what he had to say. We'd collected together around five hundred of our salespeople to listen to his words of wisdom. He launched into his presentation by saying, "Telephone marketing is vital and what you are selling is an easy pitch. I could get on the phone, and I bet you in an hour I could make two or three sales." Standing at the back of the room, I sensed this was not going down well—our sales team were all professionals and were not going to take such hyperbole easily. "Excuse me," I interrupted, "that's very interesting. I'm going to take you up on that bet. I'll arrange for a phone to be brought in so our salespeople can see firsthand how you make those sales." He actually ran out of the room like a scared rabbit.

Training excellence was a founding principle back in 1971, and it remains at the core of everything Paychex does today. The company is recognized as one of the top 125 training organizations by *Training* magazine—as it has been for the past nineteen years.

During 2019, the company delivered more than one million training hours to nearly 16,000 employees. I would like to believe this is why Paychex is one of the most respected payroll processing companies in the country.

ACQUISITIONS, NEW MARKETS, AND MORE DIVERSIONS

Between 1991 and 2000, Paychex achieved revenue growth of no less than 17 percent annually. Earnings growth was never less than 30 percent year over year.

It was our TaxPay product that was mostly responsible for that growth. In addition, in the late 1990s, we started doing the same thing with salary direct deposit. We'd take the money out of the client's account and deposit it into the employee's account. In between these two actions, the money would be "floating" with us for a day or two. This gave us an opportunity to invest it in the interim. Some skill was required to watch and assess the daily check balance in the fiduciary account over a four-week period, to calculate the amount we could safely invest. The balance could never be allowed to drop below what was required to make all required client/employee transactions. It was a powerful skill we had learned.

This period was also a busy one for acquisitions. Adding acquisitions to supplant organic growth made a lot of sense and created many new opportunities. We developed new software to expand into new sectors, new products and services to increase revenue and profits, and acquired new client lists by buying other companies wherever possible and prudent.

Olsen Computer Systems Inc.

In 1996, we decided to buy a payroll software company, which ended up embroiling us in years of legal battles as we fought with our adopted licensees. I learned a lot about how unfair the legal system can be and made the decision to never buy a company that has licensees ever again.

The company in question was Olsen Computer Systems Inc. At that time, Paychex's software wasn't designed for larger companies. It simply wasn't flexible or comprehensive enough to meet their needs. Olsen was a sole proprietorship providing PC-based software to payroll service companies in the fifty- to two-hundred-employee sector. We purchased the company for about $22.5 million and immediately changed its name to Rapid Payroll, Inc.

After three years, because of the lack of growth in the number of licensees as well as minimal revenue growth, Paychex decided it would end its software agreement with them.

There was no real benefit to Paychex in the license arrangements, and we really just needed the software to help us compete on more even terms with ADP. We decided to send them all termination notices to cease using our software, giving them twelve months to effect the change—a timeline we thought was fair. By 2001, we no longer licensed nor supported the software.

The licensee contract we inherited from Olsen stated that in case of default of any terms in the contract, the most the other party could recover was the amount of any fees paid over the period a licensee had been using the propriety software. Very simple language, very straightforward—however, the contracts had no end date, nor any provision to raise prices.

Unfortunately, twenty-seven of the licensees decided to sue us for breach of contract and claimed punitive damages. The number of disputes later grew to seventy-six. To avoid prolonged and potentially expensive court cases, we settled with most of them for between $20,000 and $30,000 each. In fact, we managed to resolve all but two of the suits. The two holdouts were in California. Licensees and franchisees start out very weak individually, but they start aggregating, talking to each other, and establishing user groups. They want to negotiate with you as a team. At that point, you have a more serious problem.

One of the holdouts was a licensee in San Francisco. We went to court before a judge (no jury) and after hearing all submissions from both parties the judge decided a settlement was appropriate and awarded the licensee $40,000, which we paid. The amount was not a lot more than we paid the other licensees in out-of-court settlements.

The second holdout was a totally different case, let's call them Mr. and Mrs. Dramatic. Their payroll company in Los Angeles was only doing about $2 million in revenue, but the judge decided the plaintiffs had a case. They were suing us for $32 million. Ominously, this court had earned the nickname as the "plaintiff's bank," due to its reputation for finding against large corporations.

Key to the decision was the fact that the judge threw out one clause in the contract as illegal. Our top intellectual property lawyer was amazed and asked the judge, "Why is it illegal? Everybody agreed to it." In the end, the case ended up going to court where twelve jurors, six of whom did not have a high school education, found in favor of the plaintiff. A complex case came down to the whims of people who probably barely understood the complicated contract law on which they were making a decision. The optics won the day, it was the big corporation with deep pockets against the poor little lady crying on the stand. Mr. and Mrs. Dramatic walked away with $11 million in compensatory damages and $15 million in punitive damages.

In summary, while one Californian licensee got a more-than-generous ruling awarding them $40,000 from Paychex based on the contract they signed, the other got $26 million to punish the corporate bully. I'm not sure the correct bully was identified in this case. So much for the legal system, especially in California.

In the end, however, purchasing Olsen was one of the best acquisitions Paychex ever made. It allowed the company to compete with ADP with software that was more applicable to larger companies of up to five hundred employees, which are now a major portion of Paychex's revenue.

Moving into 401(k)s

An important milestone in Paychex's history was the moment Gene Polisseni and his associate Tony Tortorella walked into my office and told me we should be selling 401(k) administration. They outlined a well-defined plan and I liked the idea. As with most of our previous entries into new sectors, we weren't going to use software initially—everything was to be done manually. It was this development that led us into other products such as worker's compensation insurance, employee handbooks, and a menu of other human resource services. Today, Paychex sells over $2 billion in payroll services and almost as much in HR services annually.

These new services were important to our growth in the late nineties, not least because they were extremely profitable. And they were profitable because they linked two products together. We could, for example, process 150,000 payroll clients on a Monday and if 50,000 of them had a 401(k) plan, we had the work and administration done and the money in the investor's hands by 6:00 a.m. on Tuesday. The other huge benefit was our level of accuracy; because we handled the payroll, what was on the 401(k) report reflected exactly what was in the payroll.

This gave us a tremendous advantage over our competition. Today Paychex sells more new 401(k) plans every year than any other company. The HR Services division is pulling in around $1.8 billion in gross revenues and is growing by 15 percent annually.

National Business Solutions

In June 1996, to facilitate a move into administering employee benefits, we bought Tampa, Florida–based National Business Solutions Inc. (NBS) for $142.5 million in stock. NBS was a professional employer organization (employee leasing). It handled 401(k) programs, employment regulatory compliance, workers' compensation coverage, and healthcare services for around 10,000 employees.

Office Romance

A few months after we made the acquisition, I wasn't convinced the transition was going as well as it should. I wanted to monitor it in person; of course, as it was winter in Rochester, the weather in Florida was also a big draw.

Arriving at the office on a Monday morning, I happened to walk into a sales operation's meeting. Across the table was this woman Heather Keys; she was attractive and personable. At the end of the meeting she was the only person who came up and introduced herself to me.

By this time, Diane and I had been divorced for about two years. I asked the CEO if I could go on a service call with Heather. He was okay with this and we set up a suitable day for me to accompany her when she visited one of our clients. The call was very interesting and informative in a work sense, but not as interesting as she was. At the end of the week I stopped by her workstation and asked, as I was here all weekend and didn't know anyone, if she would like to accompany me to the Tampa Bay Buccaneers football game. At first, she said she didn't think it was a good idea, but the next morning she called to say she had changed her mind.

We ended up spending the entire day together, had a great time, and a relationship started. I stretched out my time in Tampa for as long as I could, but eventually I had to return to Rochester and I sort of left her in the dust. She was not very happy with the situation and sent me all the clothes I had left at the condo we had shared while I was in Tampa.

The following winter I found myself in Tampa again and decided to visit her. It didn't go well, and it was obvious it wasn't going to go anywhere—or so I thought. Back in Rochester sometime later, the head of HR walks into my office and said, "Tom, we have a person we want to work in the training department in Rochester." I asked him why he was telling me this and he said, "Because it's Heather Keys." I was shocked, "She won't want to move up north, she's a warm-weather girl," I said. Three weeks later, however, she was working in Paychex headquarters. We'd often say a polite hello in the hallways, until one day as I was leaving the office, she put her hand on my arm in a way that sent a clear message—to me anyway. I asked her what she was doing for the weekend and suggested she might join me on a trip to see Bob Sebo in Naples. The rest is history, our romance reignited. We were together for eight years and eventually got married.

Gaining an Advantage

Paychex's next major acquisition was in 2002, when we bought Advantage Payroll Services Inc., based in Chicago, for $240 million in cash. It was a significant purchase because Advantage had almost 50,000 clients that were good prospects for our human resources and retirement services. Advantage's forty-one offices nationwide, and fifteen independently owned associate offices, became an important asset to Paychex. The acquisition also reduced the competition in many of our markets where they were becoming bigger and stronger.

The story behind the purchase tells a lot about how business doesn't have to be as complicated or difficult as it is often made out to be. I knew that Advantage was owned by a venture capital firm and that there was talk of them going public. So, while I was in Chicago attending an investment conference I put a call into the general partner of the venture capital firm and arranged a meeting with him. Within minutes I got the information I wanted, which was that he didn't want the aggravation of taking the company public.

Within forty-five minutes, I'd made him an offer for the company. He accepted, proving once again, what lawyers make complicated can be achieved by two businesspeople if they are both on the same page. Of course, both parties carried out considerable due diligence before the sale was finalized, but the negotiation and basic deal took less than an hour to consummate. This was a case of my "good deal for everyone" philosophy in action.

One of the negative sides to this acquisition was that because we paid a healthy premium for the company, it set a higher value expectation with other payroll processing companies open to being bought by Paychex.

I guess it might appear that Paychex got acquisition, happy in the late 1990s—and I'd have to concede that we did. One of the big lessons out of that period of our corporate history is that I've never been very aggressive or very happy when it came to potential acquisitions for one reason. In all my experience, and I think it happened in each of the acquisitions I've just discussed, the management of the acquired entity always say they want to stay and work for your company, but in reality, once they receive payment they generally leave within a year to eighteen months.

This means when you make an acquisition, you better have available personnel with the skill set to replace them or you can run into major problems, particularly with a proprietary software company. The reality is when it comes to acquisitions, management will leave.

HAVING FUN WITH A PUBLIC COMPANY

I had a great time during this period. Running a public company seemed to fit my temperament and the way I operated. As I mentioned in the last chapter, Paychex was a predictable company with the advantage that during the 1990s and early 2000s it was growing at an amazing rate. We were the darlings of Wall Street during that period.

One of the ways to measure the success of a company and its attractiveness to investors is the PE ratio, or profits-to-earnings ratio—or to be more accurate, earnings per share to stock price. During this period Paychex enjoyed a very high PE ratio. The average on Wall Street was 20 to 1 at that time, but at one point Paychex reached 105 to 1, a rate that was unrealistically high. Unfortunately, you can have too much of a good thing, and when a PE ratio gets too high it can result in investors getting burned because it's not sustainable. I called all our analysts and said, "What are you guys doing? Stop buying the stock, people are going to get hurt." I am sure that when I called, many of the analysts heard this rare request for the first and maybe the last time in their careers.

I enjoyed hanging out with Wall Street analysts, and as I mentioned before, many became friends. I did a road show with one stock analyst, Dave Farina, from an investment banking firm in Chicago. We hit five different cities to present Paychex as a good investment opportunity to institutional investors.

I did about seven or eight presentations in four days and Dave would then answer questions from the clients' perspective. The last stop was back in Chicago and Dave said to me, "You know, I've watched your presentation so often, I could probably do it myself." I smiled but didn't say anything. When we arrived at the final venue we were given lunch and afterward I stood up to make the presentation, but instead of launching into my slide show, I said, "Folks, I know you're expecting a presentation from me, but I've got a tired voice, and Dave Farina is going to make the presentation to you today." Dave looked at me with a stunned expression. I wasn't sure what he was going to do, but he got up there and did a great job. I think he may even have enjoyed it.

The key to stock market success, as I've mentioned before, is consistent results. I still hear CEOs say things like, "Quarterly earnings are a joke—there are so many ups and downs, it's hard to run a company on quarterly earnings." I agree—it is tough, but it's the greatest management discipline there is in running a business. Provide consistent results and you will get your best stock price. Stock analysts are professional investigators. That's why the general public doesn't have a chance against institutional investors. Analysts may spend their entire time working with as few as eight companies, so they are supremely knowledgeable about what makes those companies tick. As I've said, the CEO and CFO have to have a good relationship with these analysts, but care has to be taken not to divulge information that is not universally available. Insider trading is illegal, but it does occur, as I witnessed myself during the Chicago road trip.

A few of us got into a limo, I think it was in Denver. There was an institutional sales rep for the company I was traveling with who happened to sit up front with the driver. He got his phone out and within earshot of everyone in the limo casually called an institutional investor and said, "I found out about 'ABC Holdings.' Now's the time." And he hung up. I was shocked. This was blatant insider training happening right in front of me, something I would have absolutely nothing to do with. I have always run my businesses to the letter of the law and I simply could not sit by and watch this occur. I looked at Dave and said, "If I don't find out he's fired by next week, I'm going to report him to the SEC (the US Securities and Exchange Commission)." Unfortunately, they didn't fire him, but they did put him on notice and monitored him closely after that.

DRESSING DOWN

Right from the outset, I always wanted my company to be professional in every way. I've talked about the dress code I instigated early on and my reasoning for it. Paychex became an exemplar for the way its employees dressed and deported themselves. Women were expected to wear skirts and dresses. Men wore suits, dress shirts, and ties. Some people say we were so strict that the shirts had to be white. That's not true—I allowed blue, too.

By the time we hit the year 2000, the very strict dress code was a bit of an anachronism and I was coming under increasing pressure from various quarters to relax it a little. As far back as 1994, the National Organization for Women had criticized me for it. I'd held out as long as I could but could see that in the long run I was probably going to lose this battle.

I decided to use our annual employee meeting to tackle the dress code issue for the final time. We had a thousand people in the room and I was due to give a state-of-the-company speech. Prior to the formal part of the event I was in my normal suit and tie, the standard uniform I'd worn for thirty years or more. I walked around the room meeting people, shaking hands, catching up with old friends, and welcoming new people to the company.

When it was time for the formal part of the proceedings, I made my way backstage. Our CFO, John Morphy, introduced me and I walked out on stage. There was silence—a thousand people looked at me standing there and didn't know what to make of what they saw. I had removed my jacket and tie and put on a sweater. I didn't say a word. Then gradually, a murmur started, which grew into a roar. People applauded. Others stood on chairs and clapped and cheered. I hadn't said a word—they figured it out. When they calmed down, I said very formally, "I just want you all to know I'm retiring," Just like that, the room let out a collective gasp and went silent. I let the silence linger for a few more seconds, milking the moment as much as I could. Then I said, "No, I'm kidding, we're changing the dress code," and the room was in an uproar again.

Who says running a public company isn't fun?

STOCK SPLITS

During the ten years of Paychex's phenomenal growth, the board of directors on ten different occasions decided that we would do a stock split. Generally, we did stock splits when the stock price rose to between $45 and $50 per share, at which point the split would bring it down into the low $30 price range.

For example, for every hundred shares held, a shareholder received fifty more shares from the company at a price that was reduced by one-third. In other words, owners of a hundred shares at $30 a share before the split subsequently owned 150 shares at $20 a share after the split. It comes out to the same value. The question is why do we do stock splits? There are two reasons: First, it's a message from management to the general investing public that the management is confident of the company's future; second, it creates a little hype in the retail market—retail stockholders like stock splits.

The retail public enjoys stock splits a lot more than institutional shareholders do because it's an additional administrative burden for institutional shareholders to constantly remember how many shares of stock are outstanding.

EIGHT

WAR AND NATIONAL POLITICS

WAR

My friend Gary Muxworthy was interviewed for a PBS documentary about my life some years ago. He recalled a story that is worth retelling here. Apparently, I held a dinner party at my house, and we were discussing the Vietnam War. Gary told the interviewer that I had asked everyone, "Do any of you trust what the government tells you is actually true?" He remembered that long before there were demonstrations in the street, and as the Vietnam War turned into a disaster, that I had not accepted the government line that the war was justified to prevent communism from spreading. I have never believed we should get involved in another country's civil wars.

In fact, I have been quoted as saying, "Every time a politician mentions war, they should be shot because politicians wage war, citizens don't wage war." I certainly have trouble with government lying to us time and time again. Look at the history of the Vietnam War. It is clear that five presidents lied to the American people about events on the ground. So did the political and military advisors who surrounded them. The release of secret tape recordings has shown that both Presidents Johnson and Nixon knew the war was unwinnable, but they continued to escalate military action because of political expediency, upcoming elections, and a fear they would be seen as soft on communism. Common sense and decent honesty seem to continually take a back seat to holding onto power at any cost—including the lives of thousands of America's young people.

I told the story earlier about how my brother, Charlie, was one of 36,574 Americans who gave their life in the Korean conflict. Another 103,284 were wounded in the three years of conflict. He died on Friday, November 2, 1951, age twenty-one. Their blood is on the hands of the politicians (on both sides) who waged an unwinnable war.

People who know me well will have often heard me expound on war—and more particularly how to avoid it—such as my theory that the Cold War could have been shorter and less expensive if we had bought every single Russian family an Oldsmobile Cutlass.

I also have great difficulty supporting the draft, which allows government to forcibly recruit people into the armed forces, while at the same time setting their salary at significantly below market rate. In my opinion, the draft is slavery at its finest. Not only are you a slave, but you are now a killer of people.

If you are raising an eyebrow at this point, I ask you to consider this: What else is it when government unilaterally sets someone's wage, locale, type of work, hours, and level of danger—all in the name of fighting for freedom—a freedom the draftee himself does not enjoy. In the case of the so-called Korean "War," Congress never actually declared war on North Korea. President Truman never sought a formal declaration of war from Congress. In my opinion, our presence in Korea was no more than an illegal police action.

NATIONAL POLITICS

The first time I became seriously interested in national politics was in 1991 when Congress had a very low credibility rating—not as low as today perhaps, but still not healthy. I'd met Gordon Black, who was a pollster, while working on an anti-drug coalition. He was writing a book called, *The Politics of American Discontent: How a*

New Party Can Make Democracy Work Again which was subsequently published by Wiley in 1994. It was a snapshot of Congress and its inept dysfunctionality. His description of an American public feeling alienated from its government, the lack of genuine competition for incumbent politicians, and the power of special interest groups over mainstream Republicans and Democrats resonated with me.

In 1991 I arranged to pay $35,000 to sponsor a poll of 1,600 American adults, conducted by Gordon's company, designed to assess American voter sentiments. My underlying reason for the sponsorship was my feeling that the political system was essentially dishonest.

Later I spoke at a news conference, outlining the results of the poll, which found significant discontent with the government. In essence, the general public agreed with my assessment of the political system's lack of integrity and honesty. My specific concerns were in the areas of limiting the terms of incumbents, the welfare system, the war on drugs, trade relations, urban problems, public education reform, and the right to referendum. One other thing had caught my interest, for whatever reason: The American public toward the end of the millennium were starting to get concerned about the national debt, and I was one of them. During those years, New York state politics were a sham as well; in fact, they always had been. The press conference drew a lot of interest, but as with a lot of these things, interest peaked initially and then faded rapidly.

The topic of moving Paychex's corporate headquarters out of New York State had come up at many officers' meetings. The state seemed to take pleasure in overtaxing, overregulating, and generally harassing its corporate citizens. I was quoted in the media as saying, "I have two choices as a resident of New York State. I can leave or I can stay here and fight." Well, I chose to fight. Gordon Black was quoted calling me, "a profoundly angry man." He was not wrong. I was not sure, however, how to take being called a "rumpled Don Quixote" or a "rags to riches scrambler" by a *New York Times* article that seemed at the time to be mixing metaphors like crazy. They were, however, correct in saying that I was not the only one concerned about economic and social deterioration and that I was on somewhat of a crusade. In an advertising campaign I stated:

> New York State is on a slow death spiral. You know it and I know it. Businesses are leaving our state and taking jobs with them. Both parties are obligated to special interest groups that spend millions of dollars on their campaigns.

My interest in electoral politics was developing fast, and I was learning the art of war in politics.

Shortly before all of this, Ross Perot had decided to run for president. At that time, Gordon and I were enthusiastic about what he was doing and loved his unique and unorthodox thirty-minute television presentations. Perot gained some traction and the American public was starting to listen. In the early days of his 1992 run we supported him in a modest way. But he made many blunders. Perot publicly accused the Republicans of sabotaging his daughter's wedding, which made him look paranoid in the eyes of the public. He withdrew from the race for a while even though he was doing well, and later reentered, never regaining his earlier momentum. He brought in Vice Admiral James Stockdale as his vice-presidential candidate. The problem was that Stockdale was not a politician and unfortunately imploded during the vice presidential debate against Al Gore and Dan Quayle. He couldn't put three words together. The result was Perot's ratings dropped to just 6 percent.

Remarkably, he did fight back and ended up with 19 percent of the popular vote, one of the strongest results for a third-party candidate in US history. Before all the missteps, he was leading Bush and Clinton for a short time. I still believe that if it were not for the mistakes, he might have won the presidency. Having said that, the electoral college might have clipped him at the end.

People were ready for something different. After Perot's presidential bid failed, he started United We Stand, a nonprofit watchdog organization. Gordon and I were interested in what Perot was doing so we hopped on a plane to meet with him and his associates in Dallas. During the meeting, we suggested they turn the organization into a national political party, but Perot told us he wanted it to simply take an advocacy role. His idea was to go around endorsing candidates. He felt this would make a difference—well, it didn't. Shortly after our meeting, the effort began to disintegrate.

NINE

MY FIRST TWO

RUNS FOR GOVERNOR

THE INDEPENDENCE PARTY

I had always believed state politics was a bit of a sham. My biggest complaint about New York State's government was how they come up with their budget. Basically, three people—the governor, the speaker of the assembly, and the leader of the senate—would go into a room and come up with a budget, and then tell all their subordinates to pass it. Well, I don't think this is the way a budget should be decided. The fact is, they actually make a joke about the "three men in the room" situation. I visited Albany once and I asked the leader of the senate, "Show me the room," and sure enough it's about an eight-by-ten room with no windows and four chairs, and that's how they decide the $170 billion New York state budget. I call that a sham.

After we came back from meeting with Perot, we realized our goal was to reshape New York politics. To do that it made sense to start a new party. From that point, our primary objective was to get ballot access for the next elections and to do that we needed a gubernatorial candidate who could bring the new party 50,000 votes. This would also give us a line on the ballot for every race for the next four years across New York State, from as low as dogcatcher to as high as US senator and president. This would allow us to make endorsements, and place potential mayors, supervisors, county legislators, and state legislators on our ballot line. We would become a political party in New York State.

In order to allow that to happen, we established a new political party that we named the Independence Party of America. It was founded in 1991 by Gordon Black, activist Laureen Oliver, and me.

In order to qualify a candidate, we had to gather a set number of petition signatures in different geographical regions of the state. The petition legally had to contain a committee on vacancies in case the candidate declined to run or was otherwise incapacitated. It's also important to note that New York law allows fusion voting, so that nominated candidates can run for more than one party and different party lines can be tabulated together. As a result, many in our new party wanted to nominate a Rochester-based Republican named Richard Rosenbaum who was running in the Republican primary for the nomination. He was a former Republican state chairman under Governor Nelson Rockefeller, and both men were very liberal Republicans.

However, Rosenbaum was not supported by the Republican establishment, which instead endorsed a Westchester County Republican state senator named George Pataki for the nomination. Pataki was supported by downstate and upstate Republicans who saw him as the more conservative candidate. Rosenbaum had asked for our party's endorsement and committed to run even if he lost the primary to Pataki. In effect, our endorsement gave him a temporary boost in the primary election. Being that he had been a longtime Republican Party stalwart, I had grave doubts whether if he lost the primary he would run against the Republican standard bearer. Sure enough, in exchange for the offer of a state appointment, he quickly dropped out of the race for governor. The politics behind all this was that nobody in New York State professional politics wanted us to become an established party.

By losing our candidate we faced losing our chance to be a recognized party for the next four years. As I mentioned earlier, the petition empowered the committee on vacancies to select a new candidate if need be. However, we only had twenty-four hours to find someone to replace Rosenbaum because he dropped out the day after the primary. As has happened so many times in my life, all eyes fell on me. There I was, the CEO of Paychex. I had never run for office and more to the point, I hated politicians and I was known for that fact. I was being backed into a corner with little time to consider the situation. We had until 5:00 p.m. to put the forms into registered mail, so I told our team at the Independence Party office that I'd meet them at the post office and make my decision either en route or when I got there—I'd either sign the registration forms or I wouldn't.

MY FIRST RUN FOR GOVERNOR

I remember that day well. I was driving to the post office at 4:30 p.m. with my wife Diane and feeling the pressure. No one else was going to step up, so if we wanted to do this thing it had to be me. I had the resources to make it happen: I could fund my own campaign. There was nobody else. It was the most important decision I'd made in twenty years, and it turned out to be an interesting turn of fate. In the end, I made up my mind with only two minutes to spare—that was how close it was. I actually signed the papers at the tiny stand-up desk in the post office. There was a small group of us, maybe four or five. Laureen Oliver was there. In the end, I couldn't crush the hopes of my friends and the nascent party.

That wasn't the end of it though. Pataki fought our right of substitution, saying we didn't have valid access. Many observers felt that my inclusion in the race would take votes from Pataki and help the Democratic incumbent Mario Cuomo. As I had already spent around $5 million in advertising even though I wasn't officially the candidate, this would have been a very welcome outcome. They fought us in every court in the state. However, the courts ruled that we deserved ballot access.

The election spanned six weeks and I spent another $6 million. All of it my own money, save for $1,000 that came from a friend, a highly successful contractor in the Rochester area. The donation somehow slipped past me and had to be listed in our reporting forms. Naturally, that person did not get another job from New York State for many years.

As an aside, one might be concerned as to the effect all this had on Paychex. I'm happy to say that in the days after I announced my candidacy, Paychex shares rose almost $4.

During week two of the campaign there was a forum at Stony Brook College for George Pataki and Mario Cuomo. It was outdoors and the candidates were high on a dais. Each spoke for between fifteen to twenty minutes, Cuomo first, followed by Pataki. This was during the lawsuits trying to prevent me from running. The press kept asking whether I was really running, and if I was going to be on the ballot. None of this exposure was helping me. I was furious that I was not up there on that stage able to put forward my views. I made my way around to the bottom of the walkway the candidates would come down at the conclusion of the forum. When Pataki walked past, followed by a gaggle of reporters, I reached out my hand as if to congratulate him. We shook hands and I held onto him with a vicelike grip and said, "Mr. Pataki, I'm Tom Golisano. Why don't you tell these reporters why you're suing me under six different jurisdictions to keep me off the ballot. Don't you believe in democracy?" Pataki pulled me over to the side and said, "We can work this out, we can work this out." I said, "Yeah, baloney."

One of the other highlights, other than being sued in six different jurisdictions by Pataki, was I found myself in a television debate against Mario Cuomo. Yes, that Mario Cuomo who became an international superstar with his inspirational speech at the 1984 Democratic convention and was considered one of the greatest orators in the history of American politics. You may ask why George Pataki wasn't also at the debate? He wouldn't recognize me as a candidate and refused to attend. His other motive was that he realized Cuomo's goal in debating me was to take votes away from him. Here I was, going up against Mario Cuomo just three weeks into the campaign. That was an intense experience.

My one ace was that I had copious files of clippings and other information I had collected over the years on New York State government. I clipped anything that mentioned bad budget deals, business regulations that didn't make sense in state or town politics, or anything that highlighted the government doing something stupid. I remember telling Laureen, "I've been keeping these because one of these days, when I have time, I'm going to finally do something about these issues."

I had lots of ammunition and chose topics to which I knew he would have a tough time responding. Overall, the debate went well and afterward Cuomo graciously came into my dressing room and complimented me. He said, "Who the hell are you? Where'd you get all that knowledge and information?" He told me I was a pretty good debater. Not bad for a last-minute stand-in, anyway.

I debated Cuomo three times and by the third debate I'd learned that he used short phrases to discredit his opponents. So, I came up with eight phrases that I would use on him. I was delighted when he fell into my trap by saying, "Well Tom, your company Paychex certainly did pretty well in New York State, didn't it?" Without a moment's hesitation I replied, "We did well in New York State, not because of it, but in spite of it."

Another zinger from the debates arose during a discussion on education. I said, "It's possible to get a good high school education in New York State, unfortunately you have to go to college to get it."

Back on the campaign, I never thought being on the road meeting people at diners and the like was worthwhile. Shaking hands, kissing babies—none of that was my style. On one occasion, however, CNN wanted to film me campaigning. The cameramen were great guys so

I agreed. On one stop we walked into a nursing home, my entourage trailing behind, and I went up to the first elderly lady I saw and asked her, "Ma'am, do you know who I am?" She looked me firmly in the eye and replied, "No, but if you go to the front desk, they'll tell you."

In the end, I received 217,490 votes (4 percent), which gave the Independence Party a line on the ballot. We beat every other minor party except for the Conservatives, which meant right out of the gate we ended up fourth on the ballot. This shocked the establishment. It also ensured the birth of the Independence Party. To this day people still fight for that minority line.

Though I lost, what I learned during my first run for governor about political operatives was: don't like 'em, don't trust 'em, and they'll spend your money any way they can.

THE INDEPENDENCE PARTY—COMING OF AGE

In our first year, we ran over 1,100 candidates statewide. We had formed organizations in 47 of the 61 counties and had over 300 state committee members. We were on a roll and we were in demand. Rudy Giuliani was keynote speaker at our first annual conference; that's when he stated he felt more at home with the Independence Party than he did with the Republican Party. The annual conference was a big party and there were more Democrats and Republicans in the same room than there had ever been before. Of course, they were there because they were hoping for our endorsement. Minority parties were the tail that wagged the dog in New York politics, and we were now threatening the other minority parties. Laureen Oliver was party chairperson and people used to say, "Be careful, she still has a thousand-pound gorilla behind her." They knew I still supported Laureen and the party, and had not ruled out running again.

They called us a fledgling party, and there was always, "He'll never run again. Tom will never run again. He's going to let the party go, and he's not going to do anything to help it." But of course, I did.

SECOND TIME'S A CHARM

Immediately after the 1994 governor's race, I received a phone call from Steve Pigeon. Steve, a former legislator from Buffalo, was working with the Clinton administration as an aide to Secretary of Health and Human Services Donna Shalala. He told me he was impressed with the issues I had raised during my campaign and would like to meet with me. Shortly after we met he became the Democratic Party chairman in Erie County (Buffalo, New York).

We developed a sort of friendship. Steve worked along with Laureen Oliver to help grow the Independence Party and recognized that I was hitting on issues that he thought the Democratic Party was missing. Of course, his real motivation was that he wanted me to run for governor as a Democrat and he saw me as a major party candidate for the 1998 race.

With the 1998 governor's race approaching, Steve came to me and proposed that I seek the Democratic endorsement for governor. His argument was that my business background, humble beginnings, upstate roots, and high profile could be combined with the Democratic Party baseline vote in New York City to defeat the Republican Pataki.

My ability to self-fund my campaign would remove any advantage the incumbent Republicans had over the Democrats. In addition, I would have access to the Democrats' sophisticated field organizations throughout the state. Bringing with me Independence Party voters would negate any votes Pataki might receive on the Conservative line. Taking into consideration that Democrats outnumber Republicans two-to-one in New York State, it made sense that I could win, given major party backing.

By that time, Steve knew me well enough to realize I wouldn't stick strictly to party dictates, as my approach had always been to do what I thought was best for the state. However, he believed the Democrats had no major candidate seeking to run and that there was a chance I could seize the endorsement. As I was not a member of the Democratic Party,

I would need the blessing of at least 25 percent of the delegates at the state convention. At that time upstate controlled 20 percent of the delegates (basically anything north and west of Rockland County).

With some reservation, I agreed to explore the candidacy. Steve arranged meetings with Democratic leaders, including Assembly Speaker Shelly Silver and Democratic Senate leader Marty Connor. They were interested in floating the idea and I met with various party chairmen, state legislators, and other elected leaders. Things moved forward and I was seen to be gaining some traction. A meeting was scheduled with the Democratic chairs of the five New York City boroughs, Long Island, Westchester, and the four largest upstate counties (Erie, Monroe, Onondaga, and Albany). These were the people who could control the Democratic Party endorsement.

I presented my belief that Pataki was a do-nothing governor who was responsible for high taxes, low job growth, and stale, ineffectual government. They seemed fairly receptive and asked some intelligent questions but made no commitment. Overall, I felt it went well. As the meeting ended, one of the longtime party bosses, Dominic Baranello of Suffolk County, asked to speak to Steve in private. On our drive back to the hotel Steve told me that Baranello told him, "Kid, I like you, so I'm going to tell you what's happening. You are right, Golisano can win and that's why these guys won't give him the endorsement. They don't want an independent Rochester guy and outsider who hasn't come up through the ranks and demonstrated his loyalty to them becoming governor." He went on to say, "Besides, Pataki gives the New York City guys appointments and other patronage, so they're happy; and Silver, he likes having a Republican governor as it makes him the top Democrat in the state."

If I hadn't before, on that day I fully understood why I was running as an independent. Politicians in New York State cared more about their own narrow, vested interests and power bases than providing a government that served the best interests of the people of New York.

While all this was going on, Steve on separate occasions brought Chuck Schumer and Eliot Spitzer to meet me at Paychex. Steve was supporting Chuck's race for US Senate. (He had survived a primary against Geraldine Ferraro to win the right to run against the incumbent Al D'Amato. Al had recruited Pataki in the first place.) Steve was also working with Spitzer, who was running in a primary for attorney general against incumbent Dennis Vacco. While Steve was supporting them in their primaries, the downstate party leaders were not. Maybe they were afraid they'd win, too! Steve called on me for my help from time to time, and I actively supported both their campaigns.

Schumer and Spitzer liked the idea of me running on the Democratic line, but also wanted the Independence line. They both impressed me and I thought they would be better than the incumbents, especially D'Amato, whom I felt was one of the truly awful political officeholders in the state. I'm glad to say, they were both elected that year.

Regardless, with the Democratic Party endorsement out of reach, we were back to square one. We needed a candidate who could give us a chance to clear the 50,000-vote hurdle to remain a political party with a ballot line. Worse, there were some in the party who wanted to endorse Pataki. That would have been too much to bear, and Laureen made it very clear to me that I was the only person who could keep the endorsement from him.

Once again, I had to step up to the plate. There was a lot to do and we would need a great deal of help. Steve introduced me to Frank Sanzillo, a Democratic operative who had been chief of staff for Senate Democrats for years. Laureen brought back Tom D'Amore to work with me on the race. Tom had helped with my 1994 run, yet he was a Republican operative who had managed Lowell Weicker's successful governor's race as an independent in Connecticut.

I should mention Ross Perot's endorsement and how I nearly blew it. I was an Independent candidate with some credibility so Perot agreed to endorse me. The night before he arrived in New York to make the formal announcement, I received a call from a reporter at the *New York Times* requesting an interview, which I granted. He asked me about United We Stand, and I said to him, "Well, I think Ross Perot has made a big mistake. He should've formed a political party. There's no interest in an advocacy organization, or not enough interest, and that's why it's dissipating." The reporter printed my words verbatim.

When Perot read the piece the next morning, he was not pleased and started wondering why the heck he was endorsing me. Meantime, Gordon Black saw the article and called me up, saying, "Tom you've really stepped in it." I replied that I'd simply told the truth but perhaps the timing was poor. Gordon suggested I needed to apologize, so hat in hand I called Perot and told him that even though I believed what I had said, it was the wrong time to say it and that I was sorry. He took my apology and still endorsed me. At the press conference, we had three hundred reporters in the room, TV cameras, dozens of microphones were pushed into my face—it was chaos. I'd never experienced anything like it before.

I got another endorsement, sort of. I can't remember exactly when it was but during one of my runs for governor the media cornered my ex-wife for a quote and asked her, "What kind of governor would Tom make?" Her rapid-fire reply was, "I can tell you, he's going to make a lot better governor than he did a husband!" I've always been grateful that I get on so well with my ex-wives.

I spent $9 million of my own money on my 1998 campaign as an independent candidate and received 364,056 votes (7.69 percent). This meant we not only met our objective of keeping our ballot line for another four years, but also surpassed the votes Pataki received on the Conservative line. The result was that we acquired the coveted "Row C" and became the major-minor party in New York State.

TEN

GOLF AND A THIRD

RUN AT GOVERNOR

A ROUND OF GOLF WITH BILL CLINTON

President Clinton's term was nearing its end and he had survived impeachment. The First Lady, Hillary Rodham Clinton, was considering running for the New York Senate seat opening due to the retirement of Senator Daniel Patrick Moynihan.

Steve Pigeon was involved in the early planning of the race and her highly publicized "listening tour" of New York State. He told me that President Clinton would like to meet me at the White House and then play a round of golf. Steve said the President wanted to call me personally to invite me and I was to expect a call. After a few days, when I hadn't received a call, I assumed Steve was mistaken about the invitation.

It turned out the White House called the wrong Tom Golisano. The White House operator had goofed and called my cousin Tom Golisano in Batavia, New York. They had asked whether he'd hold for the President of the United States. My cousin was a deputy sheriff and thought it was one of his friends playing a joke so he said, "Yeah, sure. Yeah, I guess I'll hold for the President of the United States." A few seconds later, Clinton is on the phone asking him if he'd like to play golf. My cousin quickly recognized the President's voice and finally said, "Mr. President, I think you're talking to the wrong Tom Golisano, you probably want my cousin." Famed commentator Paul Harvey made a joke about the incident on his iconic national radio show.

It all got sorted out in the end and I received the call from the President. I agreed to meet and play golf and it was quite a day to remember. We met at the White House and then left for the Army Navy Country Club. It took an entourage of no less than twelve vehicles to dispatch four of us to the golf course. Terry McAuliffe, fundraiser and later governor of Virginia, was one of the other golfers. On the journey, Clinton offered me a cigar and I didn't take it. I wasn't smoking them back then, but I now wish I'd taken it as a souvenir.

There was all sorts of lore that I'd heard about, surrounding Clinton allegedly calling his number of shots before even finishing a hole, the implication being he was less than honest with his score. My experience was that he simply didn't keep score. He didn't cheat, but if he hit a bad shot he'd just hit another one. My impression was that he just enjoyed the game and wasn't being competitive. I remember he talked constantly, even during my backswing, about politics in general and more specifically about Hillary running for the Senate. On the first hole, I hit the ball 220 yards right down the center. It surprised the heck out of me. For my next shot, I pulled a four iron out of my bag—a club I've never had any luck with—and put it ten feet from the hole. I was Bill's partner and Terry looked at me as if to say, "What kind of a hustle is this?" I two-putted for par and everyone else got sixes and sevens— they were saying Clinton had brought in a ringer. Unfortunately, that was the only par I made all day. In fact, on the last hole I duck-hooked my drive straight into the side of a Honda in the parking lot. I can't remember if I took it as a mulligan. After the game, we returned to the White House and talked for an hour and a half about politics in general, including but not limited to the government of the state of New York. He was kind enough not to mention the Honda.

Over the years I got to spend a lot of time with him, and he is one of the most personable people I've ever known. You never feel like he's rushing through a conversation with you to get to the next person. For example, a few years after the golf game he came to speak at a function in Naples and I invited him to the house for dinner. At the time, I was working with a young businessman named Dale who had impressed me greatly. So, I asked him if he'd like to have dinner with the President. He of course was excited at the prospect. Dale and Bill seemed to get on well and during dinner talked about the business environment relative to the construction industry. Two years later Dale and I were at a conference that Clinton was attending; I'm talking to Bill, and Dale walks up to us and immediately Bill said, "Hi Dale, how are you doing?" Dale was stunned. Not only did Clinton remember Dale, he also recalled the topic of dinner conversation from two years previously. Clinton has an extraordinary memory that clearly served him well throughout his political career.

I've never met anyone like him. When Heather and I broke up and Bill found out about it, he called me up one Sunday morning to offer his support. It wasn't long before he was in full matchmaking mode— but that's another story.

2002 TO WIN

While I might have enjoyed the invitation to the White House and the attention I received as the founder of the Independence Party, not to mention being a newly minted member of the *Forbes* 400 list (Paychex stock continued to soar), I was distressed with the continuing decline of New York State. I felt Governor George Pataki was a disaster.

The state was suffering population decline and job losses due to high property taxes and out-of-control state spending. Everywhere I looked there was mismanagement, negligence, and what many viewed as corruption. One example was New York's Medicaid, on which spending was higher than that of California and Texas combined. The governor and state legislature continued to give sweetheart deals to the public service employee unions to placate downstate interests, all to support the governor's Republican administration in what was a very Democratic state. The governor, along with the Democrat assembly speaker and Republican Senate majority leader had complete control over the state budget. They oversaw, and shared equally, a billion-dollar pork/slush fund disguised as economic development. Politically connected project dollars were strategically awarded to ensure these powerful men continued to maintain their iron grip on the state government.

While New York City's economy has always been large enough to survive, its social problems and educational system declined along with the rest of the state as the upstate economy slowed to near depression levels.

My relationship continued with newly elected Senator Schumer and Attorney General Spitzer. I believed they were doing good work but in reality, their influence on New York state government was no match for that of the governor.

My friend and colleague Laureen Oliver had become so disgusted with the party and the state government, she stepped down as the chair and moved out of the state. Pataki meanwhile had allied with the Fulani wing of the party and spread patronage to other members. His machinations were allowing him to close in on obtaining the coveted party endorsement, in the upcoming 2002 governor's election. People were wondering, and some were asking, would I run again?

During this time, I got a call from Joel Giambra, the Erie County executive. He had defeated Dennis Gorski in the last election. Gorski had previously been named County Executive of the Year and was an excellent county government manager. I had endorsed him during the campaign so I was surprised when Giambra called me. What intrigued me more was that he said Governor Pataki had asked him to reach out to me. Pataki was going to announce in his upcoming State of the State address that he was creating a commission on consolidating local governments to save taxpayer money and create more efficiency. This was an issue on which I had been vocal. Pataki wanted Giambra and me to cochair the commission. He was calling to ask me whether I was interested, and without hesitation I told him I was indeed interested. Then the conversation went downhill fast as Pataki's true motive started to become clear.

Like a cobra's head rising from a fakir's basket, Giambra said: "There's just one thing. The governor is worried that it would look bad if he names you to the committee and you turn around and run against him." My reply was, "Are you saying that in order to be named, I need to commit to not run in 2002?" Giambra hesitated a second and said, "Well yeah." I hadn't considered at that point whether I would run or not, but I told Giambra I would absolutely turn down his offer to cochair the committee. Now, do you see what I mean when I said I never met a political operative I could trust?

Coincidentally, or perhaps not, about the same time I got a call from a prominent Rochester businessman who asked whether I was running. He had been told by the Monroe County Republican chairman that if he got me out of the race, he could get the casino license he had always coveted. Another close business friend called and said he had been promised construction contracts if he convinced me not to run. Do you see a pattern here? By this time, I was getting a little tired, to say the least, of these political maneuverings. I also recognized people were beginning to be concerned about the possibility of my running for governor once again.

When I finally announced I was running, the press called and asked whether I had been offered anything not to run. I told them the Giambra story and reporters called him; he vehemently denied the story, of course. Interestingly enough, I had kept the phone records to show the phone call between myself and Giambra. Years later, after I'd purchased the Sabres, I saw him at a mutual friend's daughter's wedding and he apologized and admitted that he had been under heavy pressure. That's what politics can do to people.

It didn't take me too long to figure out why Pataki was so worried, but let me tell you how I worked it out. It started with another Steve

Pigeon plan that he thought would provide a route to electoral success, or at the very least see Governor Pataki defeated. I'm not sure what I wanted most at that point. Pataki's personal poll numbers were dropping as overall voter dissatisfaction was climbing; increasing numbers of people felt the state was on the wrong track. Andrew Cuomo, the son of former governor Mario Cuomo, called Steve and requested a meeting at my convenience. Cuomo had been Secretary of Housing and Urban Development for President Clinton. He later served as governor of New York.

Shortly afterward, I was visiting the city and Andrew came to see Steve and me at my suite at the Waldorf Towers. He had an interesting proposition: He asked me to run for governor again. He was obviously well informed and expertly outlined the problems facing the state, while eloquently detailing the failings of Governor Pataki. He went on to announce he had lined up the Liberal Party's minor line and was going to run for governor in the Democratic primary against State Comptroller Carl McCall. McCall was attempting to be New York's first African American governor.

Cuomo believed he could win the primary. His thinking was that taking into consideration Pataki's declining popularity and my strong upstate following, I might either run up the middle to win or take enough upstate votes from Pataki to allow Cuomo to win with the tide of New York City's vote. I wasn't sure what to think. Although I followed, even accepted, Cuomo's reasoning, I wasn't sure he could defeat McCall in the primary to make it any more than a moot point.

Steve then explained that if McCall did win, he would not poll well outside of his New York City base. More importantly, he would be out of campaign cash after the primary, with little prospect of raising a lot more. With my self-funding, on the other hand, I would be in a position to outspend both major party candidates. Furthermore, taking into consideration the fact that Cuomo's name would continue to appear on the Liberal line, the Democratic vote might split widely enough to give me a shot to win in a four-way race. What was exceedingly pleasing was that either scenario presented George Pataki with a challenging and tricky race.

Cuomo's goal of course was to win rather than to present me a possible path to victory, but that's just what he was doing. I firmly believed that as an independent I could clean up politics in the state starting in Albany. The bottom line was that if all my candidacy did was help defeat Pataki, that in itself would be a good outcome. Either Cuomo or McCall would do a far better, more honest job of being governor than Pataki was doing. Or so I reasoned.

The thing was, this time I really wanted to win. After the meeting with Cuomo I was still undecided. It was the next meeting Steve arranged that clinched the deal. We went to see Bill Delmont, the Conservative Party chairman in Erie County—a wily old-school politician who told me that many rank-and-file Conservatives were fed up with Pataki's high spending and his sellout to the downstate Democratic politicians.

Bill laid out a scenario that saw him gather enough Conservative support for me to run against Pataki in a Conservative primary. He based this belief on the fact that many rank-and-file Conservative voters were disgusted with Pataki's record and would warm to my business background and outsider profile. Bill believed I could win the primary.

The facts were starting to stack up in my favor. No Republican had ever been elected without having the Conservative line. Remember I mentioned earlier that New York allows fusion voting? By combining my Independence line with the Conservative line, my chances would not only increase exponentially, but totally eliminate Pataki's ability to win a multi-candidate race with just the Republican line.

You might now be starting to believe me when I talk about the impenetrability of New York's political system—it's the strangest in the United States.

If you are thinking that I was feeling good at that point, you'd be correct. I asked Laureen Oliver for her opinion and she gave me the unsavory news that Pataki had basically bought the Independence

Party line. She did, however, have a plan to get my name on the primary ballot. All was not lost. What we needed to do was to get 25 percent of those attending the state convention to put my name on the primary ballot. If we failed at that, I could gather enough petition signatures to qualify.

She was one of my biggest supporters. She believed I could make a difference as governor and she would move back to Rochester and work full time to support the effort. Once again it seemed the path was getting clearer. There was light at the end of the tunnel, I was just hoping it wasn't an oncoming train.

It was around this time that Donald Trump called me to talk about the race. I'd met him several times and had been impressed and entertained by his character and personality. He had contacted me in my previous races and encouraged me to keep up the fight. He told me he felt people were getting tired of politicians and might turn to an outsider businessman to clean up the mess the political class had left for the rest of us. Trump urged me to run and said that if I did I should bring into my campaign Roger Stone, who had been his longtime friend and advisor. He told me he was a brilliant strategist who disliked Al D'Amato and George Pataki as much as I did, especially the way they had sold out to downstate public employee unions.

Steve, a Democrat, said he believed that Stone was brilliant. Steve was a counsel to the New York Democrats in the State Senate. He had personally seen Trump working with Stone and our friend Frank Sanzillo, as they lobbied to stop the legalization of casino gaming even though the powerful "three men in the room" had wanted (and later got) casinos into New York. Steve did, however, think we should additionally get a Democratic strategist. He recommended Eric Mullen, a young consultant who had worked for Bill Clinton and whose wife was a top aide to then Senator Hillary Clinton. I made the decision—I was going to run.

My announcement was professionally managed and we attracted extensive media coverage. First, I had to get qualified to run at both the Independence and Conservative Conventions, both of which were held in late May 2002.

We held the event at Rochester Institute of Technology, as I had been a big benefactor of the college, donating $14 million the previous year toward the creation of the B. Thomas Golisano College of Computing and Information Sciences. The president of the college was happy to host us, but again, it was not without controversy. He got a call from the governor's office saying if they held the announcement at RIT, the Institute could forget about ever getting any financial assistance ever again from the state. A phone call that I am pleased to say he ignored.

The Independence Party Convention

My first hurdle was the Independence Party Convention. If I thought this was going to be easy, I was soon to learn otherwise. Pataki's operatives (a polite word for *well-dressed henchmen*) confronted my team members and denied them access to the floor of the convention. Bear in mind this was the party I had founded—you can imagine how it felt to have the people who worked for me barred. Pataki's people even blocked independent state committeemen who had proper credentials. So much for democracy. As the former chair of the party, Laureen was able to get herself onto the convention floor and actually pulled state committeemen out to meet with me in my suite.

Knowing from previous experience that Pataki would use the courts to try to block my candidacy, I had hired Senator Martin Connor, the Democratic leader and experienced election lawyer, to work with Laureen and the county chairs to get my nomination to the floor of the convention. Marty was an expert on convention rules, so I was in good hands.

By this point, Pataki had packed the hotel lobby and floor with so many Republican operatives (one could easily call them something else) that our state committee supporters were physically being blocked from accessing the floor. The strategy was to cause them to miss their names when announced at the roll call. So much for integrity and gentlemanly conduct in politics.

We unfortunately had to meet force with force. Luckily, we had a young aide, Gary Parenti, who was agile and physically athletic. Roger and he acted like NFL linemen to open a pathway through the throng of—let's use a polite phrase "political operatives"—to help our delegates to their seats so they could cast their votes. In the end Laureen, during an hour-long roll call, was able to line up the 25 percent of votes to qualify my candidacy.

Pataki had no grounds on which to justify the way he acted. It was, when it came down to it, basic thuggery. He then tried to sue us, just as he had in 1994 and 1998—this time ridiculously claiming I hadn't achieved the required 25 percent and attempting to get my access to the ballot disallowed. All, of course, to no avail.

The Conservative Party Convention

If I thought the Independence Party Convention was tough, it was no match for the Conservative Party event. As a small teaser, the *New York Post* reported on a late-night bar fight between Steve Pigeon, Roger Stone, and Mike Long, the chairman of the state Conservative Party. I suppose a little background is in order. Roger and Steve came up with the idea that I choose a Conservative running mate as my pick for lieutenant governor.

Now for more of that complex, arcane, nonsensical New York election law: The primaries for governor and lieutenant governor are separate races, meaning we would only be joined together as a ticket in November. The idea was to run a known Conservative against Pataki's very socially liberal Conservative lieutenant governor—who was woman. If we could beat her in the primary, the fact she was on the Republican line but had lost the Conservative line meant the two lines could no longer be fused together. The bottom line was that if we could pull this feat off, Pataki would have no chance of winning because he needed the extra votes on the Conservative line to seal a victory. This explains why Mike Long was itching for a bar fight with the two people who came up with the plan.

The press, realizing this quirk in election law, began to look more seriously at our potential to win. Unfortunately, all this attention from both the Republicans and the press led to the untimely exposure of a major flaw in our plan.

During the Conservative convention, we were forced to nominate a candidate for lieutenant governor with great urgency. We found someone we thought could win but did not have a chance to carry out a comprehensive background check. After the candidate was selected, Marty Connor discovered that our candidate had voted twice in the 2000 election. It seemed that he hated Hillary Clinton so much he registered from two different addresses in the city to double up his vote against her! While some might give the man credit for his passion in defeating Mrs. Clinton, he had also committed felony fraud under the election law. Marty predicted the Republicans and the ravenous New York press would soon discover the guy's deception; this would result in him having to drop out of the race and become a major embarrassment right at the outset of my campaign. Ditching him early meant we could limit the damage, but little else.

I licked my wounds and began to campaign for the Independence primary. I also announced a write-in challenge for the Conservative line at the Conservative Convention. My team launched our campaign with a multimillion-dollar television and radio media blitz coupled with a relatively inexpensive direct mail campaign that targeted the small number of registered Independent and Conservative voters in the state.

As the founder of the Independence Party, I was an attractive alternative for party members who signed up initially as a protest against the two major political parties and their unsatisfactory candidates. In any event, polling showed that I could win the primary, and that alone could threaten Pataki's general election chances. It could also give me the momentum one gets from a victory, which would in turn boost my media campaign and catapult me into contention.

Recognizing I was doing well with Independence Party voters, the Republicans hired people to sign up new registrants for the Independence Party. The idea was to add new voters to reduce the effect of my built-in vote. Their mistake was to pay these workers for each new registration they delivered. That would have been fine except some of the overzealous ones signed up Elvis Presley, Marilyn Monroe, and Mickeys Mantle and Mouse. I suppose I should have been happy to have such illustrious people—and a famous rodent—in our party, but instead we decided to go along with it and ran hilarious statewide television advertisements that proved highly effective. They depicted Pataki's need for more voters but questioned the need for Elvis Presley and Marilyn Monroe. The idea was to subtly promote the fact that his campaign was cheating.

It was Pataki's turn to feel the burn of embarrassment.

During the lead-up to the primary I was busy on the campaign trail doing press conferences and events throughout the state. I made several proposals to garner media interest, one of which was zero-based budgeting. This is where all expenses require prior justification for each accounting period. Everything starts from a zero base and every activity an organization undertakes is analyzed based on its needs and costs. I also proposed that every student who maintained a B average could attend state college and pay no tuition. The cost would be funded by utilizing lottery revenues that were originally promoted to pay for education; those revenues' true allocation, however, was questionable. That particular idea got a lot of positive attention. I was having fun.

After all the hard work, campaign stops, and very creative and often funny campaign ads, primary night came and I won the Independence primary. As I had suspected, Carl McCall won the Democratic nod. In fact, a week before the primary and sensing defeat, Andrew Cuomo withdrew from the primary and threw his support to McCall. He did this while standing beside former President Bill Clinton. Far from bringing unity, many McCall supporters were incensed that McCall was denied his big, sensational victory night and the resulting "bounce" from all the attention it would have garnered.

All eyes, the night of the election, were on my big win over Pataki. It dominated the 11 o'clock news and the front pages of all newspapers the following morning. I beat Pataki by 546 votes, a significant victory. The win gave me a huge boost and soared my name recognition to new heights—aided by heavy media buys throughout the summer.

A Good Friend Dies and I Take a Stand

After the primary win, I kicked up my media exposure a few notches with rotating advertisements featuring me presenting a new idea or proposal to the camera each week.

On a more personal note, my closest friend Gene Polisseni had recently died from cancer. I watched him suffer greatly during his final weeks, and people told me that pain could be reduced by using medical marijuana. I investigated these claims and became one of the first candidates in the country to propose legalizing marijuana for medical purposes. Today, it is legal in dozens of states, but back then it was a risky stance to take politically. I really didn't care, I just wanted people in need to be able to use it under medical supervision without suffering any legal repercussions. I held a press conference alongside people suffering from epilepsy, Parkinson's disease, cancer, and other painful and debilitating ailments. I was visibly moved as they spoke about their illnesses and the benefits of marijuana. It was the first time I had ever seen tears in the eyes of reporters. I'm proud that I might have had a little to do with medical marijuana now being legal in New York.

Good Press, Bad Press, and Negative Attack Ads

As we predicted, while Pataki and I were spending millions on advertising throughout October, Carl McCall's funds were drying up. He had no money to make any significant media buys. I was gaining on both major party candidates. Fred Dicker, the veteran political reporter for the *New York Post*, took notice and wrote a column titled "Upstate Aflame," in which he stated that "Thomas Golisano has transformed Upstate into 'Golisano Country' with an audaciously expensive media campaign and a tough anti-Pataki message widely seen as right on the mark." In the same piece, a well-known GOP stalwart was quoted as writing in a memo, "I'm convinced [Golisano] can win Upstate." Not all reporters were so friendly, however.

The worst was Bob McCarthy, a reporter for the *Buffalo News*. For some unknown reason, he seemed to hold a grudge against Steve Pigeon, the top Democrat in that town and my friend and now supporter. In my opinion, he singled Pigeon out and treated him unlike any other politician. If Steve had found a cure for cancer, McCarthy would have found something about it that was disreputable. He also seemed to hate Dennis Gorski, who I'd endorsed for reelection to the Erie County executive against the *Buffalo News*–backed Joel Giambra and seemed on a mission to defeat Gorski. The fact that I supported these two people meant I was a target, too. McCarthy wrote a damning front page profile featuring a huge headline, half the size of the paper, stating, "Serious Candidate or Vain Billionaire?"

In the story, he cited several unnamed sources, one of whom said about me, "He's been looking in the mirror for a long time and really thinks he's the messiah." I found this amusing and tried to figure out who on earth was watching me shave in the mornings. It was a hit piece without question—what some people today would call fake news.

I am sure it was no coincidence that Pataki pulled damning quotes from the article to use in his campaign advertisements. Quoting the

Buffalo News as the source gave him third-party validation. As far as I was concerned, it was a complete and nasty setup.

Later during the campaign, I confronted McCarthy in front of other reporters at a press conference. I pulled out the Pataki campaign literature and asked him, "Did you and the campaign coordinate your story?" He didn't deny it, but he did have enough common decency to blush a rather unattractive shade of red.

There were other events that made me raise an eyebrow. For instance, the *New York Times* called me up one day and asked for an editorial interview. I took Steve Pigeon with me and almost immediately they tried to trick me. One of the reporters asked, "How much does it cost to ride the New York City subway?" I countered with, "How much is it to drive the Thruway?" And when he didn't know, I'd proven my point. This line of questioning originates from people living in New York City believing that they are the center of the universe, when in reality New York is a big state and more people drive the Thruway than ride the subway.

As I was leaving, one of the four editorial board members said, "You know something? You're the best candidate, but we can't say that." Maybe it was just a coincidence that Pataki had just given the paper $92 million to build a new headquarters in Manhattan. Or perhaps it was simply good economic development. Or maybe . . .

Polling began to show that I was in a tight three-way race, but there were still challenges ahead. There is a phenomenon that works against independent candidates. It's called the "wasted vote syndrome." People who would otherwise be inclined to vote for an independent get cold feet as election day draws near because they start to fear the candidate couldn't possibly beat both the Republican and Democratic candidates. They begin thinking they are throwing their vote away on a candidate who has no chance of winning. No one wants to back a loser, but I think voting for someone you really don't want to win is truly a case of wasting your vote.

Now, independent candidates do on occasion win; this usually happens when they reach a tipping point—that is, when the polls show them above 25 percent. At that point voters believe they have a good shot at winning. When my poll figures hit 28 percent, things got serious. Pataki recognized this and his advertising became increasingly negative—the attack ads started. On one occasion, he targeted some of my earlier positions and took them out of context; one ad ran, "Golisano favors legalizing drugs and prostitution"—untrue of course, but still damaging. In the same advertisement, he published the telephone number of the Paychex switchboard urging people to call and tell me I was wrong. The first morning it ran, our switchboard was jammed. We were one of the biggest employers in Rochester and he was attacking the company—so much for the state helping business. Pataki was quite happy fighting in the gutter, and perhaps that's where he belonged.

On the Road and Debating

The attacks continued, misquoting and fabricating my views on television, radio, and in direct mail. I was slightly above the tipping point and they were nervous. I began drawing crowds when I was out and about in New York City. The competition was attacking me. I could feel victory.

On one occasion at a bowling alley in Brooklyn, I was shaking hands and meeting people when a young lady asked if I would join her and her friends for a few frames. I hadn't bowled in years, but my campaign team and the press traveling with me urged me to accept. I have to say, I was nervous on that first roll but amazingly I bowled the ball right into the pocket for a strike. At the end of the frame, after the cheering and laughing subsided, I decided discretion was the better part of valor, thanked them, and moved on to the next event. The last thing I wanted to do was flub the next frame.

The campaign continued to gather momentum. I was slated to walk the Columbus Day parade in New York City with a group of supporters. While I was doing interviews in a nearby hotel, my aide Gary Parenti was preparing the group on the street below. He called me and said, "Tom I'm here with Bernard Goetz, the subway vigilante. He wants to endorse you at the start of the parade." While I appreciated this gesture, I was concerned that Pataki could really do a number on me with negative advertising if I was seen with Goetz. He had shot and seriously wounded four alleged muggers on a New York City subway train in Manhattan in December 1984. I asked Gary to wait while I gathered my thoughts and then asked him to hand the phone to Goetz. I thanked him for his support and asked whether he thought opponents might use it to try and hurt my campaign. He agreed they might and was nice enough to promise not to say anything publicly, but to get all his friends to vote for me. Another bullet dodged, if you'll excuse the expression in this particular case.

Another interesting endorsement I received shortly after was from Al Lewis, who had previously run for governor on the Green Party ticket. Al had played Grandpa Munster in the 1960s television series *The Munsters*.

As incumbent Mario Cuomo had done to him in the past, it was now Pataki who wouldn't debate his major party opponent unless all the minor party candidates were included. However, this time there were six of us, and as the seventh candidate, McCall was odd man out. Later Pataki refused to attend a debate, and Carl and I debated alone.

In the first televised debate, from a Syracuse television studio, I was able to score a stinging blow. Roger Stone had researched Pataki's campaign donations and found that several large donations came from people associated with prisoners—prisoners who conveniently received parole shortly after the donations were received by his party. There seemed to be a pattern that suggested that some paroles were bought and paid for. As soon as I got an opportunity, I laid out the names, amounts, and those paroled and asked, "George, are you selling paroles?" Pataki was visibly shocked, and furiously denied my accusation. He was, however, thrown off balance for the rest of the debate. Afterward, he stormed offstage without shaking hands and left the studio. In the lobby of the television station, Pataki's media consultant, Kiernan Mahoney, challenged Eric Mullen to a fistfight. A shouting match ensued, which had to be broken up by security staff. The gap was closing and it wasn't just the Pataki people who were feeling the heat.

Opponents Running Scared

Let me explain why my opponents were so fearful of my momentum, when in reality I was only a minor party candidate. My apologies, but I have to take you back to the arcane election laws at play in New York. The party with the most votes in the election gets Row A (the top line on the ballot). The party with the second-highest number of votes gets Row B (the next line). These two lines are always Republican and Democrat. The minor parties line up below. The key is they are less noticeable, and less attractive psychologically to voters.

To make matters more complex, and I would say more sinister, New York law states that parties on Rows A and B control the two commissioners and staff on the sixty-two county boards of elections. This means they control all non–civil service, politically appointed, high-paying jobs that receive state pensions and health benefits. All these people serve at the pleasure of the party leaders; they can hire and fire on their whim. This situation is a patronage gold mine for the two main parties. They can build their local organizations on the backs of taxpayer money under the guise of administrating "fair" elections. You are probably by now starting to spot a major flaw in New York State democracy.

How did this affect me? The fact I was matching dollar for dollar the Republican candidate's spending while dwarfing that of the Democratic candidate made me a major threat to the comfortable life

Tom's father, Sam, always had his eyes open for a business opportunity; in this case, he saw the potential in the furnace in his own basement and started a coal-to-oil furnace-conversion business.

Tom's sister, Marie Graham, and their parents, Sam and Anna Golisano, standing with Tom.

Tom as a young professional and entrepreneur on the verge of a good idea.

Tom Golisano, Steve Pigeon, and Bill Clinton at Clinton's home in Chappaqua, New York.

Tom, as a political figure, founded the Independence Party of America with Gordon Black and Laureen Oliver in 1991.

Gene Polisseni, instrumental in Paychex's sales and human resources development, was one of Tom's closest and lifelong friends.

Tom and his son, Steven, spending time together at a family gathering.

Tom and his grandchildren standing outside of the B. Thomas Golisano Archive Collection at Rochester Institute of Technology. Left to right: Jordan, Corey, RJ, Tom, Renee, Randy, and Amy.

Tom, as CEO and chairman, standing over the Paychex sign at the Rochester, New York, office. This photo accompanied a Paychex article featured in the Rochester Business Journal *in 1989.*

being experienced by both parties, regardless of which party owned the governorship. It was starting to look like even if I couldn't win, I had a real chance of coming in second, so Democrats who heretofore had been encouraging me, started to fear me. Horror of horrors, if I came in second, I would push them down to Row C below the Independence Party line. This would make life very difficult for their candidates at every level statewide. Not only that, the Independence Party would have the power to appoint the sixty-two commissioners of elections and their hundreds of clerks. This would be a catastrophic blow to the Democratic Party.

Sabotage or Two Simple Mistakes?

The first objective of the Independence party was to get 50,000 votes to obtain ballot access for all offices for the next four years. As I mentioned earlier, to actually win, voters had to believe a candidate had a chance to win. It was this weakness that my opponents exploited.

At this crucial juncture of the campaign, with less than two weeks to go, I had been spending millions of dollars a week on television commercials. Trusting my media consultant turned out to be just the opening my opponents were looking for to exploit voters' fears.

During those final days, Eric Mullen made a massive media buy amounting to tens of millions of dollars more than I had approved. (He always claimed it was approved, but I never greenlighted it.) When I discovered what he'd done, I was outraged and ordered him to cut back to the spending levels of previous weeks, which were already quite high for any campaign.

That's when things took a very strange and ominous turn. Mullen did as I told him, however, he cut back to previous levels in a very strategic manner, by pulling all television commercials in downstate markets where two-thirds of the state's population lived.

My headquarters was in upstate New York where our commercials were still running, so it took a couple of days for us to receive word that we'd gone dark in downstate New York. The press pounced on this like Pataki on a rumor. They reported that I must be losing confidence I could win. The important tipping point I'd reached burst like a soap bubble. I was being painted as an unsure, unsteady candidate. I hastily bought live television time to explain what had happened with the canceled advertising, but that just caused more confusion and my poll numbers dropped several points overnight.

To this day, I question Mullen's motives for the hugely elevated but unnecessary media buy at such a crucial point—not to mention canceling the spots in only downstate New York rather than cutting back proportionally across all markets. It never made sense—unless his real plan was to see that I finished last.

My campaign was devastated. Now, the Democrats' hold on Row B was safe and along with it the statewide patronage they enjoyed. Mullen went on to have a wonderful high-paying career as a consultant to the Democratic Party—make of that what you will. By now, like me you may be somewhat cynical about the politics of New York State.

On election night, I still managed a respectable 14 percent for an independent candidate and we retained the C line for the Independence Party. I was proud of the way I ran the race and of the many issues I raised that helped define future campaigns—issues such as high property taxes, out of control Medicaid, education choice, and balanced budgets.

On the other hand, I was disgusted with the politics and politicians in New York who cared more about their power than their people.

ELEVEN

FORGET THE STOCK OPTIONS,
I'LL TAKE THE CREDENZA

In 2003 I first started to seriously consider retiring from Paychex. I'd floated the idea a few years previously, but the board convinced me to stay. But this time it was different, I'd been running the company for almost thirty years and over the previous nine years had run for governor of New York State three times. As a result, I'd been spending less and less time in the office running the business. During my last run in 2002, I only managed to get into the office once a week, on Fridays, for almost five months. My conscience started to bother me and truthfully, I was getting bored dealing with Wall Street. I felt the need to spend more time on my other interests. Once again, I was asked to stay, at least until I could find a suitable replacement.

In the end, the board accepted my resignation and we began looking for someone to run a company, which at the time had around half a million clients. The executive search came up with about ten candidates, and the board and I interviewed them extensively. One of the candidates interviewed particularly well, IBM executive Jonathan Judge, and he was eventually appointed as my successor. During one of the interviews, he had raised a concern that as I had founded the company and had run it for over three decades I would have difficulty letting go. He was worried that I would interfere with the way he managed the company. I could see his point and agreed it could be a problem. That is why from the day I left as CEO I didn't return for three months except for one occasion where I had to handle a legal matter. Furthermore, even though I am still to this day chairman of the board, I do not have an office at Paychex headquarters.

Many business experts and writers have shown surprise about how I chose to handle my retirement. I'm surprised they are surprised because I have always demonstrated a different approach to the corporate world. For instance, I think CEOs are paid too highly in America. I always took a modest salary when compared to my counterparts in similar-sized corporations. In fact, my total remuneration package was substantially lower. (A CEO's salary reflects only a portion of their true earnings. One needs to take into consideration bonuses and stock options and other benefits.)

In my case, I never once in all the years I ran Paychex took a stock option. I always felt I had enough to keep me motivated in the original shareholding I retained as founder. When I retired, the board offered me stock options, and I could have taken advantage of what is often called a golden parachute. What I did take was two treasured items, my desk and my credenza. No stock, no cash, no pension—just some furniture that I arranged to have taken to my personal office. This is almost unheard of in the annals of corporate history, but I think it's the way it should be. I had the shares I'd held onto from the beginning and that was enough. The other thing people find strange is that I didn't have a retirement party. It simply wasn't something I felt I needed. Besides, I was still chairman of the board, I wasn't divorcing myself from the company.

KATRINA, GROWTH, AND LEADERSHIP CHANGE

Shortly after I left, Paychex helped out with Hurricane Katrina relief. It was another example of how a successful company can give back. The company partnered with the American Red Cross and Hibernia National Bank and processed, printed, and mailed over 270,000 disaster relief checks for victims in Louisiana. Philanthropy has always been an important facet of success for me.

Over the next few years, Paychex steadily grew its business through acquisitions and in particular by bringing in 2,000 new clients a week through traditional sales methods, the way I used to do when it was just me on the road.

Paychex's relationship with CPAs continued. Remember, CPAs had been an important element of my original sales strategy. A year before I retired, the American Institute of Certified Public Accountants (AICPA) Business Solutions Program chose Paychex as its preferred payroll provider. Two years later we began offering 401(k) recordkeeping services and major market services. These programs benefitted CPAs by enhancing their offerings to their clients, which in turn helped them strengthen their client relationships. It made me think back to all those years ago when the management at EAS said the CPAs would be upset with us for going after their clients. Now they were our clients, too—who would have thought it? Well, not to be too modest, I did actually.

Five years after he joined Paychex, Jon Judge left. It was during the summer and I was in Rochester, so I went back to run things for a few months. After interviewing several candidates for the job, I suggested to the board that I felt Martin Mucci was the person for the job.

A NEW CEO AND PRESIDENT

Marty Mucci had shown his interest in the position previously when we hired Jon Judge, but at that time he didn't have the requisite knowledge of the payroll processing industry. Originally he had called me when he was the CEO of Frontier Telephone of Rochester, New York. Things were changing at his company and he was looking for a new opportunity. This was early 2002; I agreed to meet with him, and we got along well—I liked the guy, but as he had no experience in our industry, I didn't have anything for him. I suggested we stay in touch, and a few months later after a second meeting, during which he impressed me even more, I came up with an idea. I asked him whether he would be prepared to work for Paychex on contract for ninety days for a modest fee. His project would be to visit four or five of our branches a week and report back to me what he thought of their operations. After week one, I felt he'd carried out a pretty good basic analysis. At the end of week two, his report was better, and after five weeks, I knew he would be a good fit for Paychex. I brought him on board as vice president in charge of all branches; by October that year he was senior vice president of operations. He was responsible for all payroll and human resources services, customer service, product management, and IT functions.

He was one of my best hires ever, so to my mind he was a perfect replacement for Jon Judge. The board agreed and we were all proved right, as Marty has done a stellar job ever since taking over as CEO and president on September 30, 2010.

THE PAYCHEX BOARD

In the early days, the board consisted of just insiders: About half of the vice presidents (my previous partners and franchisees) sat on the board. As we grew and went public, we started to bring in outside representation. Today, the board consists of nine highly qualified people: me as chairman, Marty Mucci, Thomas F. Bonadio, Joseph G. Doody, Joseph M. Tucci, Joseph M. Velli, Kara Wilson, Pam Joseph, and David Flaschen.

It's a highly professional board that meets quarterly. Two meetings are held in Rochester and two in Naples, Florida. Phil Horsley and Grant Inman, who recently retired, had been on the board for almost forty years and both live in California. I mentioned Phil in chapter five in regard to his role at the University of Rochester, where he was instrumental in purchasing $2 million of shares on behalf of the university. It was Phil who introduced me to Grant Inman, who at the time worked for Hambrecht and Quist and who also bought shares shortly before Paychex went public. In all the time they were on the board, Phil only missed a handful of meetings and Grant perhaps two; they have been stalwart supporters of me personally and Paychex and deserve recognition in these pages.

TWELVE

OWNING AND MANAGING A

HOCKEY TEAM

The next episode in my life was unexpected, but very rewarding. Although I'd had a successful career playing baseball in high school, I had never considered purchasing a sports team as a business venture. In fact, I would go so far as to say I had no interest at all. Then during a campaign meeting, Steve Pigeon mentioned the pending bankruptcy sale of the Buffalo Sabres. I remember my answer was, "So?" Undeterred, he told me about the dedicated Buffalo fans and the $125 million public-private investment in an arena that would be shuttered if the team left town—an event that would be devastating to the people of western New York. I asked whether anyone else was interested in buying the team, and while there was, their financial resources were questionable at best. Steve added that no one else with adequate resources was likely to step up to the plate.

Over the next seven years I applied everything I had learned in business, along with what people often referred to as my unique way of looking at things, to managing a sports team. Before that, however, I had to be convinced it was even something I should consider.

So, in the midst of my run for governor, I agreed to an initial meeting with Larry Quinn arranged by Steve and Carl Paladino, a Buffalo businessman who would later run for governor. Quinn had been president of the company that helped build the arena where the Sabres played from 1992–1996. From 1996–1998 he was president of the franchise, but didn't last long once the Rigas family, founders of the Adelphia cable company, bought the team. The Rigas family later imploded in a fraud scandal, which was why the Sabres were now facing bankruptcy. The team had been taken over by the league and put up for sale. There was a concern that most potential buyers would want to move the team out of Buffalo to a more profitable, larger city.

Initially, we met casually over drinks, but Larry and I agreed to meet in a more formal business setting to go over the franchise's numbers and explore further my initial but guarded interest in the team. He brought along Dan DiPofi, his colleague and later partner, and they walked me through a series of projections. They were taken by surprise when I took out my ruler—the one I have with a magnifying glass in the middle of it—and started going through the numbers line by line. I don't think Larry and Dan had ever seen a potential investor in a sports team go into this level of detail themselves, especially at such an early stage. I have always believed due diligence is the responsibility of the investor and should be hands-on, not delegated to accountants and the like. Although of course, that should also take place at a later date.

As we went through the numbers, I said, "There's something wrong here. You're showing projections that the company never makes money." Larry's one-word reply was disconcerting, "Yeah." I was confused, "Well, why did you do that?" And he said, "Well, I don't see how the franchise can make money under the current circumstances." He went on to explain there were current labor grievances and other problems and he didn't want to blue-sky me. I told him he was the first person to come to me asking me to invest in something that was bleeding so much red ink. I appreciated his honesty but told him I was not interested. Yet afterward, I couldn't get the team's predicament out of my mind.

As I traveled to Buffalo more often with the campaign, it became very apparent to me that the Sabres were vital to the long-term viability of western New York, and more specifically, to downtown

Buffalo. It was also clear to me that there was no real white knight on the horizon to save the team. I knew in my gut that if I didn't take on the project, there was a good chance the team would leave. I decided one August night to give Larry a call and ask if he would join my team. He said yes immediately, and together with Dan, we went to work.

I agreed to meet with league commissioner Gary Bettman in his New York office late in the summer of 2002, squeezing the meeting in between campaign stops. He told me the team had a good history of filling the arena. What was needed was financial stability and a team that could play well. He told me later that he had expected me to arrive at the meeting with a horde of press in tow, or at least waiting for us outside when we left the meeting. The fact that I wasn't using the Sabres as a vote-getting ploy made him take me more seriously than he otherwise might have.

Bettman proceeded to give me a lesson in running a hockey franchise. First, he told me there was going to be revenue sharing (a system of moving revenues from high-revenue teams to low-revenue teams) and that as Buffalo was a small-market town the Sabres would be a beneficiary. Second, a salary cap was going to be introduced and this would also be good for the franchise. The team's payroll at that time was $29 million, while the New York Rangers and Toronto Maple Leafs were both paying $80 million in salaries. He explained that the salary cap would limit the amount any team could spend on players' salaries. This would restrict wealthier clubs from signing far more top players than their less-wealthy rivals and in essence level the playing field—or ice, in this particular sport. Bettman ended the meeting by asking me to submit a proposal for the purchase of the team.

During this time, I was once again confronted with dubious political practices and what I considered misuse of taxpayers' money. Not surprisingly, it involved my nemesis Governor George Pataki. He was adamant I should not be allowed to buy the team. He enlisted the help of some of Buffalo's business elite, the mayor, the Erie County executive, all supported by the editorial weight of the *Buffalo News*. Basically, he planned to use $50 million of taxpayers' money and other incentives supplied by county and city governments to back the bid of Buffalo businessman Mark Hamister. Hamister owned the Buffalo Destroyers football team and two other minor-league football teams. The *Buffalo News* backed this irresponsible use of public money and went so far as to publish an editorial with the headline "Golisano Go Home," calling me an outsider, even though I only lived sixty miles away. And ignoring the fact that Rochester was a huge fan base for the Sabres and the Buffalo Bills. Just try traveling the New York State Thruway west from Rochester to Buffalo on any Bills home game day!

Once again, I had a fight on my hands, not only to buy the team but against unwarranted misuse of public funding. I managed to get media coverage from my old friends at the alternative weekly papers (from my *Bidders Guide* days) and through internet news channels and blogs, all of which stimulated a groundswell of public support opposing the enormous Pataki giveaways.

By now I was used to fighting campaigns against devious opponents, and enlisted the help of some honest and ethical politicians (they do exist) in the State and County Legislature as well as the Buffalo City Council, including State Senator Byron Brown (now Buffalo's mayor), County Legislature Chairman Chuck Swanick, and Council President Jim Pitts, all of whom passed legislation opposing the sweetheart deals being offered by Pataki and his cronies.

In the end, my efforts failed, and the league accepted Hamister's bid, which was higher, in large part because it was backed by so much taxpayer money. However, he had thus far failed to get all his financing in place. I told Larry to keep his powder dry and that I'd had a lot of experience with deals of this kind, and they had a habit of coming back around.

In the end, the league gave him three weeks to get his financing in order. They then extended it for a further three weeks, and subsequently another four weeks.

When it became crystal clear in January that the Hamister bid was in trouble, I wrote an open letter to Commissioner Bettman that pledged I would not use a penny of taxpayer money in my bid. That got picked up by the national news and the sports networks.

Eventually, the Hamister deal fell through in February 2003 and Gary Bettman called Larry to ask whether we were still interested in buying the team. Larry told him he thought I might be, but it would not be the deal Hamister had on the table. Gary asked whether it would be the same one we had been talking about earlier and Larry told him, "Oh, I don't think we're going to even make it that good for you." Bettman laughed sheepishly, but made it clear he was open to negotiation. We started negotiations and then one night I called Larry and told him I needed six concessions. We were dealing with the NHL, Adelphia Cable (the previous owners of the team), the federal bankruptcy court, and the franchise's creditors. Larry, being a good foot soldier, battled for the concessions and came back to me disappointed he had only managed to get three of them. I hugged him and exclaimed, "Really? I didn't think you'd get any of them! I guess we own a hockey team. There's only one thing—I don't like hockey and I've only seen three games in my entire life." Of course, in the end I grew to like it a lot.

I told the press I wanted to accomplish three things: first, stabilize the team and make it profitable; second, make it a winning team; and third, ensure the team remained in Buffalo permanently by eventually finding an owner who would commit in writing to taking the team long-term and keeping it in the community.

The media talked about me having several partners, but in the end I went it alone on this occasion. I wasn't entirely sure I knew what I was getting into, plus with a sports team, everyone wants access to high-end suites to entertain their friends, which I felt might become a problem down the line. Not only that, you have to have very deep pockets to own a sports team. I remember asking one potential partner, "How much can you afford to lose a year?" He replied, "I can probably lose a million to a million and a half a year." My next question was, "What if we lose twenty million?" Different reaction altogether. So, it's not surprising that bringing in partners who don't have deep pockets can cause problems, especially if you go through a tough financial period.

Having said that, I had a gut feeling I could make the franchise successful after my talks with the commissioner about salary caps and revenue sharing. As he had promised, the Rangers' payroll subsequently dropped from $80 million to $35 million, so I knew we could be more competitive. That, combined with receiving $4 or $5 million in revenue sharing, made all the difference to our financial situation and the team's opportunity for on-ice success.

The team owed $21 million to HSBC, which was fully guaranteed by Delaware North, our concessionaire, and net $7.5 million to the NHL's bankruptcy lender. With regard to Delaware North, owned by prominent Buffalo businessman Jerry Jacobs, who also owns the Boston Bruins, we released them from their guarantee and reset the loan with me as the guarantor. Many people thought at the time this was far too magnanimous of a gesture; it's true that it's doubtful any other prospective buyer would have let him off the hook.

Although the bankruptcy proceeding would have eliminated all of the team's unsecured creditors, I also posted approximately $2 million with the court to pay mostly small businesses that had supplied services to the team. Sadly, the bankruptcy court lawyers gobbled up most of the unsecured creditor deposit in fees, leaving only 50 cents on the dollar for the small business owners. I also had to pay $10 million to the league in escrow to fund potential losses in the event of a work stoppage.

In addition, the day after we signed the asset purchase agreement, the commissioner asked for a $10 million deposit to show good faith. Considering all the trouble he had with the prior group, you could hardly blame him. Yet Larry was nevertheless surprised when my secretary Eileen called him the next morning asking where to send the check. I always drive an exceptionally hard but fair bargain, but once an agreement is reached, my word is my bond and I move things forward quickly. We had an asset agreement in a little over a month after Bettman's call. From that point, we were given operating control of the team.

I brought in Larry as CEO and managing partner and Dan DiPofi as chief operating officer. This immediately gave me a qualified management team. The general manager of hockey was Darcy Regier. Once the deal was done we held a press conference but pointedly did not invite the business elite or any politicians, except for those who had sponsored resolutions opposing Pataki's public subsidies. Amazingly, the very people who opposed me so vehemently, and who had pushed hard for taxpayer money to be spent on purchasing the team, later invited me to join "the gang of eighteen," a group consisting of the top business leaders in the region who regularly met at the Buffalo Club. I attended one meeting with the express purpose of declining their invitation in person and walking back out of the club. As one last and exquisite piece of old business, when I made it clear to the *Buffalo News* that we were not going to spend much on advertising with them, they canceled their luxury suite in the arena. No worries, we quickly sold it to another business. I now owned a hockey team.

MANAGING THE SABRES

When I signed the asset purchase agreement, the Sabres were in last place in what was then the Northeastern Division of the NHL's Eastern Conference, and we needed to make some radical decisions. During an in-depth management meeting I asked the same questions I ask when diagnosing any ailing business: "What's right with this business? What's wrong with this business? What's missing? What's wrong with the team?" The latter question elicited Larry's response that the team lacked leadership. He said we had talent, we had good players, but we didn't have enough people who were passionate enough about not losing. Everyone likes to win but champions are players who absolutely, utterly cannot stand to lose. Surprisingly, he told me there weren't that many people like that in professional sports. I asked him to make a list of players we might be able to get who fit that criteria and go get them. The two players he targeted were Danny Briere and later Chris Drury. They became cocaptains of the team and became the leaders the team so sorely needed. My management philosophy from the outset was to guide my management team, not tell them what to do. I was determined not to be a "fantasy hockey" owner. I had people who knew the game, so from my standpoint, it was always, "Find the problem, fix the problem—that's your job."

That doesn't mean I wasn't hands-on, I just made sure they took responsibility for their decisions. People often ask me about my management techniques or remark on how different they are to other successful owners of companies. Owing the Sabres was different from anything I'd done before. I was not an expert in the industry but I did know what questions to ask, and what worked and what didn't work in any business environment. How did those management practices translate into turning a bankrupt, perennially losing team around?

When I was working with Larry and Dan I'd tell them I was coming into the office, or to watch a game, or simply that I'd like to get together with them. I wouldn't have an agenda, but I would have a topic in mind, for example, ticket prices. I never gave them time to prepare a presentation, I just wanted to know what they knew and how much of a handle they had on the business. And I never told them what to do. Instead I challenged them on how well they knew what was going on in the business at any moment in time.

Ultimately, I left them to run the business and make decisions, but along the way I would challenge their thought process. After a long debate early in my tenure, Larry once asked, "So, what do you want to do?" My answer was always, "You're the CEO of this company. You're going to decide what you want to do. If I don't like it or I don't like the way you perform, then I'll deal with you as the CEO. But this is your business to run, not mine." I always found it a highly effective management style.

An Outside Perspective

As I mentioned earlier, the team did not do well during the bankruptcy period and, despite adding Drury and Briere, showed little improvement at the start of 2003. I recall we were in the bottom third of the league standings, in the bottom three or four in scoring, and just a little better in team defense. Larry was obliged to take some time off for medical reasons and the team seemed simply to lack the ability to win. When Larry got back I called a meeting in the third week in December. Larry opened the meeting with a simple question for Darcy and Lindy Ruff, the team's coach: "What's your plan? Their response was less than inspiring. "We've got to shore up our defense, we need a better goalie, we need better defensemen, we should trade Miro Satan (who at the time was our leading scorer) for a goalie and another player." I listened to this for a while and then asked, "Why do you want to do that?" I may have been new to the game, certainly from a coaching perspective, but I'm analytical and I'd been looking at the numbers and asked them whether they had looked at our shooting percentage? I could see they were losing patience with me, so I explained, "We're not scoring goals. Let's improve our players' shooting accuracy."

At that time, no one in the NHL was looking at shooting percentages and here my management team had an owner harping on about something they didn't see as particularly relevant. So, I said, "Look guys, I'm so sick of losing 3–1, 2–1, 1–0. If we're going to lose, I want to lose 6–5. I want something that's fun to watch. You tell me we have all these great players. I want to score goals!" I went on, "I know what I'd do. I'd extend every practice twenty minutes, and those guys should do nothing but practice shooting until they can do it blindfolded." Darcy said, "Well I don't know if the players union would like that."

My response was, "When the players union brings us revenue, let me know."

Lindy was a little belligerent, but he was a good listener and loyal and said, "You want to score goals? Okay, we'll score goals." To give him his due he changed his whole system. The next day he made our goalie coach lie prostrate in front of the net and forced the players to keep rushing the goal and lift their shots over him. This evolved into a very exciting system where all five players entered the rush as a unit and we quickly became known as the most dynamic offensive team in the league.

I was impressed that they would completely change the style of play based on me, a non-hockey guy, asking basic questions based on studying game analytics. What's interesting is that today the game is all about analytics. One system is called the Corsi Rating. This rating takes into consideration the number of shots attempted, the number of shots that reach the goaltender, the number of shots blocked by your team, and then the number of goals scored, instead of a vaguely simplistic tally of shots on goal. Back in 2003, no one was looking at that kind of stuff.

The lesson here is that there is huge value in looking at things from new perspectives. No matter whether you are managing a small business, a massive corporation, a sports team, or a political campaign, thinking differently almost always pays off. In terms of the Buffalo Sabres, the new focus on our shooting percentage meant we jumped from around twenty-seventh in league scoring in December, to fourteenth by the end of the year. If you discount the games prior to our meeting, the Sabres were in the top five the rest of the way. Not bad for a two-hour discussion.

How Come You Earn More Than Me?

During another management session, I got a little more serious. It was Darcy Regier's job as general manager to select players, sign contracts, handle discipline, all that kind of stuff—pretty much anything to do with player personnel. On the day we closed the deal and made the press announcement, I told Larry that I'd like to come to Buffalo and sit down with everyone and talk team strategy. It was set up for a Saturday morning and Larry, Dan, and Darcy (Lindy was in Boston with the team) were all there. We talked for several hours about the players, where we thought our strengths and our weaknesses were. I was just taking it all in because I didn't know much about the sport. At one point, we decided to go out and get a hamburger. We sat down at the table and ordered. Then I looked to Darcy who was sitting opposite me and said, "Darcy, I have a question I want to ask you. The Buffalo Sabres does 50 or 60 million dollars in revenue. Paychex does maybe twenty or thirty times that. You have about 300 employees in the whole franchise, Paychex has 10,000 employees and made something like 700 million dollars last year. You guys lost 25 million dollars. So, why do you get paid more than I do?" I had seen that Darcy's salary was $900,000 a year.

There was dead silence. In a way, I felt sorry for him because I'd just nailed him. He hesitated for a few moments and he said, "Well, it's sort of what the other team managers get." I wasn't going to let him off the hook that easily and replied, "But there doesn't seem to be a foundation for that." After a more-than-normal lull in the conversation, Darcy responded by saying, "But I'm sure you get stock options." At that point, I offered him a piece of the team provided he would agree to fund his share of the losses. That was the end of that discussion.

Who's Going to Pay the $250,000?

One thing I learned while owning the Sabres was that whatever the industry or type of business, constant vigilance is required on your bottom line. A simple mistake can cost hundreds of thousands, as in this story of allowing a lackluster player a little more ice time.

In hockey, there are addenda to hockey players' contracts. They can be tricky things, as I was to find out as my first season as owner was coming to a close. At that time most players had these addendums to their contracts, which meant that the standard contract didn't tell the whole story. If you were going to buy a player, for instance, you had to carefully study what additional financial responsibilities you were buying into.

To give you an example, a player might have had written into their contract that if they score more than a certain number of goals in the season, they would receive a bonus. If they were traded to your team halfway through the season, you were expected to assume the remainder of the responsibility. It's confusing, I know. Basically, if in this case they had already scored 50 percent of the goals when traded, their old team would agree to pay 50 percent of the total if and when they were awarded the bonus. Today such arrangements are not allowed, but when I was an owner it could make life difficult.

Unbeknownst to me, we traded for a player in our first year that had such a rider on his contract. He was a young player and, to be truthful, not playing that well. My management team had missed the fact that there was an addendum to the player's contract. It specified that if he played a certain number of games during the season, he would be awarded a quarter-million-dollar bonus. Larry wasn't aware of the mistake until the season ended and chose not to tell me immediately.

Once the season ended my senior managers, Larry, Dan, and Darcy came to my home in Florida for a two-day meeting to discuss how the season had gone for us. On the first day it was just Larry, Dan, and me as we were discussing corporate matters. We had a great day and decided on several initiatives including significantly reducing the price of our season tickets. We also agreed to introduce variable pricing for single tickets. Once we were finished, I suggested watching the playoffs at a nearby restaurant. Over dinner, Dan told me about the missed addendum. Larry had specifically told him to leave it for the following day, but it had been gnawing away at Dan all day. I was furious and immediately confronted Larry, who defended his decision by saying that he just wanted a nice evening and to leave work until the following day. I demanded to know what he planned to do about it, but he again said we should leave it until after Darcy arrived and we'd spent time talking about the team.

The first words out of my mouth the next morning when gathered in my sunroom were, "So, do we owe a games-played bonus for Jeff Jillson?" The room was silent, until Darcy eventually agreed that was the case. I asked how much of the bonus his previous team, San Jose, was going to pay. The answer was none. So I asked who was responsible for reviewing the contract and therefore who was responsible for missing the addendum. No one answered, so I asked who was going to pay me back the lost money.

What happened then could almost have been a farce on stage. There we were in my glass-walled sunroom sitting around a table, bathed in sunlight, in silence. The discomfort in the room was palpable—at least it was for them. I was happy to sit in silence—I'm good at it. The others fidgeted and looked as if they'd like to be anywhere but there with me in that increasingly hot sunroom. Everyone knew that it was Darcy's department that had missed the rider, so he was feeling particularly uncomfortable. I let the silence go on for forty-five minutes—I just sat there. Larry was the first to break. He decided to escape to the patio but due to the stressful situation had not noticed that the glass doors were in fact closed. He walked into the door headfirst, bounced off, and ended up prostrate on the tile floor. Embarrassed, he quickly got up and poured himself a glass of water. The bump on his head was red and very obvious. After that, the silence only lasted a minute or so; Darcy blurted out, "Tom, do you want me to reimburse the Sabres for the loss?" I looked at him and said that it wouldn't be necessary, I just expected someone to at least offer. After that the meeting continued as if nothing had happened.

I've used the pregnant pause, or its close cousin the extended silence, throughout my business career. It is an excellent entrepreneurial strategy that can be employed in a wide range of situations. In this case, I needed to emphasize that my money, my investment in the team, should not be taken lightly. I wanted them to respect our resources and use them wisely. It's the same with the charities to which I give money and to the young businesses in which I invest both my money and time.

Thoughts on Scouting

Too often, businesspeople get stuck into a rut of doing things the way they've always been done without questioning why. I walked into the office one day and asked a simple question, "How do we scout?" Larry gave me the stock answer, but I wasn't satisfied so we brought Darcy into the office and I rapid-fired questions at him, too. "How do you scout? Who do you have scouting for us? Where do they live? Where do they scout? Who do they go to see?" I soon discovered we had a part-time scout in Ontario and two in Saskatchewan. That seemed strange to me so I asked how many players we had on the team from Saskatchewan and the answer was zero. Pushing it further I asked how many had we had in the last ten years and got the answer, "Maybe two." I went in for the kill, "So, why do we scout this way?" Darcy gave me the worst possible answer, "We've always done it that way, but if I had my druthers . . ." To which I answered, "Darcy, you do have your druthers—how do you want to do it?"

To his credit, Darcy changed the way we scouted and once again it became far more analytical. Instead of getting bland advice from a scout that a player was "good," Darcy would gather all the scouts and coaches in a video conference and ask, "Why should we get a particular player?" He would make them debate and ask tough questions such as, "Okay, if we get him, where are you going to play him? And, who are you going to remove from the lineup?" Scouting at the Sabres became a collaborative affair—there was a critical review element. Darcy even took it a stage further and built a computer system that evaluated players in various circumstances. For instance, how well did he play with different team members, or in different lineups? How good was he defensively when playing with a specific player?

From a simple question on scouting and the discovery of "in-a-rut thinking," we developed a sophisticated system of analyzing players. Today, most teams do this, but in 2003 it was revolutionary; old-school coaches actually criticized us in the press, saying we were cheap and only doing video scouting. Not true, of course, we were just changing the analytics behind our scouting. We never answered our critics in the press because we didn't want other teams to know what we were doing. I was continually trying to differentiate us from the competition, and the only way we could do that was through how well we scouted, coached, analyzed, and developed the team. All of this I brought from Paychex where we were big on training, personnel development, and growing from within. These were business principles being used in a hockey arena to great effect.

MAKING HOCKEY AFFORDABLE

In the early days, before we had fully taken over the franchise, I went to a game with Larry and we sat in the arena. He had tickets and I asked to look at them. I commented, "How can anyone afford this? The average Joe can't pay this." That stuck with me, and after the first year I noticed that every time we played the Toronto Maple Leafs their fans would come down and buy all the tickets. It was like being at a Toronto home game every time they came to town. What was worse, their fans would all be in the lower section and our fans would be up top, as those seats were the only tickets they could afford. Over the years, the Sabres had systematically increased ticket prices, and the price for a season ticket was very expensive. This was the reason we were only selling 5,800 per year.

One very serious problem was that season ticket holders were paying anywhere from $50 to $80 per game whereas someone could pick up a ticket in a promotion from Pizza Hut for $15 and get a free pizza—and that person might only come to one or two games a year. In effect, we were rewarding the casual fan at the expense of our most loyal customer.

My plan was to lower the season ticket prices by 25 percent. In addition, in July 2004 we were the first professional franchise in the four major sports to institute variable pricing for all home games. Each game was designated by one of five classifications (Platinum, Gold, Silver, Bronze, and Value). The classifications were based on the opponent, time of the year, day of the week, rivalries, and games against marquee players. Our objective in developing this pricing structure was to find a way to make the game affordable for more fans. This in turn enhanced all patrons' experiences by filling the arena, while at the same time protecting the pricing of our season tickets. One great spinoff to implementing this new pricing schedule was that within three years we went from last in the league in merchandise sales to number one.

OTHER EVENTS

The Winter Game

One of the things that Larry pulled off, which I think has been a tremendous help to professional hockey itself, was hosting an outdoor game, the first of which was held on January 1, 2008. There'd been a game some years previously but not for many years. NBC thought if we staged an outdoor game on that day it would generate good ratings, as there was little to no on-air competition. The league backed it, but there was a lot of doubt it would sell well. We decided to donate all revenues over and above normal ticket sales to a sellout game to the league.

The game set an NHL record for attendance with 71,217 people. Another 11,500 watched on TV at an HSBC Arena house party. It is still considered the benchmark for this now annual NHL event. The game was televised nationally on NBC in the United States, and CBC in Canada. This was the highest-rated NHL broadcast in eleven years in the United States, with an estimated 2 million viewers. We sold 47,000 tickets in fifteen minutes. To support our season ticketholders, we held back 27,000 tickets for them.

2011 IIHF World Junior Championships

We hosted the 2011 World Junior Championship (WJC) in Buffalo from December 26 to January 5, 2011. Over 330,000 people attended the event in Buffalo, making it the second most-attended WJC event ever.

OFF-ICE ENTERTAINMENT

Over the period I was owner, we held more than eighty concerts starring celebrities such as Celine Dion, Faith Hill, Bruce Springsteen, Justin Timberlake, Elton John, Simon and Garfunkel, and dozens more. There were two individuals who came to watch hockey, however, who stand out in my memory.

One of these occasions was when Larry got a call from Senator Chuck Schumer's office. We were playing the Rangers and he wanted to come to the game and drop the puck. Larry told him that any politician attending a game gets booed, so he sort of invited himself for dinner instead. I wasn't pleased when I found out he was coming and asked Larry whether he was paying for his own meal.

On the evening of the game he appeared in my box. I wasn't keen on socializing with people in general at matches, in part because this was one of my businesses so I used to watch the game intensely. He then did the unforgivable: He sat in my seat. No one does that. Larry wouldn't even dare to sit in the box, let alone in my seat. I told Larry to get him out of the box, he was driving me crazy. So, Larry coyly asked him if he'd like to be a guest on our radio broadcast during the game. Larry had read him perfectly; Bob Dole once said about Schumer, "Now be careful; the most dangerous place to be in Washington, DC, is between Chuck Schumer and a microphone."

A Presidential Visit

Bill Clinton once made an unofficial visit during the height of the Iraq War when George W. Bush was president. He hadn't announced it and we didn't alert the press, he just came into my box and sat next to me. This of course was fine with me, he was by now a close friend. Suddenly there was a buzz; people were telling the people next to them to "look in the box, look in the box." The fever grew to a point where there was a spontaneous standing ovation. Clinton had to stand up and wave to the crowd. They showed him on the jumbotron and then a chant arose, getting louder and louder, "We wish you were still there, we wish you were still there." It was a moving moment. Especially, I would say, for me, as I was so against Bush taking us into the war. It was all the more powerful because it was so natural and so organic. We hadn't announced he was coming, there was no press presence per se, just a personal visit.

FIGHTING TALK

I went to war with league commissioner Gary Bettman for a short period. Traditionalists felt the game was a man's game and that fighting was part of it, but I always thought it was unnecessary. After our player Chris Drury took a brutal late hit from an Ottawa player and suffered a concussion, I wrote a letter calling for a ban on hits to the head. It stirred up all sorts of strong feelings. I was vilified for quite a while. It was even covered by ESPN. At the next Board of Governors meeting, one of the other owners got very excited and said hard hits and fighting were a part of the game and my proposal would ruin the sport. Players, he proclaimed, should be allowed to drop their gloves and duke it out. I stood up and roared, "Would you like to step outside?" I was joking but half the people in the room thought I was serious. However, I think it got the point across as to how ridiculous fighting in the game truly is. This is a sport, after all, in which goalies originally refused to wear protective facemasks and the wearing of helmets by line players was also resisted for years. These days there is a lot more concern about head injuries.

TURNING THE FRANCHISE AROUND

In the first year, we lost $10 million and sold only 5,800 season tickets. The second year we lost another $10 million, in part because it was a lockout year and we had all the expenses and no revenue. In years three and four we made back those losses, and during years five to seven we made money every year. Within two years we acquired 15,000 season ticket holders and there was a waiting list.

When we bought the franchise in 2003, we were mired in last place and after a late-season surge climbed to twenty-fifth. In terms of playing well, things really started going right for us in the 2005–06 season. The NHL had instituted a number of rule changes that favored speed over size and strength. And our roster was built for speed. Come the middle of November, after a slow start, Chris Drury and Danny Briere rallied the team and the players started to work in harmony and we couldn't stop winning. We had one of the best lineups in the league and we began to dominate the competition—we were simply faster and better than anyone else. That year and the next we reached the Stanley Cup playoffs with fifty-win seasons. For the first time in the Sabres history, in 2006–07, we won the Presidents' Trophy. Not only that, we became one of just five teams to make consecutive appearances in the Conference Finals since the lockout.

During the 2005–06 season the excitement in Buffalo was palpable; everybody was talking about the Sabres. The games were selling out so often that we used outdoor screens to enable thousands more to watch key games.

Not only that, on a regional basis our television ratings were the highest in the league. In 2007, we were rated as the best-run sports franchise in professional sports by ESPN, ahead of 122 major professional sports teams in North America. This, even though the *Buffalo News* had said I couldn't run a 7-11 store. My reply was, they sure as hell couldn't run a hockey team.

CHRIS DRURY AND DANIEL BRIERE—THE TRUE STORY

Although it's an imperfect analogy, buying a sports team is a little like asking the love of your life to marry you and then demanding that she sit down right away and negotiate the prenuptial. Winning requires a level of trust and commitment among a group of people that engenders great emotion and feeling. This is true within a team but also extends to the fan base, management, and believe it or not, the owner. But as much fun as winning can be, there is always the day of reckoning at the end of the season.

The thrills and excitement of our two Conference Finals, the division titles, and the Presidents' Trophy also created very difficult business decisions that had to be addressed.

After our miraculous run in 2006, thirteen players filed for arbitration. This meant that over two-thirds of the team would receive a substantial raise. Two key players, Mike Greer and Jay McKee, left as free agents, and several other players without arbitration rights still required contracts with significant raises. More importantly, Daniel Briere won a one-year arbitration award of $3 million and a second award a year later of $5 million. The cost of keeping the team together had gone up dramatically, pushing us against the salary cap.

We knew that our success was the by-product of great coaching, team cohesion, and remarkable depth at the forward position. After successfully navigating the arbitration minefield during the summer and adding defensive depth with the acquisition of Jaro Spacek, we started the 2006 season with the previous year's team largely in place. It immediately paid off. The team won its first ten games, and Stanley Cup fever was running high.

Despite the excitement, every Sabres fan and certainly the management and I were painfully aware that our two cocaptains, Chris Drury and Daniel Briere, would be eligible for free agency at the end of the season. Although we wanted to keep both players, we knew it wasn't a realistic option. Briere had asked for $6 million in his previous arbitration and would certainly command more as a free agent.

Although Chris Drury didn't have the offensive upside of a Briere, we viewed him as an essential leader who could play a key role in developing our up-and-coming players. With our aggregate salaries within less than $100,000 of the salary cap, it was clear we couldn't keep both players. We decided to try to sign Chris Drury.

There is a Buffalo columnist who insists that we subsequently reached an agreement with Drury and then reneged on it—this is pure fiction. Although we had discussions with his agent that at one point appeared as if they might lead to a contract, they never reached fruition. When it became clear that Chris was headed toward the best offensive season of his career, ultimately finishing with 37 goals, his agent asked that we defer further discussion until the postseason.

In the final analysis, both players left for very large contracts. Although I have great respect for both of them and fully understand a player's need—and right—to maximize his earning potential, their departure was a huge blow to the community and, of course, to the franchise. I am grateful to both of them for helping us achieve such success and rebuilding the franchise after the bankruptcy. To this day, people play the *what if* game as it relates to these players. Why didn't we give them more money? Why did we let them leave for nothing? Would we have finally won the cup if they had stayed?

Obviously, those are unanswerable questions. All I can say is that we were all in to win in 2006–07 and worked hard to keep the 2005–06 team together. We gave the team all the support possible. We were certainly not going to disrupt the team by trading Drury or Briere for future assets, as some Monday morning quarterbacks suggested. In the end, we won the team's first Presidents' Trophy and took one hell of a shot at the Stanley Cup.

With or without Danny and Chris, our window started to close a little at the end of the season. The run-and-gun style that we embraced was becoming less effective. Although the value of quickness and skill is returning today, people forget Anaheim won the cup in 2007 with big forwards and the old pre-lockout system of play. We were able to rebuild our team quickly and won the Northeast Division in 2010, the last year of my ownership. Most fans forget that our group brought Drury and Briere to Buffalo in the first place. And although I regret that our exciting run with the team is so often overshadowed by the Drury and Briere departures, it was an incredible ride.

In terms of team success, we went to the Conference Finals twice and went to the playoffs more years than we didn't. Not only that, we never missed the playoffs by more than four points.

BUFFALO SABRES FOUNDATION

When I took control of the franchise in March of 2003, there was $13,000 in a charitable fund known as the Buffalo Sabres Foundation. A little over seven years later we had over $300,000, and hundreds of organizations in western New York benefited from the fund. The Foundation has generated over $4 million in revenue and donated almost $2 million back into the community.

CAPITAL IMPROVEMENTS

Over the seven years I owned the Buffalo Sabres we made over $10 million in capital improvements to HSBC Arena. No public taxpayer money was used to fund these improvements. Some of the major upgrades we did were a state-of-the-art high-definition jumbotron, a ribbon board, a high-definition production facility, the Poor Man's Aud Club, club seating in the 200-level, and a new team locker room.

TIME TO MOVE ON

In the fall of 2008, I decided to give Larry and Dan a total of 13 percent minority interest in the team. They had worked hard to build the franchise and were not the highest paid executives in the league by a long shot. I wanted to be sure that when I sold the team they would be rewarded.

By 2010, other business was pulling my attention away from the team and I'd had some interest from potential buyers. My number one proviso in selling was that the team must stay in Buffalo. I could have put the franchise up for sale and stimulated a bidding war without that proviso, but I had taken over ownership of the team specifically to keep it in Buffalo and I wasn't going to allow it to be taken away now that it was successful. The owner of a cell phone manufacturing company showed some interest and offered $165 million if he kept it in Buffalo, but $235 million if I helped him to move it. In the end, I decided not to sell.

I then got an offer from Terry Pegula. He had founded the Pennsylvania energy company East Resources Inc., which he had recently sold to Royal Dutch Shell. At first, I turned his offer down, but a little later I decided it was a good deal, especially as he was willing to sign a clause that the team could never be moved out of Buffalo. The offer was $189 million, a lot less than I could have commanded without the clause, but I was happy. I'd had a great seven years. I'd bought the franchise for around $7.5 million and when the dust settled I'd made about $150 million. And in between, I'd helped make the team a major league contender.

There's one more thing that happened, which I'd like to mention to close out this chapter of my life. At our first outdoor Winter Game, I met Monica, who later became my wife. The Buffalo Sabres were indeed good to me.

THIRTEEN

MORE POLITICS AND CGI

ROCKEFELLER DRUG LAWS AND HIP-HOP

Not long after I'd purchased the Sabres, I became involved in some other issues that interested me. Steve Pigeon and Roger Stone, who had worked with me on the governor's race, told me about a movement in New York State to reform the "Rockefeller Drug Laws" originally signed into being in 1973. These draconian laws meant anyone caught selling two ounces of a prohibited drug, or in possession of four ounces, would be given a minimum sentence of fifteen years, and potentially up to twenty-five years to life in a state penitentiary. What was surprising, even then, was that the sentence was the same for cannabis as for hard drugs. In 1979, however, sentences for possession of marijuana were reduced.

These new drug laws followed Governor Nelson Rockefeller's introduction of the Narcotic Addiction and Control Commission in the late 1960s and later the Methadone Maintenance Program. The goal of the former was to help addicts get off drugs but in the end, it proved too costly. Neither actually resulted in a significant reduction in the proliferation of illegal drugs on the streets.

My interest, as I mentioned earlier, was primarily in seeing medical marijuana made legal after watching Gene Polisseni suffer debilitating pain while fighting and losing to prostate cancer.

Putting that aside, these almost zero tolerance laws were exceptionally regressive. Generations of people (mostly men) were locked up for extended periods for relatively minor infractions, when what they needed was medical treatment for addiction, not imprisonment as criminals. The social impact, not to mention cost, of broken families and of children not being raised by both parents was significant. What's more, these laws did nothing to curb drug addiction or neighborhoods infested with drug dealers and open-air street dealing.

I was asked to cosponsor a rally in New York City with Andrew Cuomo and entertainment executive Russell Simmons (the CEO of Rush Communications and the cofounder of the hip-hop record label Def Jam Recordings). Thousands attended the rally, including many hip-hop recording stars, to call upon Governor Pataki to finally reform these devastating laws. We asked that nonviolent drug offenders be treated as addicts requiring treatment rather than criminals deserving imprisonment. After sustained pressure from both activists and legislators, Pataki signed the Drug Law Reform Act, which amended sentencing guidelines. The act relaxed the possession amounts and reduced the mandatory minimum sentence to eight years, rising to twenty. However, many advocates felt the new laws were almost as harsh as before and still relied on prison sentences instead of rehabilitation, particularly in the case of users rather than dealers. I'll tell you how I'd deal with it in the final chapter.

PRESIDENT BUSH AND IRAQ

There was a lot of dubious politics taking place during the early 2000s, and in particular I was not impressed with the way President Bush was handling global affairs. In the run-up to the invasion of Iraq, I was both publicly and privately against the United States taking any offensive action. I didn't believe that Iraq had anything to do with the

9/11 attacks and furthermore thought the evidence Saddam Hussein had weapons of mass destruction was weak at best.

In my opinion, terminating Hussein's rule without knowing who might take his place was risky. I was convinced we would be seen as occupiers rather than as liberators, despite the offensive being called *Operation Iraqi Freedom*—a replacement for the mission title prior to March 19, 2003, which was *Operation Enduring Freedom*. Good PR in the United States, perhaps, but meaningless to the Iraqis on the ground.

My concerns that Hussein's absence might be filled by an even more dangerous individual or fanatical groups were well-founded. Bush's decision to attack was one of the worst made by a president in our nation's history. It led to mayhem on all fronts and the loss of far too many lives. It also resulted in the emergence of ISIS and a more brutal, radical Islam, which still proliferates and bedevils the world to this day.

During this period, we met with John Edwards, a senator from North Carolina who was a Democratic presidential candidate in 2004 (he would also run in 2008). We arrived a little early for our meeting and were shown into the front office where we could, however, see his reflection in a mirror. We watched him spend five minutes preening his hair. I'd seen enough, the guy was totally self-absorbed, so I said to Steve, "This guy doesn't need us, he loves himself too much." In truth, I found him a little ridiculous.

Four years later, when he was running as a candidate for the Democratic presidential nomination against Hillary Clinton and Barack Obama, he was forced to drop out in humiliation because he was having an affair with a staffer with whom he'd fathered a child out of wedlock. What made things hideously worse was his wife was dying of cancer.

Of all the candidates I met, I was most impressed with Dick Gephardt, a moderate who had good ideas on the economy. He was convinced that Bush was not only wrong with regard to the war but that he had emboldened Saudi Arabia to a degree that was detrimental to American interests.

I supported his campaign financially and Steve worked full time for him in Iowa. Unfortunately, Howard Dean's emergence weakened Dick and John Kerry was able to run up the middle and win the caucus. In the end, Gephardt dropped out and Kerry emerged as the nominee. Kerry didn't impress me, so I decided not to become involved.

ANOTHER RUN AT GOVERNOR—MAYBE

Meanwhile Governor Pataki's popularity continued to decline and there was a belief that he would not seek a fourth term. Attorney General Eliot Spitzer, whom I had supported in the past, was gaining national attention with his investigations of corruption and securities law violations on Wall Street and was frequently mentioned as a possible future governor.

Around this time Republican New York State Senate Majority Leader Joe Bruno contacted me. He told me that while Eliot Spitzer was gaining national press with his investigations of Wall Street, he was also making many enemies. There was a prevalent belief that his charges lacked merit and were hurting legitimate businesses just to garner personal and political press attention. Bruno went on to say that Spitzer's ego was out of control and his thin skin might mean that his overhyped candidacy might have clay feet. Bruno told me he would support me for the Republican nomination and also help me receive the Conservative line. I could still obtain the Independence line in my role as founder. Like Pigeon before him, Bruno believed that my life story, my attractiveness to independent voters, combined with a major party line could be a solid path to victory. At that point, he had my attention.

Around this time, President Clinton called Steve to ask whether he could arrange a meeting with me. He wanted to ask me to work with him on a bipartisan charitable endeavor, for which he felt I would be a perfect fit. He asked Steve to invite me to lunch with him as soon as possible at his home in Chappaqua. The meeting was arranged, quite coincidentally, at the same time the press had been reporting that the Republican Party was wooing me to be their nominee in the 2006 race.

As I mentioned earlier, Steve was Erie County Democratic chairman and had worked closely with Spitzer in the past. I made a point to see Spitzer frequently in his office in New York City to hear his views. Spitzer's right-hand man Rich Baum, who had also worked with Steve, called him to ask whether they could set up a meeting between Eliot and me as soon as possible. The topic of conversation was to discuss whether there was more we could work on together—rather than competing in a race for governor.

It was an odd coincidence that I had Bill Clinton and Eliot Spitzer both wanting to see me urgently in New York City, both with sensitive issues to discuss. I certainly felt in demand.

The Spitzer and Baum meeting was scheduled as an early breakfast at Oscar's in the Waldorf Hotel. I was then scheduled to meet President Clinton at his home for lunch about an hour's drive from Manhattan. We arrived at the Waldorf and Baum stood to greet us—he was all smiles and firm handshakes. By contrast, Spitzer stayed seated, looked angry, and barely nodded. I knew immediately he was in an adversarial mood and not interested in small talk. His opening salvo was, "Joe Bruno and the Republicans are using you to try to go against me because they have no one else and are afraid of losing the Senate." I said, "Did it ever occur to you that I might be using them?" I smiled—he grimaced. He was about to respond when the waiter appeared and I said, "Come on Eliot, let's order." As we placed our orders I could see he was visibly agitated. His face was red and he was barely able to contain himself. Once the waiter left he blurted out, "Do you really want to get in a comparison of records with me?"

I have to admit at that point I was a little confused as to the reason for his hostility, so I said, "Steve and Rich here wanted us to talk to see if there are things we can work on together. One question I have is, while I see a lot of reforms you have brought to Wall Street, I haven't seen you do much on State Street" (the home of the state government). I thought this was a logical question, and one that the state's political observers had been asking. For a while, Spitzer's record was one of focusing heavily on the financial industry rather than on state government reform. Surprisingly, he seemed to be blindsided by my questions and shouted, "If you want to compare my reform credentials with yours, I'll have that battle any day!" He was obviously losing control, so I decided to try to calm things down. I said gently, "Eliot, calm down, I'm just looking for a reason to support you."

That's when things took a bizarre turn. He snarled, "I'll give you a good one, because if you fucking run, I will fucking crush you!" Steve's and Rich's jaws dropped, and I swear they both spat food on the table. I stood and said, "That's it, Steve, we're out of here." As we walked away Spitzer fired a parting shot, "How much do you want to bet I win in a 65-35 landslide?" I turned just enough to look him in the eye and say, "Oh, Eliot, I have no money to bet because I'm going to need every cent to beat you."

Now on the other side of the aisle, I'd been flattered by Bruno's offer of Republican support, but having recently bought the Sabres and preparing to retire as CEO of Paychex, I wasn't thinking seriously of another run at governor. Besides, I had thought Spitzer had done a decent job as attorney general. But now I was wondering whether he had the right temperament to be a successful governor of New York. The state's problems had only worsened since 2002, and as I had implied at breakfast, he had not done much on state government reform.

As I mentioned earlier, Spitzer had become known for investigating violations on Wall Street. Many thought he was a bully and a press hound. Some said he would investigate companies, or leak that they were being investigated, to threaten their stock prices. And that this was a ploy to get them to agree to pay a fine or admit an infraction for the express purpose of making him look like a defender of the public good. A *Time* magazine headline read: "Eliot Spitzer: Wall Street's Top Cop." Other headlines called him the "Enforcer" and the "Sheriff of Wall Street."

I mentioned earlier that I had supported some of his initial Wall Street initiatives. However, in many quarters it was felt that he was far too vigilant and investigated companies on no more than a rumor, or a hunch that something untoward was taking place that was somehow hurting business and the economy. As I have said, I thought he was doing a good job until I saw his Rambo performance over a breakfast that was never eaten.

The bizarre breakfast did, however, give me second thoughts—should I take another run for governor? The ride out to Westchester to the Clinton residence was almost surreal. I even said to Steve, "I wonder if Clinton would still work with me if I decided to run again?" Steve knew Clinton well and assured me that he was a political junkie and was almost certainly aware that the Republicans wanted me to be their gubernatorial candidate. As Hillary was a Democratic senator, he was very attuned to state politics. He was also interested in forming bipartisan relationships. Steve also informed me that the Clintons weren't fans of the sharp-elbowed Spitzer.

Meeting with a former president is always somewhat of an event, and I always enjoyed Bill's company. We were greeted by Cindy Testa, the former president's aide, and waited in the living room for him to arrive. His first words were, "How did breakfast go with Spitzer?"

I recounted the story—it was still very fresh in my mind—and he looked stunned. He said he thought Spitzer would have said, "Let's work together to make the state better, no one knows more about upstate than you do; in fact, you should be my economic development czar!" This was a moment where I realized what a skillful politician Clinton was and that Spitzer wasn't even in the same league.

THE CLINTON GLOBAL INITIATIVE

Over a health-conscious lunch in the Clintons' kitchen, Bill shared with me his plans for post-presidency. His concept was to create something he wanted to call the Clinton Global Initiative (CGI). He said that many of us have sat on committees and commissions and attended conferences where everybody talks about solutions to global problems and there's lots of goodwill. The problem is attendees leave feeling better about themselves and their good intentions, but nothing happens until the next conference when it starts all over again. I hate anything that is a waste of my time, so to me this was a very familiar and all-too-common and frustrating scenario.

Bill's vision was to hold a more practical conference, one where leaders of industries, nongovernmental organizations (NGOs), and governments at all levels representing all countries would come together not only to discuss global challenges and solutions, but also commit to take specific actions and provide the necessary financial resources. He said he would actually get them to sign a commitment in front of the other delegates. He wanted the conference to focus on finding solutions to issues in five main areas: poverty, religion, conflict resolution, climate change, and enhancing governance.

What would make CGI different was that people and organizations that made commitments would work with CGI staff to implement their pledges. They would then come back the following year to report on specific outcomes or results. If they didn't follow through on their pledge, they would not be invited back and their failure would be obvious to all other members. This was a way to keep honest people honest.

Sitting there in his kitchen he emphasized that time was of the essence. It was March and he wanted to hold the first event to coincide with the United Nations reopening in New York, which was to be held in September, so that world leaders could easily attend.

The challenge, as is often the case, was raising money to cover the cost of the first year as there was not enough time to hold a fundraising event to raise money for the main event. The crux of the matter was that he was looking for someone to underwrite the conference and the organization's first fledgling year.

He wasn't looking for just any sponsor, he wanted someone with a bipartisan background who would relate well to leaders and problem-solvers from across the political spectrum. Now I knew why I was having lunch with a former President of the United States.

The event would feature prominent speakers in plenary sessions and breakout groups. The bottom line was that he felt I would be the perfect founding sponsor. His enthusiasm was impressive and I really liked his concept of making people put their money where their mouth was, while also having a plan to ensure things actually happened to mitigate pressing and serious real-world societal issues. I was sold and agreed to give him $3 million to get the initiative off the ground. I'm not sure what I would have said at that time if someone had told me I would continue as the major underwriter and sponsor for eight years.

Once I agreed to be founding sponsor and underwriter of the CGI, I worked with Cindy Testa and a few others to review the topics they were planning to cover at the conference. We discussed panels and who should sit on them, and I made suggestions wherever I could.

When Bill Clinton had said preparing for such a major conference in a little over five months would be a Herculean effort, he was not exaggerating. Major speakers had to be approached and booked, the agenda created, media had to be alerted and provided with press packs, and potential participants had to be identified and sent invitations.

We achieved it all in record time and the first annual CGI conference launched on time in September 2005. On the first evening, I sat at the president's table with King Abdullah and Queen Noor of Jordan, Colin Powell (the first African American appointed as US Secretary of State), Madeleine Albright (the first woman to become US Secretary of State), and Tony Bennett, who has always been one of my favorite singers. Not bad for an Italian kid from West Irondequoit!

FROM MOVIE STARS TO HEADS OF STATE

As I had one of the largest suites in the hotel, I thought it might be a good idea to invite some interesting people to an after-dinner party just to hang out. I asked Steve and Gary Parenti to wander off and see who they could invite; the only instruction being to make it large enough so we could have some fun, but small enough that we might stimulate some thought-provoking conversations.

Gary was a New York State legislative staffer who had worked as an advance man and event organizer for my Governor's race. His outgoing, friendly disposition attracted people to him. He could talk to anyone, so rounding up people for an impromptu party was a perfect job for him. He and our friend, attorney John Bartolomei, purchased a large amount of food and beverages and amazed me with the cast of celebrities they managed to invite at such short notice. Cindy had confirmed that Bill Clinton would come, and Steve had asked Hillary and Andrew Cuomo to stop by as well.

The invitation list grew to include: Senator John Glenn and his wife Annie; General Wesley Clark and his wife Gert; former Health and Human Services Secretary and Miami University President Donna Shalala; former Israeli Prime Minister Shimon Peres; Al de Benedetto (one of the top businessman in Italy); Carlos Slim from Mexico; Donna Karan the fashion mogul and founder of DKNY; entertainers Usher, Alicia Keyes, Chevy Chase, Matt Damon, Ben Affleck, Julia Ormond, Brad Pitt, Angelina Jolie, Ashton Kutcher, Sarah Jessica Parker, Matthew Broderick, and of course Tony Bennett. And many more I either can't remember or never got a chance to meet.

Gary also managed to bring along one of my favorite actresses, Daryl Hannah. He had told her that I'd love to meet her. When she arrived, I was sitting at the head of the big open room in a leather chair and there was another one next to mine. She saw me across the room and came over. She gave me a hug and kiss and I of course invited her to sit with me. She had some very well thought-out views, which she expressed very cogently, and as a result we hit it off. As others left, we drifted into our own conversation—I have to say, there was chemistry. It wasn't until many years later that my friend and Independence Party colleague Laureen Oliver informed me that my wife Heather was in the kitchen, hurt and crying at all the attention I was showing Ms. Hannah. I've always felt badly about that.

However, not all female superstars were quite as enamored with me, nor I with them. The evening before the opening event of the first CGI conference, President Clinton held a small party for sponsors and some of the major corporate leaders and entertainers who were participating in the conference. I took my team with me and was standing at the hors d'oeuvre table with Gary when we saw Barbra Streisand walk into the room with her husband James Brolin. Everyone who knows Gary, knows he's a teenager in a man's body and he said, a little too loudly, "Oh, there's Dr. Kiley." He was referring to the character Brolin played in the well-known television series, *Marcus Welby, M.D.*, which aired from the late 1960s to the mid-1970s. Gary then greeted Brolin with his infectious smile, extended a handshake and said, "My mother loved you in *Marcus Welby*." For some reason, this greeting irritated Ms. Streisand; she peered over her granny glasses and said very sternly to Gary, "Well, he's done so many things since then—come on now, buddy."

I felt bad for Gary and felt the put-down unnecessary, so I retorted, "Come on, Barbra, he was just complimenting your husband." At this point Brolin jumped in to try to make things right, "Yes, really dear, I don't mind at all." Apparently, she didn't like this either and stormed off, leaving us to have a pleasant conversation with her very likeable husband.

That might have been the end of it, but of course it wasn't. The next morning, we were gathering for an opening talk from Bill Clinton and I was seated in an aisle seat. Those who know me well understand I am a little claustrophobic and uncomfortable when hemmed in by people. Russell Simmons was talking to Streisand in the aisle and pushing her closer and closer to me, to a point where she was invading my personal space and people were hitting me in the head with their briefcases and purses. It was at that point one of Clinton's young aides approached and asked me if everything was all right, to which I angrily snapped, "I'd be fine if someone wasn't in my way." Ms. Streisand quickly spun around at the sound of my voice, undoubtedly remembering me from the previous evening and gasped, "Well!" With that, she flounced out of the room and never took her seat for the opening speech.

I did feel a little bad about my comment and said as much to my team. Later in the day, Bill grabbed Steve and Gary and told them, "We need to do something about this Tom and Barbra thing." It was decided that Bill would bring Barbra to my suite party that evening and that I would greet her as if I'd never met her before and he would ask her to do likewise. It was all set. That evening, President Clinton escorted Ms. Streisand into my suite and as they walked up to me, Bill with utmost congeniality said, "Barbra, let me introduce you to our sponsor Tom Golisano." She said, "Great to meet you," and I said the same. I've always marveled at Clinton's diplomatic and personal skills.

The party was a hit. Substantively, we discussed why the Iraq War was failing with the help of a great deal of inside knowledge provided by Senator Glenn and General Clark. All of which confirmed my original gut instincts. At 3:00 a.m. the party was still going strong as Russell Simmons and his friends drifted in for last call.

The next day Cindy, Clinton's aide, told us she had gotten into trouble with the Clinton staff and the hotel. The former because they weren't invited and felt snubbed; the latter because we'd brought in our own food and drink. This apparently contravened the catering contract the hotel had with CGI.

The party was well intentioned, but perhaps we could have thought it through a little more than we did. But then it wouldn't have been the impromptu fun it turned out to be.

In the ensuing years "Tom's suite party" became a scheduled official event held on opening night. Of course, I always ensured there was an after-after party where a smaller group could remain behind and informally discuss interesting global issues.

One of my favorite guests was Goldie Hawn, who was simply delightful. She was heavily involved in doing good and still continues to do great charitable work. I also really liked Geena Davis, and Tony Blair, Britain's prime minister at the time, was very interesting.

Clinton also wanted to introduce me to President George W. Bush, but I politely declined because I was concerned I might mention my feelings about him taking us into the Iraq War. However, on another occasion I met his father, President George H. W. Bush who I thought was a gentleman. There was one other person I preferred not to meet when offered the opportunity, and that was Mick Jagger—I'm not a big fan of his type of music.

CGI PHILANTHROPY

The first conference resulted in around $1 billion in pledges, which I thought was an excellent return on my $3 million seed money. It's great when a plan comes together.

In 2007, through CGI, I donated $10 million to create the Golisano Institute for Sustainability (GIS) at the Rochester Institute of Technology. GIS is a global resource for education, research, technology transfer, and outreach in sustainable manufacturing processes.

Over the next few years things grew beyond our wildest dreams and we passed $25 billion. And it wasn't always about major global initiatives. On one occasion, I arranged an invitation for an employee from Paychex to attend. He and his wife did a lot of charitable work in Africa and he wouldn't normally have been invited. On the first day at lunch, he apparently looked for me but couldn't find my table. Later I bumped into him and he was excited and beaming. "You're not going to believe what just happened!" he said. "I was at this table because I couldn't find you and I started talking to this guy and he's going to give me 6,000 bicycles so that the people we are working with in Africa can use them to deliver medication and water." It was things like this, especially in the early days of CGI, that made me feel it was all worthwhile.

While I talk more extensively about my involvement with and financial support of Special Olympics in chapter fourteen, it deserves mention here as it took center stage at the CGI Annual Meeting in 2012.

I announced that my foundation would be giving $12 million to the Special Olympics for the launch of the new Healthy Communities initiative to end health disparities for people with intellectual and developmental disabilities (IDDs). I chose the CGI annual meeting to announce the gift because I wanted to underline the need for action, rather than just words, on a world stage.

It was the largest gift Special Olympics had ever received from an individual donor, and it was also my first international gift. Since it is a global organization, Special Olympics has the infrastructure in place to reach more than a million people with IDDs. No other organization could touch so many people with IDDs or leverage the partnerships needed to break down barriers in complex health systems that are preventing people from accessing care.

Being the father of a son born with developmental disabilities, I had been extremely active with organizations serving those with developmental disabilities. I have always been dismayed that people with intellectual disabilities and their health needs and status remained largely invisible to practitioners, systems, governments, and the larger global health community.

By supporting Special Olympics, my vision of a different world— where dignity and access to care would be possible for everyone who, like my son, would need support throughout their lifetimes—would become a reality.

Due to the success of the Healthy Communities initiative during the four-year pilot phase, I donated an additional $25 million to continue this work, bringing my total gift to Special Olympics to more than $37 million since the beginning of our partnership. Once again, it was the largest gift Special Olympics had ever received and the largest single gift I have ever made.

We had a lot of fun at the CGI conferences, all while tackling some of the most challenging global issues we face as human beings. One memorable moment occurred when I got into a bidding war at a fundraising auction. I was bidding against Frank Giustra, founder of Lionsgate Entertainment, for a painting that Tony Bennett created specifically for CGI. Although I secured the painting, I always felt Frank let me win in the end because I was the founding sponsor. No matter, it was all money directed to a good cause.

A few years later, I was honored when President Clinton presented me with an award recognizing my support for CGI. In a press release after the event, Clinton was kind enough to say:

> The Clinton Global Initiative may not exist today if not for Tom Golisano. Tom made the initial commitment of several million dollars to make CGI a reality and has been there ever since. I was proud to present Tom with a commitment certificate at the Global Citizen Awards at Carnegie Hall. His commitment to create a sustainability institute at RIT is an important contribution to RIT and to the international community.

The Clinton Global Initiative provided me with an opportunity to expand my philanthropy on a global level—as well as to make a significant impact on millions of lives around the world. I closed my acceptance speech with these words, "The only wealth that you get to keep is that which you give away."

Around year three, I noticed that most of the projects we worked on were in Asia, Africa, Latin America, and the Middle East. By contrast, I felt that, right here at home in America, we were beginning to have severe societal problems in education and other areas. I brought my concerns to Bill Clinton's attention and he wholeheart-edly agreed and started a separate CGI American conference. He and I became friends and he was gracious enough to stop by a few Sabres games; it was before one of these games that I confronted him with a budget issue at the CGI conference. I had noticed that his staff were laying on an extensive, sumptuous buffet in the breakout sessions and the food wasn't being eaten. Delegates would eat at the plenary session prior to attending their breakout groups and therefore were in no need of further sustenance. I asked him to explain the catering bill and put him to work analyzing the budget. This was during a period when I was considering my next commitment to CGI. He looked at the budget and asked his staff why we were paying so much. They had thought it was going to be a fun day out and I put them to work; I'm sure they would have liked to kill me. Bill, however, was fine and agreed it was an unnecessary expense. I've always felt it important that people respect the money I either invest or donate and never take it for granted, even if it's a former president of the United States. From a personal perspective, he was a good friend to me after my breakup and divorce from Heather.

Over time, CGI seemed to become less bipartisan, especially during Hillary's second presidential campaign. Politics seemed to creep into everything. And then at one point, the director of CGI and my foundation director could not come to agreement on the terms of my continued involvement. The writing was on the wall. With the 2016 presidential races looming, I decided to pull out as the major underwriter and founding sponsor. I don't regret my eight-year involvement in the least, although I raised an eyebrow at how quickly my name was removed from the website as founding sponsor.

FOURTEEN

NATIONAL POLITICS AND THE
NEW YORK SENATE COUP

TO RUN OR NOT TO RUN . . .

After my thoroughly unpleasant experience with Eliot Spitzer, I strongly considered running for governor again. I believed that if I had a major party line and was fighting a clearly thin-skinned and arrogant Spitzer, I had a good chance to win. On reconsideration, however, I realized that in recent months I had gotten remarried, bought an NHL hockey franchise, and sponsored and underwritten the CGI. I was also enjoying my other many philanthropic activities and was quite happy. I had to seriously ask myself, at this point in my life did I still really want to be governor. Naturally, Steve Pigeon and Laureen Oliver were excited and encouraged me to run again. They believed I could win and believed I would make a great governor. Steve, who was a staunch Democrat, was even willing to support a Republican candidate (me) for the first time in his life! And then there was State Senate Majority Leader Joe Bruno, who committed the entire apparatus of the Republican Party to support my run for governor.

In a surprising phone call, Senator Chuck Schumer, a Democrat, while not offering to publicly endorse me, encouraged me to run. He told me he felt Spitzer was an immature bully with a glass jaw. Chuck said he'd do nothing to help Spitzer, and in fact would tell his friends that I would make the better governor.

Part of me looked forward to the competition, and victory would certainly have been sweet, but I wasn't sure I was ready to devote the next four years of my life to what would be a 24/7 commitment to being governor. If I was going to run, I had to be ready for the consequences of winning, because if I won, I knew I would give the job my full attention and do my very best for the people of New York State. I knew I had to make a decision quickly, so that if I didn't run, another suitable candidate would have time to mount a viable challenge.

It was a tough decision; Steve and Laureen came over to the house one evening and the four of us went over the pros and cons one last time. Of course, they were in favor of me running again so they were in essence making their case as strongly as they could, reiterating that I had a great chance to win this time and would be a transformative governor. I really appreciated their faith in me but in the end, I told them at this point in my life I simply couldn't commit to four more years of that level of responsibility. Another factor was that I knew that four years would turn into eight, as I would want to finish whatever I had started. They were extremely disappointed, but I knew as my close friends they would understand my rationale.

THE FALL OF ELIOT SPITZER

Thirteen months into his term, the former tough prosecutor and straitlaced perfectionist Spitzer was identified in a federal indictment as "Client Number 9." This was a bizarre situation, and like most New Yorkers I was interested in watching the spectacle unfold from the sidelines. He was being accused of violating banking laws by using family company money to disguise payments to a high-class escort (prostitution) service. This was, apparently, bank fraud. By all accounts, federal agents followed a young woman to the Mayflower

Hotel in Washington, DC, where she met Spitzer in a hotel room that he had booked under an assumed name. The indictment outlined that he had paid for her to travel by train from New York to Washington, DC, for the purposes of prostitution. Paying for a person to cross a state line for the purposes of prostitution is a federal offense. He resigned as governor in a deal to avoid prosecution.

OUT OF THE FRYING PAN . . .

With Spitzer's departure Lt. Governor David Patterson immediately became governor, making him the first African American governor in New York history. He had been the leader of the Senate Democrats and Steve had worked with him in the past. I'd had some very productive meetings with him and found him a fun dinner companion; however, I wasn't sure he was up for the top job.

It turned out my concerns were justified. Within days of replacing Spitzer after his sex and fraud scandals, Governor Patterson decided to hold a press conference where he said that he would make it easy for the journalists in attendance and disclose the skeletons lurking in his closet. In a bizarre confession he admitted to having numerous extra-marital affairs, both while married and separated from his wife. If that was not enough, he also admitted to being a longtime recreational drug user. He announced that he used to use marijuana regularly in the past and also admitted to using cocaine once or twice. I couldn't believe it; we'd just got rid of one joke of a governor and now we had one that was making New York State a national laughingstock.

Senator Joe Bruno and I maintained a good relationship after he courted me as the Republican candidate for governor. I was therefore surprised that he made a deal with Speaker Sheldon (Shelly) Silver that saw services union 1199 get a sweetheart deal that skyrocketed the already huge New York State budget deficit. It raised already-too-high taxes and drove more jobs and people out of New York State.

The collusions and maneuverings of New York State politics were at play once again. When I called Bruno to complain, he told me that the only way he could keep the majority in the Senate was to re-elect his New York City members. In order to do this, he needed to be "joined at the hip" with 1199 leader Dennis Rivera. I can't say I was happy with his answer and asked him, "What good is a majority if it leads to such an unholy alliance that breaks the state bank?"

Heavily embroiled in New York State politics, I also became more involved in national politics. I was vehemently opposed to President George W. Bush's disastrous invasion of Iraq. But I also thought he was an ineffective leader on the domestic front. He was mismanaging the economy, his response to Hurricane Katrina was pathetic, and overall, I thought he was a lousy president.

SUPPORTING BARACK OBAMA

When Barack Obama announced his candidacy for the presidency, I was impressed with him. Although I wasn't enthusiastic about Hillary Clinton, I liked Bill and didn't want to embarrass him by supporting Obama in the primary. I was working with him on the CGI and saw him at meetings throughout the year, so I sat out the primary election. Besides, with the exception of Dick Gephardt's race, I usually didn't get involved with presidential politics. Once Obama defeated Hillary Clinton, however, Steve suggested we talk to Obama's people who he knew from working on previous campaigns. The reason I considered supporting Obama was that I believed he was different than other politicians. In particular he seemed to be more thoughtful and wasn't one to beat the war drums. I also felt he was in an excellent position to do something to improve race relations in the United States.

It was my belief that in spite of the many changes in law promoted by activist lobbies, there were still far too many social issues that were not being addressed. The United States had too many people living in poverty, too many single parents and absentee parent households, and poor schools surrounded by gang violence. The war on drugs was being lost, while at the same time we were punishing and incarcerating too many young people.

THE 2008 DEMOCRATIC CONVENTION

For these and other reasons I decided to give $1 million to help put on the Democratic Convention. My donation and support of candidate Obama was reported on the front page of the *New York Times*. We attended the convention in Denver and brought a great group of people along with us. Our little informal gang included Buffalo's African American mayor Byron Brown and some other western New York Democrats. In fact, like they did at the CGI events, Gary Parenti and John Bartolomei managed our suite and scheduled our attendance at other fun events. We hosted interesting guests to our suites and transported our entourage to events we organized across Denver. I even took my grandchildren, who had a blast watching the big music stars of the day provide the major entertainment event of the convention. I also ensured they got a lesson in civics along the way. My friend Laureen Oliver, who had helped me set up the Independence Party also came along. She was as sick of Bush as I was.

We had hospitality suites for three days at the hockey arena where the convention was held and also at the football stadium for the last night where Obama was nominated. We were suite neighbors with the likes of Jon Corzine, George Soros, and Bill Gates, which gave the whole event quite a party atmosphere. At times it became a little like a CGI reunion. Ben Affleck and his wife Jennifer Garner popped in, as did our friends John and Annie Glenn. Even Bill and Hillary stopped by to say hello. Another person who stopped by impressed me a lot at the time, Denver mayor and subsequently Colorado governor, Jon Hickenlooper. On one particular night Parenti told me that over twenty senators had stopped by the box including Democratic stalwarts like Daniel Inouye, Dianne Feinstein, Sherrod Brown, and

Tom Harkin. That was 20 percent of the US Senate—I thought, perhaps we really could make a difference.

Steve Pigeon and Dick Gephardt had arranged private meetings with Obama's economic and foreign policy advisors, and I was pleased with the discussions. Bill Clinton and his assistant, Cindy Testa, were also a great help in setting up meetings with people like San Francisco mayor Gavin Newsom, and Los Angeles mayor Antonio Villaraigosa They also connected me with many other leading Democrats who they felt I should meet.

The night of Obama's nomination was exciting, and I was proud I could share such a historical moment with my grandchildren and so many friends. After the nomination, Obama's campaign asked me to make several television appearances to explain why as an independent businessperson, I supported Obama. I remember one strange incident when Congressman Rahm Emanuel, who later became Obama's chief of staff, threw a hissy fit because the interviewer wanted to interview me before him. He actually made Spitzer seem polite. It's beyond me how such a rude, crude, mean, arrogant person, who treats everyone around him like lesser mortals can be elected to anything. He was mayor of Chicago; my friends tell me he did a less-than-stellar job, which is no surprise.

My convention experience was mostly very positive, but this was politics and the gloves always come off at some point. Steve told me that Bob McCarthy of the *Buffalo News* wanted to interview me; this was the hack journalist who had written so many biased stories on Steve over the years. He also did the "vain billionaire" hit piece during my 2002 governor's race. He'd given Steve a line about wanting to write a nice profile on me as a former Independence Party gubernatorial candidate and owner of the Sabres becoming so politically active nationally. In spite of the many slanted and rotten stories McCarthy had written about him over the years, Steve thought this might be a positive story and perhaps start a new relationship with the *Buffalo News*. I reluctantly agreed—something to this day I regret doing. The festive atmosphere of the convention must have weakened my defenses.

McCarthy, true to form, wrote another hit piece painting me as an elitist billionaire. He interviewed Steve's enemies in the local Democratic Party—people McCarthy socialized with—and printed all the nasty things they said. I vowed that day I would never talk to Bob McCarthy again.

FINAL THOUGHTS ON PRESIDENT BARACK OBAMA

As for President Obama, once he was elected, I was asked at the last minute to attend a transition meeting in Chicago—a meeting I could not attend. I found it odd that I never heard from anyone in his administration again. More to the point, I was never thanked for my donation nor my personal support.

Our paths crossed again at the CGI conference, which he attended just as his reelection was approaching. I had mentioned to Bill Clinton that I wasn't pleased with Obama because, among other reasons, I never got so much as a thank-you note from him. Clinton asked me if my wife Monica and I would like to be with him and Bill Gates when he greeted President Obama backstage on his arrival to address the CGI opening session. This was my moment; when the President came over to shake my hand I grasped it firmly, pulled him in close and said, "I donated a million dollars to you and endorsed you, and I never received so much as a thank-you from you or any of your people." He said something like, "Oh my God I don't believe that. I don't know how it happened, I'll call you next week and set up a meeting." Bill Clinton was surprised that I was so blunt with the president, but equally shocked I'd been treated so poorly by Obama.

He said he would try to arrange a golf game with the three of us and another guest. Needless to say, I never got the call. Not that I really cared.

BACK TO NEW YORK

I had started an independent committee called Responsible New York. The idea was that we would support candidates of either party, as long as they shared our goals. We would subsequently announce our endorsements and donations, to boost those candidates who best supported our defined principles for better state government.

When we got back to New York, Steve and Laureen and I sprang into action for the election races for the candidates we were supporting in the upcoming elections.

We created a series of commercials where I personally endorsed the candidates; other commercials focused on what we felt were flaws in their opponents. We also carried out an advertising campaign by direct mail, on radio, through social media, and in the free press. In a step above what anyone could have expected, we set up field operations similar to a presidential campaign, where we went door-to-door and made phone calls to voters in key districts.

At the end of the day, we won some and we lost some, which is par for the course. The big win however was that the Democrats won thirty-two seats, which gave them a one-seat majority in the Senate. This was the first time the Democrats had held a majority in forty years—and they won largely with the candidates we supported. I was excited and so was our whole team. Everyone had put in so much hard work.

I soon met with the prospective incoming majority leader, Malcolm Smith. I'd never met him before and the first thing he asked me was how much time could I devote to helping him get state government under control. My answer was, "How about full-time?"

I immediately wanted him to listen to my big beef, which was that politicians thought the needs of upstate and downstate New York were the same, when in fact they needed parallel but different policies. What made sense in Rochester did not work in Queens.

I also told him I had ideas on how to cut waste, save money, and reduce mismanagement when delivering developmentally disabled services while at the same time making them better. This was something close to my heart. He said he'd work closely with us and at least give serious review to all our ideas. He would especially ask for our input on all things upstate New York. Then there was a major glitch; Steve got a call that three recently elected Democrats were considering supporting the Republicans. The holdouts were Pedro Espada and two of his allies, Carl Kruger and Ruben Diaz Sr., a conservative Hispanic Democrat. The situation was dire: We had helped the Democrats win thirty-two votes on election night but here we were in a situation where they couldn't bring those votes together to elect Malcolm Smith as majority leader.

Smith asked Steve, who knew Espada, if we could help get his vote back along with his three allies. However, when Steve talked to him, Espada told him that he had known Smith for thirty years and didn't trust or like him. He did agree to meet with him, but only if I agreed to accompany him. His thinking was that Smith might lie to him but that he would be more cautious with me, because we had been instrumental in helping win the majority in the first place.

I was somewhat of a neophyte when it came to backroom politics back then, but it was bread and butter to Steve. I didn't want to get involved in any petty personal power brokering, but reluctantly said I would agree to meet with the three senators. In the end, I was pleasantly surprised by Espada. He told me he was concerned that the Democratic conference was too liberal. He felt that there was one particular senator who would totally decimate the New York City real estate markets, by rolling back previously agreed increases in the amount charged for rent-controlled apartments. He and his allies would only vote for Smith, therefore, if a moderate from their group was named housing chair. There were other housekeeping requests, but that was the gist of the deal.

Up to that point, not a word had leaked to the press, so I agreed we'd meet Smith together. A few days later we met, and Smith agreed to appoint Espada chairman of the Housing Committee. There were other assignments for the three holdouts who agreed to support Smith.

Smith said he had to bring other Democratic leaders to the meeting to bless the arrangement. I guess he also leaked to the press. Tony Bergamo, who worked for real estate magnate Howard Milstein, had arranged for our use of the University Club for the meeting, and I don't think they were prepared for the swarm of press, cameras, and microphones that descended on the club. The top Democratic officeholder turned up, and several senators arrived with Governor Patterson and Congressman Joe Crowley, who was the Democratic chairman of Manhattan, along with the chairs of Brooklyn, the Bronx, and Queens (the same guys that wanted Pataki back in 1998). Soon the club had the feel of a three-ring circus.

Smith, Espada, and I outlined what had been agreed, and there were a few side meetings before everyone went in front of the cameras to announce the Democrats would take the majority of the New York State Senate. The new Senate started out well. I got on very well with Smith's top aide, Angelo Aponte, who not only kept me abreast of developments but also kept watch for upstate issues in which I might be interested. Coincidentally he had a developmentally disabled son, so we talked about some positive reforms in a state that already had a good record in this field.

During the spring of 2009, it became increasingly difficult to reach Malcolm Smith. And Aponte seemed to have little time for me. Then, the Senate passed a budget that saw a 9 percent increase in the state budget. It was also completely biased toward downstate New York and seriously hurt upstate New York. It was so full of wasteful spending I literally saw red. Everything I had discussed with him had been ignored.

IT'S A COUP, IT'S A COUP!

At that point, a couple of senators also felt that he was not living up to the promises he made and on which they had based their support. We agreed to work with them to attempt to change the rules of the Senate to make them fairer and more democratic. It became known publicly, in the summer of 2009, as the coup. I won't go into the incredible and complex machinations that happened behind the scenes as it would take a dozen pages or more. But as it was such a historic moment in New York politics, with reverberations across every state in the land, it's a story worth telling.

In short, what happened was that we were able to oust Malcolm Smith, who was majority leader at the time, and vote in a new majority leader, thus creating a breakaway caucus of centrist Democrats called the Independent Democratic Conference (IDC).

The mechanics of this was that we had to get a motion made and seconded on the floor of the senate to ask for a new vote on majority leader. We knew the Democratic presiding officer would rule the motion out of order because the rules required that leadership votes be announced at party conventions. What we were counting on was that rules are not laws and can be changed by a majority vote. The trick was to get the rule-change motion on the floor and seconded, so when it was ruled out of order there could be a challenge to the chair. If the chair's ruling was defeated with enough votes, a vote for a new majority leader could take place. Our belief was that no court would tell a legislative body they can't change their own rules.

Everything went to plan. A move to change the rules was put forth by Republican Senator Tom Libous and seconded by Democrat Pedro Espada. At this point Senator Ruben Diaz, a Hispanic conservative, began running to his seat with a huge smile on his face yelling, in a high-pitched voice, "It's a coup! It's a coup!"

The Democratic presiding officer, Neil Breslin, tried to rule the motion out of order. However, the senator who had put forward the motion brandished Robert's rules saying that a motion properly made and seconded must be voted on, as did a challenge to the chair.

The Senate parliamentarian then ruled there must be a vote on the challenge. There was then a vote to overturn the ruling of the chair, which passed. At that point, all hell broke loose in the senate.

The Democrats knew the chair's ruling was going to be over-turned. What happened next would have made politicians in the Kremlin proud. Rather than announcing that the chair was overruled, Breslin banged his gavel and screamed, "We are adjourned." This was outrageous, since his party was in the minority and you can't adjourn without a motion that passes with a majority.

The Democrats walked off the floor, turned off the microphones, turned off the lights, and ordered the state police to remove the Republicans and the two renegade Democrats. The police of course knew it was not their place to remove elected representatives, so the Senate secretary locked the doors. It was in the dark with no microphones that thirty-two members of the state legislature voted Dean Skelos their new majority leader. We were all euphoric. History had been made and the result was historic rule changes that included, for the first time, allowing the conference to be budgeted equally in staff and chairmanships to the Democrats and Republicans.

As a founder of the Independence Party, I got to have an independent conference. And more importantly, it gave back members' powers and weakened the position of majority leader. It allowed for committee chairmen to bring bills to their committees. Previously no bill went to a committee or the floor without the majority leader's approval. This allowed committee chairmen to run their own legislation without the agreement of the majority leader.

It also allowed for members to get a bill on the floor to be voted, whereas before this the majority leader could keep any bill from the floor. Furthermore, the rules changes allowed chairmen of committees to have power over their committees. It empowered the backbenchers and committee chairs and lessened the power of the leader for the first time in the history of the New York state legislature. It is interesting to note that since the coup, the assembly has adopted similar rules.

POLITICS IS NEVER DULL AND NEVER SIMPLE

Politics is never dull and my final foray into politics involved Mike Bloomberg, who was ending his second term as mayor of New York City. Bloomberg, however, felt he had not finished what he had started and wanted to run a third time. Unfortunately for him, the city had a two-term limit on the office of mayor. So he was trying to change the law.

The stage was set for another political showdown. From what little I knew of him at the time, I thought he'd done a decent job, but I remember thinking that it seemed a little over the top to change the law for one person. I probably wouldn't have thought any more about it but the public advocate, Bill de Blasio (who is the current mayor of New York) asked Steve Pigeon to arrange a meeting with Responsible New York. He flew up to Rochester and we met in my office with Laureen Oliver and Steve. He told us about the deals being made in city council to overturn the term limits law, and how this would hurt the city and the state. He felt it would probably doom Bloomberg's third term, even if he should win in that hardball way.

He asked for my help. I had rarely involved myself in New York City politics, but de Blasio made a good case and I thought it was a little unfair for city council to change the rules midstream without a citywide referendum. In my opinion it was the citizens of New York City who should decide whether to change the term limit.

I thought it over for a few days and then got back to de Blasio and agreed to appear with de Blasio, Mark Green, and other top public officials in the city at a press conference where I would urge the city council to vote against changing the limits. I also took out full-page ads in the major newspapers. I felt I'd done what I was asked and didn't plan any further involvement. Of course, politics is never that simple.

Within twenty-four hours Deputy Mayor Kevin Sheekey called Steve Pigeon asking for a meeting with the mayor at Gracie Mansion.

Laureen Oliver, Steve, and I soon found ourselves eating popcorn at Gracie Mansion with the mayor and deputy mayor while they explained their achievements in improving public schools and creating charter schools in the city, along with budget and government reforms. They emphasized that the economy was on fire and that they had rebuilt downtown and increased tourism. Bloomberg felt he needed more time to complete his vision and solidify his many improvements to city government.

He reminded me that he was first elected as an independent and always ran on the Independence Party line. He flattered me, saying he admired me for founding the party but felt it had grown too parochial and was only interested in government jobs for its members. Given a third term, he proposed he and I could combine resources, and Sheekey, the deputy mayor, Oliver, and Pigeon would be able to work with Independence activists to help organize the party and actually push reform and issues like we first intended.

I listened intently and appreciated where he was coming from but told him I wouldn't change my position. I did, however, want to work to bring the Independence Party back to its true mission and mandate.

Sheekey said that he was not asking for a change in my position, but only that we not turn our newspaper ads into television spots. Steve agreed without hesitation. Of course, this was because I had told him weeks previously that I would never buy ads in that market on a local issue! We did however, work together to improve the Independence Party.

MOVING ON, AND OUT OF POLITICS

Shortly after that diversion, I'd had enough of New York. Its state policies were driving out residents who were no longer able to afford its taxes. It was driving out business with overregulation and taxes, costing us more jobs and decimating upstate regions. Paychex would remain in my hometown, but I was now retired and spending more time at my Florida home. My final political statement, perhaps a grand gesture, was to become a resident of Florida. I call this a "grand" gesture because it saved me thirteen of them every day. That's correct, I saved $13,800.00 per day by leaving and not paying New York State taxes. I highly recommend all New Yorkers check it out. It wasn't the amount as much as the principle: I give those savings and far more to colleges, hospitals, and my foundation for the developmentally disabled. More on this work in the next chapter.

MY ALMOST RUN FOR PRESIDENT

There was one moment when I was almost tempted out of retirement. I was asked by Peter Ackerman, one of the founders of the group Americans Elect (the other was Kahlil Byrd) and Doug Schoen, the well-known pollster who handled my polling in my governors' races, to consider running for president.

They came to my home in Naples and we had a very productive and positive conversation. Steve and Laureen loved the idea and were enthusiastic for me to throw my hat in the ring. They were realistic about my chances as an independent, especially given how the electoral college operates. But they felt I could help set the tone of national discussions and present strong reasons why people should rise above party politics and allegiances and put national interests first. They put forward a convincing argument, and I have to say, I was tempted.

They also noted it would be a short campaign, which would allow us to build a new national independent reform party, like we wanted Perot to do years before. Tempting me further, they said if I could get into the debates with Obama and Romney I would be in my element. Pollster Schoen was convinced I would be polling enough for a spot on the stage. I have to say, I would have loved that opportunity.

In the end, although I was very flattered, I was beginning to realize how much I enjoyed my new life. I just felt I couldn't give the commitment it would require to do even a short sprint at the presidency. I was in an amazing relationship with Monica, the sweetest, most humble person I have ever known and whom I planned to marry.

Although I said no, I was convinced Americans were looking for something or someone different. A candidate who would be authentic, not managed by consultants and lobbyists. A person who was not part of the Washington political class, but who had enough credibility to be seen as a leader. Americans Elect said all their studies showed that people were tired of the same old Tweedledum and Tweedledee candidates both parties were promoting.

That's why I was one of the few people not surprised by the success of Donald J. Trump!

FIFTEEN

THE ONLY WEALTH YOU GET TO KEEP IS THAT WHICH YOU GIVE AWAY

"In my entire career, I have never seen someone who applies the same degree of competitive rigor to the work they want to do on behalf of others as they apply to the work they do on behalf of themselves."

—TIM SHRIVER, SPECIAL OLYMPICS

Over the last twenty years I have donated more than $300 million to worthy causes personally and through the Golisano Foundation, which is my family's foundation. People often ask me why I am such an active philanthropist. I suppose the simple answer is that you can't take it with you, or perhaps because I applied for immortality, but I didn't get it. I've already ensured my family is well taken care of, and I want to continue chipping away at the many other social and community challenges I see out there. In fact, I want to do more in all the areas in which I'm interested. Money is a responsibility that can be difficult to handle, so distributing it to individuals or to charitable causes is a responsibility not to be taken lightly.

From a corporate responsibility standpoint, as the chairman of Paychex, I believe all businesses are an integral part of their community, whether that community is local, national, or international. As such most, if not all, businesses give back in some way or another to one or more of the communities with which they interact. The owners of successful businesses also give back, both through their companies and personally. It is a key ingredient to their success, both corporately and as members of society.

Looking deeper, there are causes that are close to my heart and people who need help to be the best they can be given their circumstances. The Golisano Foundation supports organizations that work with people who have IDDs, and on a personal level I support other initiatives through contributions to hospitals, colleges, universities, and even a children's museum.

Paychex also has a foundation, which we set up in 2014 to support entrepreneurship/education, health and wellness, improving the economic health of the community and its workforce, and corporate citizenship.

MY PHILANTHROPIC PHILOSOPHY

The title of this chapter uses the closing words of the speech I made when I accepted a commitment certificate from President Bill Clinton at the Global Citizen Awards at Carnegie Hall. When I said, "The only wealth you get to keep is that which you give away," I had tears in my eyes.

My philanthropic beliefs have deep roots for me and my family. It's never been just about supporting good causes financially but more about, "How can I fix a challenge and solve a community issue?"

Tim Shriver's quote that opened this chapter accurately reflects my philosophy on charitable giving. I have never believed in simply donating money to nonprofit organizations without both accepting responsibility for how that money might be used, and ensuring the organization accepts a similar level of responsibility. The story of me going line by line through the CGI budget with Bill Clinton, along with my hands-on work with Special Olympics in its healthcare initiatives are good examples. Someone once called my rigorous examination of how money was being spent as being "Golisano'ed." I hate waste and mismanagement; I expect to see respect for hard-earned money. I want to ensure as much as possible goes directly to help those it was intended to benefit. In that vein, we often offer matching challenge grants, where the organization must raise funds that we in turn will match.

To that end, I support organizations that demonstrate they are getting to the bottom of issues and identifying solutions—organizations that are not only efficient at what they do but are also cost-effective. I admire efficiency and directness and look to help those groups that demonstrate a sense of urgency and have a firm call to action to get down to work.

I don't believe we ever have to live with the status quo, and I don't like it when people accept it as a given. I enjoy getting to the bottom of complex issues and identifying solutions. That's why it's never just been about the money, but about rolling up my sleeves and working with the organizations I support to make things better.

When it comes down to it, I believe any donation has to make sense both to my heart and to my head. It has to make economic sense and those in control have to be accountable. Not only that, my personal philanthropy has to expand what is being offered to those in need and make the community a better place in which to live.

THE GENESIS OF GIVING

Philanthropy has been an important part of my life and my business career. My particular interest has been focused on people with IDDs, although education and global health issues have also played a significant part in my charitable giving.

Reports have shown that almost two-thirds of people choose a charity based on direct experience. For instance, if someone survives cancer or has a friend or family member who suffers from or died from the disease, they are more likely to financially support or volunteer at an agency that works with cancer patients.

My story is no different. My second child Steven had an uneventful birth. He was a normal weight and looked like any other healthy baby born to loving, expectant parents. However, at three or four months old we noticed he was not as responsive as our first child Cynthia had been, or the babies of other parents we knew. At first, we didn't think a lot of it. Friends and family told us all kids are different and they develop at their own pace. But, at six or seven months he wasn't sitting up by himself and well after his first birthday he was still not walking.

During his first year we took him to our family doctor on several occasions, but nothing definitive came out of the consultations. It wasn't until we visited a pediatrician that we were told that Steven was "mentally retarded," a phrase that thank goodness has been replaced by IDD. For the past several years, our foundation has promoted National End the R-word Day of Awareness. We encourage individuals and organizations to take a pledge to stand against using the word *retarded* and to instead consider another R word—*respect*.

Having a child born with an IDD is a frightening experience for young parents. There are so many unknowns and Gloria and I were no different. Steven was small, he wore glasses, he couldn't talk, and it seemed everyone was looking at us, feeling sorry for us. But, we didn't let that bother us—he was our son.

Throughout Steven's childhood, Gloria became very active in the field of developmental disabilities. She was a tireless advocate, working for parents of children with disabilities as well as the children themselves.

I remember her telling me once about a trip she made with some of her colleagues to a New York State developmental center caring for the developmentally disabled. One of the first things she noticed was that many children were missing their front teeth. She questioned this and was told they had been removed because, "they bite." The sad reality was that this radical and cruel treatment of children was all too common in the sixties and seventies. We were determined it would never happen to Steven.

Steven's IQ ended up at about 64—average is considered to be between 90 and 110—so when Steven became an adult, we had to consider what options were open to us. He could have gone into a group home and become a ward of the state, but after seeing the way children with developmentally disabilities were treated at the time, we were not going to see him institutionalized. In the end, we were fortunate enough to be able to afford to purchase a house and hire qualified house parents to look after him. He's been living in this environment for about thirty-two years and in all that time we've only had two sets of house parents. They love him, and he loves them. Today he is fifty-five and works in a sheltered workshop doing assembly line jobs for companies in the community.

Twenty years after Steven was born, we started the Golisano Foundation with an initial $90,000. It was 1985, and at that time Paychex was still in its infancy. Today, the foundation is one of the largest private foundations in the United States devoted exclusively to supporting programs for people with IDD. Its mission is to help them achieve maximum potential by integrating independence, self-determination, and productivity into all facets of their lives. Today, it has more than $40 million in gross assets and has awarded over $24 million in grants. It continues to award around $2 million annually to nonprofit organizations in western New York (including the Finger Lakes region) and southwest Florida.

I see the work of my foundation as one of opening doors and changing negative perceptions and stereotypes. We want to create partnerships that ensure individuals with IDD have pathways to self-sufficiency, personal dignity, and the best possible expression of their abilities and talents throughout their lifetimes.

PROJECTS THAT MEAN A LOT TO ME

It would be difficult to list every single organization or project I have supported, whether through my family foundation or personally, but the following projects are ones that stand out in one way or another. I am proud to say I was, and in some cases still am, involved with these endeavors and I would like to thank and salute the incredible people who helped make them happen.

Our foundation, under the leadership of Ann Costello, has worked with multiple organizations in recent years to create some remarkable facilities and communitywide initiatives including the Pediatric Behavioral Health & Wellness Center, the Golisano Autism Center in Rochester; the Golisano Center for Community Health at Niagara Falls Memorial Medical Center; dental care accessibility through the Eastman Institute for Oral Health (URMC); and transitional housing for young adults with autism at CP Rochester.

Reaching out to a wider population, I am particularly proud of the cutting-edge work and lifesaving care being carried out by the staff at three Golisano Children's Hospitals in Rochester and Syracuse, New York, as well as Fort Myers, Florida. The Golisano Neurology and Rehabilitation Center at Unity Hospital in Rochester is making significant advances in improving patient outcomes, and I am excited about the joy the Children's Museum in Naples, Florida, brings to so many families.

And, we don't only fund buildings and centers; we also help train medical professionals to treat Special Olympic athletes, thereby increasing access to quality care in local communities and improving the health of thousands of people with IDD through timely follow-up treatment. My global health work with Special Olympics led to me being recognized as one of *Forbes* magazine's *Philanthropy's Big Bets for Social Change of 2015*. I was honored to be in the company of Bill and Melinda Gates and Michael Bloomberg, among others.

We also established the first-ever global Leadership Award for Exemplary Health Care Services. The awards recognize healthcare professionals who demonstrate extraordinary work to improve healthcare, and access to care, for people with intellectual disabilities.

My passion lies in answering a community need whenever I can. One such need was to provide effective transition information, programs, and services for young adults with disabilities and their families. In this case, we partnered with the Warner School of Education at the University of Rochester to launch an Institute for Innovative Transition. Its aim is to improve the quality of life of young adults with IDD and their families, as they transition from school age to adulthood.

Providing services to people with IDD is important, and so is supporting movements that help change the way people think about these members of our community. That's why we've been keen to provide financial backing to the National End the R-word Day of Awareness, and in partnership with WXXI public broadcasting corporation, the *Move to Include—It's Up to You!*—a multimedia initiative with the goal of promoting inclusion for people with intellectual and physical disabilities.

Perhaps one of the benefits of my political activity is that I was able to get in front of New York State leaders to put forward the concept of providing financial assistance to parents of people with developmental disabilities, rather than putting them into group homes. My observation was that it cost more money to place someone in a group home than it would to support the guardians financially and keep that person in a home where they would very likely get better and more personal care. The savings to government could be as much as $100,000 per person per year. I'm pleased to say that some other states followed New York's lead.

It may seem that my philanthropic activity is limited to healthcare in one way or another, but I am also a keen supporter of education and have worked with Rochester Institute of Technology to make possible the Golisano College of Computing and Information, and the B. Thomas Golisano Institute for Sustainability.

In addition, I have been happy to support the efforts of many other colleges and schools along the way including St. John Fisher College, Niagara University, Robert Wesleyan College, Ava Maria University, Nazareth College, Hartwick College of Oneonta, and Bishop Kearney High School.

PAYCHEX

Through its foundation, Paychex provides financial resources to initiatives that support economic development in the communities where the company has operations, while also enhancing the quality of life for those who work and live in these communities.

The company also provides each employee with eight hours of paid time off every year to volunteer for a community organization. The United Way, Salvation Army, American Cancer Society, and the American Heart Association are just some of the groups supported at the local level.

Paychex has participated for many years in United Way's *Day of Caring* event where local businesses and individuals volunteer to work on selected community projects. In 2017, the Paychex office in Rochester fielded the largest company team in the area—850 employees on 53 different teams who spent the day working at 50 nonprofit organizations.

Without Paychex and all the people who have worked for the company over the years and who have made it so successful, I couldn't possibly have been able to help the hundreds of organizations who have received donations from the company, my family foundation, or from me personally. My thanks go out to them on behalf of all the people we have assisted over the past forty-plus years.

HURRICANE DORIAN

I'm fortunate to own a motor yacht called the *Laurel* which over the years we've used to travel throughout Europe and the Caribbean. Recently my captain, Roy Hodges, contacted me with a request. He asked for permission to support relief efforts after Hurricane Dorian passed through the region. A relief association needed help in delivering fifty tons of food and other supplies to the region and to bring back sixty-four dogs (in crates) to Palm Beach, so they could be reunited with their families who had been evacuated and forced to leave them behind. Monica and I have always been dog lovers, and over the last twenty years I've always had at least two dogs in my life at any one time. Currently Monica has three or four around the house as we also look after her mother's dogs on occasion. I was therefore pleased to be able to help by donating the services of my crew and, of course, the *Laurel* for such a good cause.

N O T   A   O N E - T R I C K   P O N Y

Most businesspeople know me either as the founder of Paychex or the owner of the Buffalo Sabres, but over the years I've invested in, and been involved with, dozens of other businesses. Along the way, I've mentored a slew of young entrepreneurs.

I'm guessing at some point, many successful entrepreneurs who have built a business probably wonder to themselves, were they lucky, or was it skill? What contributed to their success—was it circumstances or business acumen? Was it being in the right place at the right time, or did they create the conditions for their success?

I'm no different. Paychex turned out to be a great company—it's still an incredible company—but I was no different to any other entrepreneur in asking myself, *was I lucky or do I have a bunch of skills that I could bring to other businesses?*

Never lacking in confidence, I decided to find out and become an investor. I was not interested in starting another business, but I was interested in supporting entrepreneurs in a general sense with advice, and most importantly capital. As Paychex became increasingly known and respected within the business community, I was never short of investment opportunities. Even today, I probably get two to three business plans a week from prospective entrepreneurs who want to interest me in their enterprise, far more than I could ever entertain.

Over the years, I've been intimately involved in about twenty-five companies as a result of entrepreneurs coming to me with intriguing business concepts. These days I have three associates who vet everything I receive. They have developed an understanding of the kind of companies in which I prefer to invest. People often ask me to define what it is I am looking for, and that's difficult, but I can say that I prefer revenue-recurring businesses. It's what I'm used to in Paychex and it makes sense to continue getting business from an existing customer base, rather than trying to constantly attract new business.

Pulling back on the lens a little, when an opportunity comes across my desk, I can either look at the idea or the business concept and back that, or I can look at the jockey—the entrepreneur—and invest in him or her. In most cases I feel better backing the jockey, but I have to admit I have backed sound business ideas in the past with varying degrees of success, even when I've not been convinced the jockey could reach the finish line.

What I look for in an entrepreneur is a thorough understanding of their business, everything from raising capital through to pricing and human resources administration, along with a strong ability to sell and market their product or service.

Back in the 1980s I was involved with several ventures that offered great promise but failed to live up to expectations. One such "great" idea was a company that rented pay-to-play opportunities for kids. The idea was simple: We had facilities in shopping malls full of games for children. Parents could rent the space for birthday parties and we'd supply cake and other refreshments. We lasted a year and lost $500,000—as the primary investor, I took a significant hit.

Another fairly short-lived enterprise during the same period was a specialized radio network that focused programming on specific communities in upstate New York. In this case three entrepreneurs approached me and I felt it was a good idea. However, we never sold enough advertising to cover the broadcasting costs. In the end, we closed it down.

One of the by-products of closing that company was the launch of another broadcasting company that was close to my heart for a long time. We still owned the broadcasting equipment, and a friend of mine came to me and suggested we use it to offer specialized music programming in seniors' residences and nursing homes. The idea was to broadcast music that came from the era the residents had lived through—music they would relate to and enjoy. This was once again a recurring-revenue opportunity; we charged a fee per bed, per month. The business got off to a good start, but we continually struggled to cover our overhead, due to the high cost of installing the equipment. We managed to build it to a point where we were broadcasting in three hundred residences, but the added high cost of sales was killing us. The challenge was a long selling cycle combined with the fact sales representatives had to travel long distances between prospects.

I kept that business going for many years past its sell-by date for sentimental reasons, but in 2017, after investing over $12 million, we had to close it down. For one thing, technology was against us; even older seniors owned smartphones and tablets that could stream music. We couldn't even sell the business to another operator.

It's through these experiences we as entrepreneurs learn what not to do; being successful in business is not about luck, it's about learning on the job. Business history is littered with people who went bankrupt in their early careers, from Milton Hershey and H. J. Heinz to Henry Ford and Walt Disney. The secret is to get back up, learn from what went wrong, and don't make the same mistake again. Of course, that's a heck of a lot easier said than done.

Some of the more notable enterprises discussed in this chapter offer some excellent lessons in entrepreneurship. It's tempting to focus on the highly successful businesses I've been an integral part of, but I'd like to share some of the lessons I've learned from the failures, too.

The following will, I hope, provide insights into not only the way I personally approach investing in businesses and advising entrepreneurs but also the many issues and challenges one can face in the early stages of launching, growing, or expanding a business.

Safe Site

Safe Site stored business documents, including client and medical records for customers such as banks, insurance companies, and doctors' offices. We knew this was a cost-sensitive market, so for a few dollars a month our clients could have safe storage while still accessing their records quickly (within half a day) when they required them. We also stored magnetic records such as computer tapes. Basically, we offered an offsite backup service.

I received a call from a friend in the early 1980s with the original concept, and once again appreciated the recurring-revenue element at the core of the business. I funded its start-up and my nephew Charles Graham managed the company.

We purchased an offsite records management company in its early stages to allow us to be up and running quickly. The capital cost was significant, but sales were good, and our revenues grew rapidly. After several months, I invited Jim Wayman to join me in the company. He had recently retired from Paychex and was looking for new opportunities. He liked the concept and subsequently opened Safe Site offices in Boston, Hartford, and New York City.

At the time I thought we could perhaps build the business like we did with Paychex, by bringing partners on board—no franchisees though. To this end, I began recruiting people in the Rochester area to move to different parts of the country. Unlike with Paychex, however, we started out with the idea of eventually consolidating and either going public or selling in the future.

At one point, we grew to fourteen offices and we had annual revenues of around $10 million. As planned, we consolidated into one company, and a little later ran into a major problem. We were losing money, not a lot but enough to be of some concern. Then one day I got a call from Jim telling me we had a serious problem. He said we owed the bank over $2 million—our account was overdrawn. Our chief financial officer had failed to mention this very salient point to us during any of our meetings. To cut a long story short, he was indicted by the FBI for kiting checks and electronic transactions. What our young controller had been doing was writing checks for nonexistent funds and depositing them back and forth between accounts, relying on the three days it takes for the bank to process the checks. In this way he was able to access what amounted to an interest-free, unapproved loan. This is of course illegal, and it wasn't too long before the bank caught on to what he was doing.

His actions took us all by surprise, and I immediately realized it was unlikely that this was his only nefarious activity. I asked Jim to check with the IRS to see if we were behind on our payroll taxes. I was correct; that call uncovered another $800,000 owed in taxes. Our predicament became public and our national competitor Iron Mountain approached us and tried to take advantage of our embarrassing situation. They offered us $14 million, which we discussed at a board meeting. I was told that if we didn't accept their offer, we needed to find over $3 million in new capital. Everyone kind of looked at me—if we were going to save the company I'd have to come up with the money. I decided the time wasn't right to sell—it's never a good time to sell when you're on the back foot. I increased my equity position and left Iron Mountain very disappointed. From that point, we started to climb our own mountain back to profitability.

A couple of years later I was attending an investment conference and an analyst friend approached me and asked whether we were interested in selling. I asked him who was interested; it turned out to be a company called Pierce Leahy. We entered into discussions and they subsequently offered us $40 million. Not a bad hike from Iron

Mountain's $14 million just a year or two before. I ran it by Jim, who was my principal partner, and he felt Iron Mountain would pay more. I contacted them and negotiated a price of $63 million. In just a few years we went from close to bankruptcy to financial success.

This is an abject lesson in perseverance. Often you need to stick it out if you're convinced it's a good idea and will succeed over the long haul. Of course, it was also demonstrated, painfully, that you need to be fully aware of your financial situation at all times. Not just the basic financial statements, although they are vitally important, but to ensure there are sufficient checks and balances on anyone dealing with the company's finances.

One more thing, I don't think I've been involved in any company where the capital required wasn't more than was originally anticipated. You have to have the resources to survive when a big storm hits hard. As an epilogue to this story, Iron Mountain invited me to sit on its board, a position I held for many years.

Pictometry

In the early 1990s another friend called me to tell me about a company he was working with called Pictometry. The company had created a technology that merged digital photographs taken by low-flying aircraft with tax records to identify properties. The market for this ranged from county governments to sheriff's departments and fire departments to real estate developers. The technology could be used by law enforcement and emergency responders to identify entrances, exits, and geographical features, and by municipal governments for tax assessment purposes.

I liked the idea. This was not a jockey situation, but one where I felt the concept itself was worthy of investment. The technology was well developed before I got to hear about it and there were several shareholders, one of whom was looking to liquidate his shares. I bought them and after a year or two the technology was working well and we needed to develop a sales organization. After my experience at Paychex, this was certainly in my wheelhouse, and I invested additional capital so we could build a national sales organization. As it had with Paychex, this helped make the company profitable within a few years and fueled healthy growth.

If you have a good idea, other businesses come knocking on your door. This was the case with a Seattle-based company that was using Pictometry technology to do roof appraisals after a hurricane or tornado ripped through a community. Our technology dramatically reduced the time it took to do damage estimates. The idea of a merger was floated, and we basically threw all our shares into a bucket and took new shares in the merged company. No cash exchanged hands.

Sometimes a good idea is simply that: a good idea. In less than two years we got an offer from a public company for a staggering $650 million. Of course, we decided to take it, but the Federal Trade Commission got involved and after about ten months they said it was monopolistic and would not allow the sale.

We as shareholders were bitterly disappointed, but it gave us the confidence to put the company in the hands of an investment banker. Within sixty days he brought us an offer of $750 million. As the offer was from an equity firm, there was no problem with the Federal Trade Commission and we closed the deal in about sixty days. The shareholders were very happy campers.

The key lesson here is to either have the ability yourself, or find someone with the ability, to identify what your company needs to be successful. In this case it was a well-organized, well-managed sales team created at just the right time in the company's growth.

BlueTie

Sometimes you get lucky and a business makes money almost in spite of itself. I'm not sure that was quite what happened with BlueTie, but I certainly made money in an unexpected way. The company was started in 1999 by a local entrepreneur name David Koretz. BlueTie stored email data for companies—a recurring-revenue business again. You may be sensing a theme here. BlueTie transformed the software-as-a-service (SaaS) industry by launching the first hosted suite of business email and collaboration applications.

I invested $25 million but we soon had a great deal of competition and had to reduce our prices to compete in what was becoming a saturated market. We never broke even, but sometime later the CEO came to me and the other partners and informed us the company had developed two new products. He felt we should spin them off into new companies. We followed his advice and launched a company called Mykonos, which was developing a highly efficient way to prevent hackers from accessing computer networks. I invested a couple million dollars to support the development work. A little later the CEO called to say that someone wanted to buy the new company. I was shocked—we didn't even have our first sale. I was even more surprised when the company, the Juniper Corporation, offered us $83 million for the technology. We took the deal and my share was $55 million. Taking into consideration my $27 million investment, this was one of my better forays into the technology world.

We spun off another company from BlueTie that I am still involved in named Adventive. I invested a couple million dollars in this one, too. The company sells a digital ad production platform that allows digital publishers to monetize and scale ad production and delivery. It's still fairly small but it enjoys positive cash flow, so I'm happy with its performance at this point.

Although I'm no longer involved, I'm pleased to report BlueTie itself is still successful and is a one-stop shop for a range of cloud-based applications to assist companies in creating, storing, organizing, and sharing and protecting documents. It also sells scalable email and calendar solutions.

Ultra-Scan Corporation

Here is a case that demonstrates the need for persistence and access to enough capital to weather the storms that affect most business start-ups. Ultra-Scan was founded in 1987. It had developed an ultrasound scanner, similar to those used in medical applications, to identify fingerprints.

I'd put in $20 million, but the cost to the end user was too high and sales were not meeting our targets. I was considering cutting my losses, but John Schneider, the CEO, approached me with a new angle. The FBI had been in contact and were interested in whether we could develop four-finger identification (at the point our technology was limited to scanning only two fingers). The caveat was that the company needed time (twelve to twenty-four months) and another $5 million to develop the new technology. As an entrepreneur you have to have an instinct for when to hold and when to fold; in this case I decided to invest another chunk of money and take a bigger interest in the company.

Time went by and I hung on, until one day I got a call from John informing me that a company called Qualcomm had offered $65 million for Ultra-Scan. My patience, persistence, and belief in the concept was rewarded with a profit of around $10 million.

Grand Oaks Resort

Sometimes a business opportunity comes to you unexpectedly, as was the case with Grand Oaks Resort. My first wife, a horse lover, became the owner of the largest collection of antique horse carriages in America and built a museum to house them in Lady Lake, Florida. She had been highly successful as a Paychex franchisee and for many years was in the fortunate position of being able to grow her collection. But, for a variety of reasons she hit some bad times and found herself real estate rich and cash poor. She had a farm that housed the museum, several other buildings, and about four hundred acres of stunningly beautiful land. Horse lovers from around the world visited to drive carriages, take lessons, see the museum, and use the Equine Heritage Institute Library. The challenge was that it wasn't commercial enough and it was losing money. She needed to sell the ranch. I'd always loved the place and liked the overall concept, so I decided to purchase the entire operation from Gloria and invest money in it to help the property reach its full potential.

Since 2011, I've invested significant amounts of capital to develop a full-blown equestrian resort targeting horse lovers of all types, not just carriage-driving enthusiasts. Grand Oaks now has a large RV park, cabins, a restaurant, and twelve arenas (including one that is 54,000 square feet and covered), and hosts weddings in its own chapel. The resort holds more than forty horse events a year; people come with their own horses and carriages and ride, watch world-class shows, take lessons, or simply enjoy the peace and quiet of this very special place.

It's taken seven years, but we are closing in on making a profit. It will take a little more time and capital, but I am confident it will turn the corner. Every weekend we have to turn away over a hundred people who would like to stay. That's where some of the new capital is required—to build more accommodation. As always, I watch the trends and one new addition to the entertainment found at the resort is pickleball. The sport is becoming increasingly popular, especially with the clientele we attract at the resort. Laureen Oliver, my friend and one of the people I started the Independence Party with, is the general manager of the resort along with Tom Warriner.

———

Since becoming a resident of Florida, I have invested in three businesses in the Sunshine State and one in upstate New York. I'm excited by the potential of all these companies.

Zoom Tan

One of my fairly recent investments is Zoom Tan, which now operates in almost a hundred locations from Florida to upstate New York. As you can guess by the name, these are tanning salons that offer both spray and UV tanning. The latter is offered in stand-up booths only, which is one of the unique selling propositions of the company. These booths are more effective at tanning—and more importantly far more hygienic.

With Zoom Tan I was definitely backing the jockey. Tony Toepfer, the CEO, has twenty-five years' experience in the tanning business. Originally from Chicago, Tony had started with a few salons but was finding it tough to expand without an influx of capital. This is yet another example of a recurring-revenue business; customers sign up for either quarterly or annual memberships. The company is profitable and enjoys a very positive cash flow. Here is a case where an experienced businessperson with industry knowledge approaches a competitive market with a new way of doing business that appeals to the target market. My contribution, other than providing capital, has been to help Tony gain a better understanding of financial statements. I can't stress how important it is in any business to fully understand the finances of your business.

Line 5

Line 5 is a company I am particularly proud of; it's a good example of where I discovered an excellent jockey who took quite a while to come to me with a concept worthy of investment and it paid off. I met Justin Lane at the Bentley dealership in Naples. In fact I'd bought several cars from him over the years and he had looked after me extremely well. He always went over and above when it came to customer service— even bringing a Bentley to my house for a test drive. Over the years,

I became friends with him. He was in his early thirties at that time. At one point I asked him if he'd like to work for Paychex, but he was the number-one Bentley salesperson in the United States so I couldn't offer him a position that would provide him a salary to match what he was earning. To put that in perspective, in the last ten months of his employment he sold 140 cars at an average price of $175,000—that's over $24 million worth of cars.

I told him that he was the kind of guy I liked to invest in, and that if he ever came up with a business idea he felt I should look at, he should call me. A few months after he left the dealership, he called me about his highly original business concept for partnering with dealers to fully fund vehicle protection plans for cars and trucks including coverage such as extended service plans, maintenance plans, road hazard, road-side assistance, appearance protection, and theft protection. One of the keys to Line 5's success is that banks won't finance a car beyond its value, whereas we will.

It's all done online very quickly. The online application gives our client's customers not just instant approval, but guaranteed approval with zero down payment. It took Justin a year to develop the software, which is the key to the whole business. Line 5 is now in its third year and doing very well; it made a significant profit in its second year. A great jockey and a groundbreaking concept originated from years of industry knowledge—a match made in heaven.

TrueFrame

Keeping with the automotive theme, I'm also invested in TrueFrame, a company that takes automobile reports such as CARFAX and Auto-Check to the next level. Both these companies provide a bare-bones, often vague report on any damage a car might have sustained. The problem is that they never actually see the vehicle. With TrueFrame, however, a full assessment is carried out by qualified automotive technicians detailing both any damage and any repairs that have been undertaken. Subsequently, a comprehensive report is written.

The primary clients for TrueFrame are car dealerships. Once a report has been carried out, a sticker is placed in the window of the car stating, "I've got my TrueFrame report." The sticker features a QR code that car buyers can use to access the full report on their mobile devices. This far more comprehensive report can repudiate negative CARFAX and AutoCheck reports, allowing a dealer to charge more for a car, whether or not it has been in an accident.

TrueFrame operates in about fifteen cities currently, and I am the principal shareholder. It's doing quite well and I'm confident it will continue to grow as more dealerships sign up to use the service. This is a case where an excellent concept won me over.

Greenlight

I recently invested in an internet service provider called Greenlight based in Rochester, New York. The company was started by local people. It currently services 18,000 residents and is growing fast. As I write this, the company is growing at a rate of 800 new residences per month, and I have a 65 percent stake in the company.

What makes it unique is that, using a fiber-optic network, Greenlight is able to provide its customers with internet speeds that are 100 times faster than what most Americans have access to today. A recent study found that homes in neighborhoods with a fiber connection can see an increase in value up to 3.1 percent, or $5,437. Studies have also shown that home buyers are choosing where to live based on access to high-speed internet service.

What I particularly like about Greenlight is that it offers its customer extremely fast internet speeds at affordable prices. We were awarded "Best Internet Service Provider" in 2017, 2018, and 2019 by *Rochester Business Journal* Readers Ranking.

INVESTING 101

Many people ask me how I make my decision as to whether I'll invest in a company. In reality, it's rarely just one thing. As I mentioned earlier, I like to back jockeys, but a strong idea is also a good draw. It might be better to tell you what the warning signs are that make me walk away.

Ownership

Before I even consider an idea, a major turn-off is when someone states in their business plan that they want to retain 51 percent of the company. What that tells me is they want to keep control but they want someone else to finance the risk. Let's explore that idea a little further. When I ran Paychex, I never owned more than 50 percent of the company. After we merged, or consolidated, I only retained about 30 percent. Did that put me in a difficult position? Not really, since there were so many stockholders that would have had to come together to vote me out, the chances of that happening were very slim. Unless I did something really dumb that hurt the company and their investment. In which case, I would have deserved to be ousted.

When it comes down to ownership breakdown, it has to be logical. It has to make sense to the investor. I have people come to me and say they want to start a business and require $3 million and they are willing to give up 10 percent of the company in return. What that tells me is they are valuing the company at $30 million, which is ridiculous, especially if they haven't even opened their doors yet. These ownership demands discredit investment seekers immediately in my eyes. I won't even start talking to them about their business concept.

The Entrepreneur

The next thing I look at is the person—the entrepreneur. I run through the following questions: Do I think they can do the job? Do they have sufficient industry knowledge? Do they have a strong work ethic? Can they manage people? Are they smart? Do I have faith they can deliver? Can they sell? Do they know how to market their product or service?

I have to have faith in the jockey. To continue the analogy, it doesn't matter how fast the horse can run, if the jockey has no idea how to ride it to victory.

Is There a Market?

The business concept has to make sense. Is there a market for the company and what it sells? What is unique about the product or service? Why is it different than what competitors are already offering? What need is it fulfilling that isn't being met by someone else? TrueFrame, for instance, built on where CARFAX and AutoCheck fell short and offered something that would increase auto dealers' profits.

Eventual Liquidity

Shareholders don't invest out of the kindness of their hearts. They are looking to earn dividends, and if not a dividend, they want to see that there is a possibility down the line of selling the company. The question of eventual liquidity has to be real. They have to see that there is a market for the company. The worst thing that can happen is to be caught as a minority shareholder in a small company that has no opportunity for liquidity.

Can You Sell What You Produce?

I find myself continually telling wannabe entrepreneurs that just because you hang up your shingle, it doesn't mean the world is going to beat a path to your door. I warn them the sales process is going to be harder than they can ever imagine.

A lack of sales ability is the biggest reason companies get into cash flow problems. If sales are low, there will be insufficient revenues to cover operating costs. People often refer to a cash flow problem, when in truth it's a management problem.

––––––

Investing in a business is about due diligence. I have to identify that there are enough positives in terms of the jockey and the concept to catch my attention. I have to have a flicker of interest and I also need to believe I can help in some way. I don't invest to make money necessarily—although I hate to lose it—I invest to help turn a business around, make it more successful, help it reach new heights. That's the challenge. Anyone can invest in a business and sit back and either see it lose their money or provide dividends. That's called gambling. I always want the deck stacked in my favor.

SEVENTEEN

MY TWO CENTS

SOCIAL WELFARE

While I was chairman of Rochester Fights Back, I became associated with Dr. Andrew Doniger. Andy was the head of the Monroe County Health Department, and during a casual conversation we got onto the topic of teen pregnancy. Obviously, Dr. Doniger knew quite a bit about the topic and educated me as to the magnitude of the problem. At that time in Monroe County there were approximately 1,400 children born to teenage mothers. I was shocked at the cost to society and the struggle it put on the young parents. Being a teenager is difficult enough; being a parent at the same time makes things exceptionally difficult, both financially and in terms of job placement and advancement. From a broader perspective, it was a grave social problem that had serious cost implications for our community.

Andy and I decided to take action and contacted the mayor of the City of Rochester, the chair of the Rochester Community United Way, and the Monroe County executive to discuss the idea of a media campaign aimed at fighting teen pregnancy through education. I put up $100,000 and asked the others to do the same. The United Way and the county executive came in with me, but the mayor didn't. I was very disappointed that he wouldn't participate in the campaign, especially as most of the problem was centered in the urban areas of Rochester.

The campaign was quite successful, and over two to three years we did see a significant reduction in the number of teen pregnancies. I always felt, however, that it never quite reached its potential. In my opinion, the campaign message was too nice. It needed to be far more hard-hitting, but maybe that is just my personality.

Teen pregnancy is often in the news and is currently at a record low. To put this into perspective, however, 229,715 babies were born to women 15 to 19 years of age in 2015. And the US teen pregnancy rate is significantly higher than any other western industrialized country.

SUBSTANCE ABUSE AND GAMBLING

During the early 1990s I had started to become more interested in, and concerned about, what was going on in my community and in the state in general. Up to that point I'd been too busy with Paychex to focus on much else. Even during the nineties things were busy, but I started clipping news items of interest out of newspapers as they caught my eye.

I got a call from the Monroe County executive asking me if I would participate in a community organization called Rochester Fights Back. Its goal was to reduce illegal drug use and trafficking locally. The executive also invited other people in the community to share their expertise including the police chief, an advertising executive, legal counsel, and representatives from schools and government. For the first two years, under the chairmanship of Dr. Richard Miller, we did a good job in bringing the issue to the attention of a wider audience; in year three the chair was handed to me.

One of the major accomplishments of Rochester Fights Back was the creation of what we called Drug-Free School Zones, a program that worked with the relevant authorities to set fines and punishment at a far higher level for people selling drugs within a certain radius of a school. We also launched a media campaign with the highly evocative and effective slogan "Drugs Lie," which we put on bumper stickers and other advertisements.

The committee also favored and promoted pre-employment drug testing, for which I was a big advocate. The general business community accepted it quite well, but we had difficulties when it came to the city and county governments. As counterintuitive and illogical as it sounds, even though the committee was set up by them, they were not willing to commit to those types of employment regulations for their own employees.

On one occasion, I did a major presentation on the importance and necessity for pre-employment drug testing for county and city officials, but my points and suggestions were not well received. After the presentation, however, the head of the food service and janitorial workers union in the school district came up to me urging me not to give up. He said, "Keep fighting for this, we need it." I asked him what his angle was and was shocked when he replied, "Who do you think is selling the drugs in the schools?" So, I told him we would keep trying. It was a real wake-up call for me.

Previously I mentioned that during my run for governor I was one of the first candidates to come out in support of legalizing medical marijuana and reforming the harsh Rockefeller drug laws.

The challenge with legalizing any drug is that often government becomes involved in its sale and distribution and subsequently becomes dependent on the tax revenue it generates. Once that happens it often begins to commercialize it to increase revenues. If you don't think governments are happy to promote poor life choices to create revenue, consider gambling.

Ever hear the expression, "A dollar and a dream" or "Hey, you never know"? They are advertising slogans sponsored by the New York State Lottery. They blatantly encourage people to gamble on the lottery. I find this strange. Why wouldn't the government want people to work harder to earn more money, or become more educated to get better jobs, or be more community oriented? Why should they choose to promote gambling?

The result of these advertisements, which have been airing in one form or another for more than fifty years (the New York State Lottery's first draw was in 1967) is astonishing. If you divide the revenue collected from the sale of tickets by the number of people in the state, every man, woman, and child spends on average $500 a year on lottery tickets. Now, not everyone plays the lottery so many people are spending way more way than $500 on this scheme. Then we have casinos: New York State recently added five new ones. You can't tell me that having them in a community does not encourage gambling. I'm only talking about one state. Wherever you live the situation will be the same. Governments promote things that create revenue, which goes into their general fund.

When I owned the Buffalo Sabres, I did not allow the New York State Lottery nor any of the local casinos to advertise in our arena or on our television programming. This didn't go down well with my management team because they wanted the revenue, but I absolutely insisted we would not promote that type of activity.

Let's return to the legalization of marijuana, or for that matter any drug. Once something is legalized, government can't help but see it as a source of revenue. Once that occurs, the temptation to commercialize and promote it becomes intense. I am against legalizing marijuana, if it is promoted by government and commercialized for profit. Where it is legalized, any revenues ending up in the government purse should be used solely to educate people as to the negative effects, discourage its use and proliferation, and to treat people suffering from substance abuse. The government will benefit from lower law enforcement costs and lower rates of incarceration due to decriminalization.

While I'm talking about poor life choices and media influence, I often think about beer commercials and the effect they have on our society. I'm not saying beer is bad in moderation—in fact it can be very pleasurable. However, the ads often use scantily clad young ladies and focus too much on consumption, in my opinion. By the time a young person reaches legal drinking age, they've seen several hundred thousand beer commercials.

It makes me consider what impact a change in the way the industry advertises its product might have on alcoholic diseases, and automobile accidents caused by drunk driving. Perhaps beer commercials could promote not drinking and driving, rather than hedonistic behavior. Perhaps the industry should stop advertising altogether.

One of my experiences during the period I was chairman of Rochester Fights Back was when I took my grandchildren down to SeaWorld in Florida for a vacation. As I was sitting on a park bench enjoying the carnival atmosphere, I heard this terrific inspirational music coming from around the corner. It sounded fun, so I went to investigate. All the excitement was coming from the beer wagon for Budweiser beer. There were the huge Clydesdale horses and gentlemen in bright-red uniforms sitting on the big carriage. I immediately thought, here we are at SeaWorld, a family attraction aimed primarily at children, and here they are promoting the hell out of Budweiser beer. I didn't think that was right, even though Budweiser owned SeaWorld at the time. When I got back to my office in Rochester, I wrote a letter to the CEO of Budweiser saying I was disappointed that a company of their stature would be doing something like that. His reaction was swift. His office sent a letter out to all the Budweiser distributors across the country and told them not to use Paychex. No good deed goes unpunished.

I'll leave you with a question: Today, is the vaping industry using a similar formula to market its product?

RACE RELATIONS

Pick up almost any newspaper, tune into a news program on television, or visit a news website and there will likely be something about how poor race relations are in the United States today. But is this really true, or is it media hype? I've lived for over seventy years and in my opinion, we have come a long way in improving race relations in this country. In reality, the tolerance levels between races has improved significantly over the years. If you think I am talking from a pulpit of white privilege, I should tell you that I was persecuted throughout my young life for being an Italian—a *dago*. I've experienced prejudice firsthand.

The media, however, continues to portray white people as racist and black people, especially, as victims. I don't understand it. Take a look at the interaction between people participating in sports, business, and in communities and you will see things are so much better than they used to be. Not perfect, of course. There will always be intolerance, bigots, and those who hate anyone who is not a carbon copy of themselves. In my opinion, however, the media seems to actually fuel the fire of racism and prejudice.

I would like to see the media report more often on all the ways people of all races, creeds, ethnicities, and religious persuasions come together in harmony. Make no mistake, this does happen more than you would ever realize from the coverage we are exposed to on a daily basis.

EDUCATION

The American economy needs to continually create jobs for its people, and in my opinion the best way to do this is through entrepreneurship. People who start businesses take risks and, assuming they are successful, enjoy the financial benefits of their endeavors. What they also do is create employment.

My question is, why doesn't the government or the educational system promote entrepreneurship? Why aren't they educating our young people about the benefits of capitalism and the many benefits of entrepreneurship to our society? More to the point, why isn't entrepreneurship part of the core curriculum? Why aren't kids in elementary school learning about business? Heck, for the most part they leave school not knowing how to read a simple financial statement.

To me, it sometimes seems like we are heading in the opposite direction. Some people might say educators actually downplay capitalism.

Knowing how businesses and industries work can be useful to everyone, not only those considering going into business for themselves. Let me give you an analogy. Say your child is interested in playing lacrosse but it doesn't exist in your community and you decide to introduce the sport. What's involved?

You'd need to develop a plan that includes attracting other parents and coaches. You'd need to form some sort of organization, open a bank account, develop a budget, raise some funds for equipment, find a location to play games, connect with other lacrosse teams and apply to join a division, and you will need to market and promote lacrosse to the community. Once up and running, there will be a need for scheduling and a need to bring on people to handle all the facets of running a lacrosse league in your community.

Sounds a lot like running a business, doesn't it? That's the thing, business skills, in effect entrepreneurship, are transferable skills. The more people possessing those skills in our communities, the better. Teach it in school and we'll see more young people take control of their lives and contribute to society.

CONGRESSIONAL TERM LIMITS

In general, I am not in favor of term limits for legislators and executives in our various levels of government. However, I have one exception and that is the leaders of the US Senate and the Speaker of the House of Representatives and their counterparts in the fifty state legislatures.

Some of those people have held those positions for a long time. Speakers control the agendas of their houses; they have a great deal of power. If a speaker doesn't want to put a bill by a member of a party on the floor for a vote, they don't have to. I think that's totally wrong. They have the ability to control the agenda for that body (the House or the Senate) for a long, long time.

Interestingly, one of the ways they manage to use their power and keep it is to control their pork-barrel funding. If they have a member of either party who doesn't agree with them, the speaker can punish them financially by limiting their access to pork barrel money in their district.

For example, a personal friend of mine was a member of the majority party in the New York State Senate, and in a recent election the minority party took over the majority. As a result, he found his office had been moved to the basement. That, to me, is kind of petty, but it's an example of the kind of power speakers have. And, it's so difficult to unseat them because, while they are in power, they can control members' staff, their pork-barrel money, and even their legislative statements. In essence they have the power to reward people by paying them more money. That's why Mitch McConnell and Nancy Pelosi have been in place for so long. Another example is Shelly Silver, who was the speaker controlling the New York State assembly for more than twenty years.

I therefore believe in term limits for leaders of legislative bodies, not the members. This would ensure there is turnover in the legislative body that would allow things to be more about policy than power.

FINAL WORDS (FOR NOW)

We all have those precious moments in our life, ones that seem to make it all worthwhile. One such moment was when I had the honor of speaking to Paychex employees at the annual employee meeting. I was a surprise guest. Marty Mucci, Paychex's CEO, had invited me and I was pleased I could attend. What blew me away was how well I was received. When I walked onto the stage, the 4,000 people in attendance applauded enthusiastically, and when I wrapped up my speech, the standing ovation was incredibly touching.

Presenting at the event gave me an opportunity to recognize the contribution people in the audience, such as Bob Sebo and Tom Clarke, had made to the company. One other employee in attendance, who deserved very special recognition, was Kathy Angelitis—employee number two and amazingly still working at Paychex. She is probably the most knowledgeable and experienced person in payroll processing in the industry today. It was wonderful to see her at an employee meeting along with several thousand colleagues, considering back in 1971 we simply pulled our two chairs together when we wanted to discuss something.

There were four things I felt it was important to share with employees. First, there are around 12 million businesses in the United States and all payroll processing companies combined only had 2 million as clients. With more than 10 million business not being serviced, the potential for growth is amazing. Second, that the company had three masters—employees, clients, and shareholders—and all three have to be kept happy and serviced well if the company is to continue to succeed and grow. Third, corporations are often criticized for not paying their fair share of taxes. I told them, I remembered the first $1 million check I wrote to the IRS and that, "Boy did that bust my hump," but in 2016 we paid over $390 million to federal and state governments excluding social security taxes, federal and state unemployment taxes, sales taxes, and real estate taxes. I went on to say, "Paychex is paying its share—we are way ahead of the game." Finally, I thanked them for all their efforts in making the company successful because it was this success that made it possible for Paychex and my personal foundation to make philanthropic gestures to the tune of almost $300 million to date.

After the event I spent two hours as Paychex's wonderful employees lined up to take a selfie with me. It's not often that the founder of a company remains as CEO for forty years, and I think that sets me apart from many of today's corporate leaders. I have a relationship with Paychex that is unique in the depth of its intimacy—a strange word perhaps when talking about a company but fitting in this case, I think.

PAYCHEX TODAY

Paychex is a very different company today than it was when it was just me and Kathy. It has grown through acquisitions, but even more so through the introduction of new products and services such as TaxPay, 401(k), HR outsourcing, and the development of increasingly sophisticated software that has made the company a technology-driven enterprise.

Today, Paychex has approximately 15,500 employees, thousands of shareholders, over 670,000 payroll clients, and a market cap of $30 billion. One measure of Paychex's success is that over 110,000 clients have been with the company for more than a decade. Not only that, the company's HR outsourcing services supports more than one million worksite employees, and Paychex is now the largest 401(k) record-keeper in America.

ON A PERSONAL NOTE

I'm incredibly fortunate. I've had a long and interesting life. I've been successful in my business life, both with Paychex and the Buffalo Sabres, and in recent years with the businesses in which I've invested.

In politics, I've been a thorn in the side of what I see as an often ineffective, inefficient, wasteful, and sometimes corrupt political system. I make no apologies. And who says I'm finished?

There are a large number of people to whom I am immensely grateful and who have had a positive influence on my life, and I thank them dearly. None deserves my thanks more than my sister Marie. She stands out as a shining beacon. She looked after me as a baby, stood by me during the hard days of Paychex, and was, and is, a constant cheerleader and continual inspiration. Today Marie is in her early nineties and very active. If you don't call her before 9:00 a.m, you probably won't reach her: She'll already be up and about, making the most of life. She still drives and spends half her year in Naples, Florida, and the other half in Rochester. We've been as close as two people could be.

I can't close this book without mentioning two of my best friends who are no longer with us, Gene Polisseni and Gary Muxworthy; I miss them greatly. We were the three musketeers until we were joined by Bob Sebo who became the fourth member. Bob stood by me for almost all of the years I was at the helm of Paychex. He's still alive and well and enjoying retirement.

I am blessed with two children, two stepchildren, six grandchildren, and three great-grandchildren. I also have three nephews and nieces and three grandnieces with whom I am very close. Fortunately, they all live in Rochester, which is my summer home. I am grateful we are a family that hasn't fallen victim to a generation choosing to move out of state. As a side note, I am pleased to say that one of my great-grandchildren is named Blase, upholding an Italian tradition that would have brought special joy to my mother.

Many people ask about Steven, my son who has a developmental disability. He is now fifty-five and lives in Rochester, in his own house, just a few miles from our home with his house parents who provide the special care he needs. I am pleased to say that in the last thirty years he has only had two sets of house parents. For the last twenty years he has worked in a sheltered workshop, the School of the Holy Childhood, a nonprofit organization that focuses on education and vocational training. They have a bakery, a wood shop, and also do simple assembly line jobs. Steven's work is a very important part of his life. He loves going there every day and has a lot of friends. In spite of everything he is a very happy person.

I can't wrap up this autobiography without sincerely thanking Steve Pigeon, my close friend, colleague, and confidant for the last twenty-six years. He has been a constant companion through many adventures and has been by my side every day during the writing of not only this book, but also *Built, Not Born*, my highly successful guide for entrepreneurs.

Last, I'd like to mention my wife Monica. We've been together now for twelve years and she has a very special place in my heart. She is one of the nicest people I have ever met, and I feel privileged that she is a part of my life. I love you, Monica.

ACKNOWLEDGMENTS

I would like to thank the many people who helped me write *The Italian Kid Did It*. Memory is a tricky thing and although I am blessed with excellent recall of the events of my life, there were still times when some of the minutiae of complex discussions and political machinations needed clarification and confirmation.

To my sister Marie, to whom this book is dedicated, for her lifelong support and love and her recall of our family's history.

To Marti Mucci and Bob Sebo for their help in writing the chapters on Paychex.

My thanks go to Laureen Oliver and Steve Pigeon. Their contributions to the chapters on my political career were invaluable.

To Larry Quinn for his valuable input on our time together running the Buffalo Sabres.

To Ann Costello, the director of my family foundation for working with me to ensure the foundation's work was accurately represented.

To Naomi Whittel, for her marketing insights and wisdom, and ongoing support and commitment to this book.

I'd also like to extend my thanks to Kevin Anderson of Kevin Anderson and Associates (KAA), and my ghostwriter at KAA, Mike Wicks. Mike listened to me talk about my life for hundreds of hours and was able to accurately transpose my words and thoughts to the written page. His commitment to helping me find my voice and tell my story was invaluable.

And finally, to my wife Monica for putting up with the hundreds of hours I spent working on the book.

INDEX

Tom Golisano

Born in Irondequoit, New York, Tom Golisano graduated from Alfred State College in 1962 with a degree in general business management. In 2009, he was presented with an honorary doctorate of humane letters at his alma mater's commencement ceremony. He holds honorary doctorate degrees from five colleges and universities.

In 1971, Golisano founded Paychex, a leading provider of integrated human capital management solutions for payroll, benefits, human resources, and insurance services. Today, Paychex services more than seven hundred thousand clients in the United States and Northern Europe. Stepping down as CEO in 2004, he remains the company's board chair.

Golisano founded the Independent Party in New York State, which acquired ballot status in 1995, and ran for governor three times. In March 2003, he purchased the Buffalo Sabres hockey team to ensure it remained in Buffalo. He took the team from near bankruptcy to being rated by ESPN, in 2007, as the best-run sports franchise in professional sports.

He was the principal underwriter of the Clinton Global Initiative Annual Meeting for eight years. His philanthropic contributions have exceeded $330 million, helping hospitals, educational institutions, and many other organizations. Three children's hospitals bear his name. He has two children, six grandchildren, and four great-grandchildren.

Mike Wicks

An author, ghostwriter, writing coach, and senior writer with Kevin Anderson & Associates, Mike Wicks has a writing and publishing career that spans more than forty years. He has worked on both sides of the Atlantic for many of the leading names in publishing, including Random House, Michael Joseph, and imprints of Hachette and the Pearson-Longman group. For the past twenty-one years, he has focused on writing and ghostwriting business books, memoirs, and other nonfiction books.